Roger Verge's Entertaining in the French Style

Photography by Pierre Hussenot

Recipes translated and edited by Stephanie Curtis

Text translated by Geoffrey O'Brien

Webb &Bower

MICHAEL JOSEPH

Copyright © 1986 Flammarion

Design by
  J.C. Suarès
  Andrea Perrine
  Diana Jones
  Virginia Pope

Photo stylist: Laurence Mouton

First published in Great Britain 1986 by
Webb & Bower (Publishers) Limited
9 Colleton Crescent, Exeter, Devon EX2 4BY

in association with Michael Joseph Limited
27 Wright's Lane, London W8 5SL

Published in the United States by
Stewart, Tabori & Chang, Inc.
Publishers
740 Broadway
New York, N.Y.
10003
U.S.A.

British Library Cataloguing in Publication Data

Vergé, Roger
    Entertaining in the French style
    1. Cookery, French
    I. Title
    641.5944   TX719

    ISBN 0-86350-127-3

Printed in Italy

86 87 88 89 10 9 8 7 6 5 4 3 2 1

First Edition

To my wife Denise
and my little Cordélia
who make of each of our meals
a special occasion

page 1
Lunch is served under the arbor.

pages 2-3
This book proposes menus according to seasons. We open,
naturally, with summer, the most magnificent time of year
in Provence.

page 4
Kir, a traditional apéritif composed of white wine and
crème de cassis, is refreshing and extremely drinkable.

above
The chef's taste also expresses itself in the products he cre-
ates: oils, mustards, herbs.

Contents

Introduction

The Feasts of My Windmill

The windmill that I've turned into Le Moulin de Mougins has made me well-known far beyond my native Provence, and even across the seas. In fact, though, you won't necessarily find recipes from the Moulin's menu in this book, but rather the dishes I like to prepare for my friends, the dishes that are so intimately linked to memories of my childhood and my apprenticeship in eating. I would like these recipes to become yours, to accompany your own special meals.

Some of these menus may strike you as overabundant, but they are scaled to my own appetite, which is not small. Moreover, it is impossible for me to envisage a feast in anything but a generous spirit. To serve guests is my way of sharing happiness with those I love.

These menus are not just lists of dishes. They also include wine suggestions and everything else that contributes to the atmosphere of a meal—the choice of tableware and silverware, of tablecloth, glasses, and so on. I also offer all sorts of advice on giving your guests a relaxed and confident welcome.

I've made a point of writing these recipes out in great detail to make them as clear and as easy to prepare as possible. I've also had them tested by many of my friends, which has led to some slight modifications.

For the Roast Pheasant with Chartreuse, for example, I had indicated that the bird should be stuffed with "two petits suisses." My friend Denis, who was testing the menu, called me up somewhat at a loss to ask: "Where do you find your petits suisses? With the ones I've got, it would take at least fifteen of them to stuff a pheasant!" Obviously he had taken my use of the word "stuff" too literally! I had meant merely to baste the interior with them.

On the other hand, my friend Jean-Marie Dubois of Champagne asked me if he could substitute fresh truffles for the onions and leeks in Grandmother Catherine's Chicken Pie. I answered in the affirmative, asking only how many truffles he planned to use. He replied, "Oh, only about a pound." You will doubtless understand why I've retained my recipe rather than adopting Jean-Marie's. All the same, you are welcome to try his version; and don't hesitate to interpret my recipes as freely as he did.

I have grouped the recipes into menus because one good dish isn't enough to make a good meal. You have to establish a "program" which puts dishes together harmoniously.

Don't make the mistake of serving a

meal such as one I had in which every dish was perfect but the menu unbalanced—a rather strong and highly seasoned fish soup was followed by a chicken in cream sauce. After that soup, we no longer had the sensitivity necessary to appreciate the delicacy of the chicken, so it ended up seeming bland.

You are free, however, to modify these menus or to select only a single dish from them. While the simplest meal can be a moment of great pleasure, don't forget that cooking also has to do with generosity. But you are not obliged to go as far as my friend Paul Bocuse, for whom nothing is ever enough. It sometimes happens that we make a simple, low-calorie vegetable bouillon (it doesn't happen very often,

but after two or three days of banqueting...). This simple bouillon not only contains every conceivable vegetable, but Paul also manages to slip in a bit of pork belly, one or two pig's tails, and a fowl. "For that matter," he'll say, "a fowl isn't much. It's one of the meats with the fewest calories. And what you really crave can't do you any harm." And—to conserve the dietetic aspect of this bouillon—he adds to our plates at the last moment an enormous minced truffle, with the comment, "You see, you really don't need much for good cooking."

Off you go, then. I think I've said enough to encourage you to make your guests happy in an atmosphere of peace and serenity. But don't forget: it's *your* feast.

Shopping

The successful realization of a menu depends on intelligent shopping—unless you are lucky enough to have a garden. Nothing equals the aroma of freshly cut vegetables, fruits, and herbs. At the Moulin, the gardener brings me fresh figs for the *fricassée de volaille*, but he has found uses for the leaves as well. In back of the restaurant, the herb garden supplies an abundance of thyme, chives, chervil, and so forth.

But if you don't have a garden, you must learn how to shop. I was fortunate to learn this art in my early childhood, and that is probably what made me a chef. Every Friday I would go to market with my Aunt Celestine. This was the most fascinating and picturesque school I have ever attended— and also the only one where I had any success!

We always began by going all around the market, while my aunt cast a seemingly indifferent eye over the

The freshest fruits and vegetables from the market in Cannes.

farmers' baskets. But once she had completed her circuit, her mind was virtually made up.

Then, with a vaguely interested air, she would stop in front of the stall she had chosen, examine a couple of chickens (they were sold in pairs in those days), and verify that the comb was a healthy red, the feet smooth and white, and the eyes bright. Then she blew on the feathers of the crop, in order to separate them, and felt with her thumb to see that the crop was slim, bright, and without any white flakiness. She checked to see that the gizzard wasn't stuffed with corn, which would have artificially inflated the weight ("Why should I pay for corn which does neither the chicken nor me any good?"). Finally, she made sure that the other chicken making up the pair had the same qualities as his corn-fed brother.

Following this minute examination, my aunt's face would express a pained skepticism with regard to the unfortunate fowls, and the farmer's wife, watching my aunt out of the corner of her eye, became convinced that she had a difficult customer on her hands.

"My little woman," she would protest (my Aunt Celestine was a "little woman" of over 200 pounds), "those chickens have never eaten anything but corn. It's been over a week since they stopped running loose and were put in the *épinette*." (An *épinette* was a wicker cage in which chickens were placed for fattening.)

"My poor woman," my aunt replied with an absolutely counterfeit air of profound commiseration, "your chickens ought to have stayed another

Even in winter I can make tarts using fruits from my garden.

week or two in the *épinette*. In any case, at my table I can't serve birds that are nothing but skin and bones."

With that, she began a false exit, knowing full well that the farmer's wife would do everything in her power to keep her from going. It was all part of an immutable ritual, without which—for the farmer's wife as much as for my aunt—the negotiation would have had no real interest.

Aunt Celestine would then announce a firm and definitive price, which she would not exceed for anything in the world. It was a question of dignity. Her price was, for that matter, perfectly honest, which didn't prevent the farmer's wife from feigning, for the sake of principle, a deep disappointment. Magnanimously, my aunt would agree to take—at the same price—two or three other pairs of the remaining chickens. The farmer's wife, in order to have the last word, would exclaim: "Very well! But it's only because it's you—I'm losing money on the deal." This didn't fool anyone, but it provided a logical ending for the transaction.

From chickens we moved on to eggs—a rather normal progression. Aunt Celestine accepted only brown eggs, whose yolks, she assured me, were fresher.

Then came the cheeses, whose grain and relative hardness indicated whether or not the milk had been heated, the cream skimmed, and if they had been carefully washed in clear water.

For the butter, it mustn't be too yellow—that would have meant that the cows had grazed on meadows full of buttercups ("Buttercups are nice to look at, but they coarsen the flavor") or that the butter had been rinsed in carrot juice. A single morsel detached with the thumbnail was enough to reveal a butter that had not been washed in well water, that had been badly pressed, or that contained "buttermilk."

All these endless examinations, and the haggling that followed, fascinated me all the more because this expense of time and energy often resulted in saving only a few centimes on the products my aunt had decided to buy right from the start. But in those days a sou was a sou, and—even more important—where would the fun have been otherwise?

While my aunt went marketing, my uncle kept busy with his vegetable garden. He too followed an absolutely immutable and sacred ritual, which forbade him to cut any salad greens that had not been blanched in advance (a week before cutting them, he would use straw to tie the leaves tightly around the heart of the lettuce so that the heart would turn white, since it was well protected from the sun), which forbade carrots beyond a certain size, or green beans or peas after the third cutting—except for feeding the rabbits. "They get too hard after that third cutting," he would explain. For whatever reason, flowers, fruits, or vegetables were never to be cut after the sun had risen in the sky.

Thus, armed with infallible rigor, age-old traditions, and a very sure taste, my aunt and uncle started in the early morning to prepare lovingly the marvelous meal that would bring together friends and family.

Of course—you'll tell me—these are stories about the good old days, and neither time nor markets are what they used to be. But I can assure you that you still can find very fine ingredients, as long as you look for them; and you still can find time, if you want to.

Having said that, I would urge you not to imitate the famous Vatel, the Duc de Condé's cook, and stab yourself with a cutlass for having failed to find a fresh-caught daurade royale at your fishmonger's. The first rule to observe about shopping for fish is to insist on freshness. Don't hesitate to replace a dubious turbot with a fresh cod.

I will go even further—at the risk of offending the purists. While canned and frozen foods are clearly not nearly as good as fresh products, they can contribute to a delicious meal if supplemented with fresh herbs, a nice tomato, a few ounces of originality, and a lot of love. Canned and frozen foods are also very convenient out of season for certain vegetables (asparagus, peas) and certain fruits (fruits in syrup, frozen strawberries and raspberries for purées only). Frozen fish and shellfish lose much of their flavor and texture; they can be used, but don't expect the same quality as when fresh.

It is important to be well organized in order to avoid unexpected shortages. The simple lack of a garlic clove at the crucial moment can spoil a dish. With that in mind, I have provided a list of all the necessary ingredients for each recipe. So, if you are inviting friends to dinner, carefully read the recipes you plan to follow two days ahead of time and make a list of what you have to buy. However, don't be alarmed if you can't find the precise ingredient indicated in the recipe. You can always replace it with something similar.

Here is some advice on how to store what you have bought:

Meat, fowl, and game purchased ahead of time should be wrapped tightly in plastic wrap to prevent its picking up off odors in the refrigerator. To prevent spoilage, do not buy longer than forty-eight hours before using.

Fish, especially fillets prepared by your fishmonger, should be stored flat; if you bend them, the skin may break. As with meat, wrap tightly in plastic wrap and store in the lower part of the refrigerator for no longer than twenty-four hours.

Shellfish should be alive when they are prepared. Buy them fresh the day you intend to use them. Oysters can be wrapped tightly in newspaper and kept for two days in the bottom of the refrigerator, but do not store below 50 degrees F.

Fruits and vegetables absolutely should be kept in the refrigerator drawer designed for that purpose. They don't need too much refrigeration, and they must be kept away from any ventilation that could dehydrate them. Furthermore, it is essential that their odor (particularly that of melons) not spread to the rest of the refrigerator. It is also important to put only clean vegetables in the refrigerator, and not to leave them there longer than two or three days.

Cheeses should not be bought too far in advance. If you buy from a qualified cheese merchant, ask him or her to give you fully matured cheeses that are ready to be eaten. Leave each of them wrapped in its original paper, or wrap them individually in plastic and store in the bottom of the refrigerator.

Take the cheeses out about an hour before serving, but do not unwrap them. If you want to prepare your platter in advance, do so, but cover it with plastic wrap or with a slightly damp cloth.

To prevent running, which can oc-

King of the Charolais is the name of the butcher shop in Cannes.

cur with a Camembert, a Reblochon, or a Brie, cut out one-inch-high strips of wood or cardboard and place them against the cut sides of the cheese.

Milk products (butter, milk, cream, etc.) can easily pick up the odors from other foods. They should be carefully wrapped or well covered.

Wines should rest for at least two days (or even a week for older wines) after being transported; therefore, don't wait until the last minute to buy them. For advice on serving wines, see "Wine" on page 15.

Bread should be bought on the day of your meal. Note, however, that big country-style breads and uncut loaves freeze very well. Take them out of the freezer a good hour ahead of time.

If you forget to defrost them ahead of time, put them in a medium oven for ten minutes or, even better, in a microwave oven. (In this latter case you must be careful, because the bread will heat from the center toward the outside; three or four minutes is enough for a country-style loaf.)

Finally, when you do your shopping, don't forget those thousand-and-one details that add charm to a meal: candles, flowers, coffee, liqueurs, herb teas, cigars, menus, and gifts, depending on the occasion.

The Kitchen

A good saucepan or skillet doesn't make a good cook; but, obviously, good equipment and a good cooking area can only make things easier and help you cook in greater comfort.

The dream, of course, would be to have an enormous kitchen with all the room in the world to move around in, a room full of cupboards and a table for family meals or, better yet, a kitchen that is exposed to the sun so that your cooking could be all the more warm and authentic.

Unfortunately, architects and real estate developers tend too often to reduce kitchens to the size of a closet. Don't despair, however—you do not absolutely need a big kitchen to make great food.

It hardly matters whether the cooking range is gas or electric. As for the oven, an electric oven or a convection oven allows you to obtain precise temperatures and uniform heat. In addition, a microwave oven can be very useful. I have achieved some excellent results with them, but it's difficult to give exact advice about using them—each brand has its own specific characteristics, leading to variations in use and cooking time.

The sink, I think, should be a double unit, and I recommend stainless steel. But when it comes to work surfaces, I am a bit more choosy. There are numerous types of materials for work surfaces. Ceramic tiles and other hard materials are attractive and easy to maintain, but they don't absorb shocks and can break glasses and crockery. Furthermore, it isn't very comfortable to cut and chop on a board placed on these rigid surfaces. You can compensate by placing a folded cloth under the cutting board.

Stainless-steel work surfaces are very functional, but they must be thick (and thus expensive) and fitted into a wooden framework that assures their stability. The ideal, for me, remains a wooden work surface complemented by a marble board for making pastry.

Kitchen cupboards should be numerous and easily accessible. Designate a precise place for everything to avoid wasting your time. Above all, keep the cupboards clean; cleanliness is a chef's most important virtue.

A large refrigerator is indispensable. The ideal, in fact, is to have two, so as not to pile things on top of one another or to mix odors. "Ventilated" refrigerators are preferable. They guarantee better refrigeration and keep odors under better control. Ideally, there should be closed compartments for foods such as fish, vegetables, cheese, butter, milk products, and meat. The freezer must maintain a consistently cold temperature, without fluctuation.

Equipment

If you have an electric range, use pots and pans with very flat bottoms that permit good transference of heat.

For gas ranges, any type of saucepans or skillets will do, but choose thick-bottomed ones. I personally prefer a stainless-steel stockpot. Stainless-steel-lined copper or cast-iron saucepans generally give good results. Enameled cast-iron cookware must be heavy and thick, but be aware of the fragility of the enamel.

In general, avoid aluminum, which loses its shape, and which can give a disagreeable gray color to your sauces, creams, and other dishes.

Food mills and grinders are still sometimes quite useful, but nothing equals today's blenders and electric mixers with optional accessories. You should also have a food processor; it is indispensable for pâtés, mousses, and the preparation of pastries and sauces. Choose a machine with a powerful motor; some cut-rate machines wear out quickly, their accessories frequently need to be replaced, and they are generally incapable of mixing firm pastry or cutting foods that are somewhat hard.

Wine

Rest assured: I am not going to give you a treatise on oenology in the jargon of connoisseurs. Their language is usually incomprehensible to the uninitiated. What would you make, for example, of a wine with "a black cherry nose," "an animal nose," "a nose with its mouth still closed," or "a nose with a hint of underbrush"? What would you say to a Bordeaux with "thick, colored legs," "a good chew," "a bit of crushed black currant leaf"; or that is described as "somewhat plump," "very straightforward," or "an outright attack"?

All these expressions seem relatively impoverished for those who, like me, had the good fortune to know Jean-Baptiste Troisgros, father of the famous Troisgros brothers of Roanne. He was a marvelous man who spoke of wines with an extraordinary richness of language, essentially based on female anatomy. In the presence of women, however, his good breeding obliged him to change registers; on such occasions, with just as much energy and lyricism, he switched his metaphor to race horses. In either case, hearing him talk about wines was almost as great a pleasure as drinking them. Since I lack his talent, my ambition is more modest.

To know how to choose a wine to go with a particular dish, you won't necessarily have, as I do, a sommelier to help you. My sommelier, Patrice Lopez, has kindly agreed to share his expertise and has assisted me in preparing these few simple pieces of advice; it would take more than a book to talk about all the aspects of this noble domain.

How to Choose the Wine

In the introductions to the menus you will find suggestions on choosing a wine to go with each dish. Here I wish only to give some general advice on buying wine.

How to Read the Label

The label of a good wine should be modest and precise. Beware of those that are vague or make excessive claims. A good label should be absolutely precise on four fundamental points:

1. *The appellation*. Quality French wines are classified AOC (Appellation d'Origine Contrôlée) or VDQS (Vins Délimités de Qualité Supérieure).

2. *The year*. In general, bottles of AOC or VDQS wine are marked with the vintage. If one of them is not, it is because the vintage is undistin-

guished—although the wine may nevertheless be good. Champagne is an exception to this rule. Aside from exceptional years, Champagne is composed of a mixture of vintages.

3. *Bottled at the château.* This usually is an indication of quality.

4. *The name of the proprietor.* The name of the proprietor, or at least of the wine merchant, should always appear on the label. By laying his reputation on the line, the proprietor guarantees the quality of his wine.

*Additional
Notes*

Labels of AOC and VDQS never carry information on alcohol content, unless intended for export.

When a label refers to a region without identifying the vineyard (for example: Bordeaux, Appellation Bordeaux Contrôlée), it is a mixture that is often very good.

The labels of the great Burgundy and Bordeaux wines always carry the name of their region. For Bordeaux, for example, Saint-Estèphe, Saint-Emilion, Margaux, Pomerol, Pauillac; for Burgundy, Côte-de-Nuits, Pommard, Côte-de-Beaune, Mercurey, Chablis.

It is thus the regions and the designation of the *côteaux* which provide the *appellation* and ownership of the wine, while the names of the *châteaux* or the *domaines* provide the classification.

In fact, within a given *appellation*, the designation of the vintner further distinguishes among the products of neighboring vineyards. Also, wine from merchants whose labels refer to a particular domain or château offers assurances of quality.

As a general rule, the designation "Château" was traditionally applied only to Bordeaux wines. However, this designation is increasingly used for wines of other regions.

The Good Years

Not all wines age in the same fashion, and a wine from the same vineyard will age differently according to its year of origin, the conditions under which it has been kept, and so on.

One fifty-year-old wine may be sublime, and another of the same age perfectly insipid; one year will be remarkable for the wines of one vineyard and mediocre for another vineyard only ten miles away. It is thus impossible to establish absolute, universally reliable rules. The indications in the table below refer only to general tendencies, subject to numerous exceptions.

*Good Years
for French
Wine*

Good*
Excellent**
Exceptional***

ALSACE			1962**	1971**	1978*
			1964**	1973**	1979**
1928**	1945***	1953**	1966**	1974*	1981**
1929***	1947***	1955**	1967*	1975**	1982*
1934**	1948*	1959**	1969**	1976**	
1937*	1949**	1960***	1970*	1977*	

Even though they are not from the same region, Roquefort and Hermitage marry well.

BEAUJOLAIS

Villages or Nouveau are consumed only in the months that follow the harvest.

Chiroubles, Juliénas, Morgon, etc.:

1928**	1929***	1934**

1937**	1962**	1974*
1945**	1964**	1976**
1947**	1966**	1978**
1949**	1967**	1979*
1953**	1969**	1981**
1955**	1970**	1982*
1959**	1971**	
1961***	1973*	

BORDEAUX

Dry whites (Graves) usually keep for only 2 to 3 years.

Sweet whites (Sauternes):

1928**	1934**	1945***
1929***	1937***	1947**

1948**	1966**	1975***
1949**	1967***	1976**
1953**	1969*	1977*
1955**	1970**	1978**
1959**	1971**	1979**
1961***	1972*	1980*
1962**	1973*	1981**
1964*	1974*	1982*

Reds:

1928***	1945***	1953***
1929***	1947***	1955**
1934**	1948**	1959**
1937*	1949***	1961***

1962**	1971**	1978**
1964**	1973*	1979**
1966***	1974*	1980*
1967*	1975***	1981**
1969*	1976**	1982***
1970***	1977*	

BURGUNDIES

Whites:

1928**	1937*	1949**
1929***	1945*	1953**
1934**	1947**	1955**

1959**	1970**	1978**
1961**	1971**	1979**
1962**	1973**	1980*
1964**	1974*	1981**
1966**	1975*	1982**
1967*	1976**	
1969**	1977*	

Reds:

1928**	1937**	1948*
1929***	1945***	1949***
1934***	1947**	1953*

1955**	1966**	1974*
1959**	1969***	1976**
1961***	1971***	1977*
1962*	1972**	1978***
1964**	1973*	1979**

CHAMPAGNE

1928***	1947***	1959**
1929***	1948*	1960***
1934**	1949**	1962**
1937*	1953**	1964**
1945***	1955**	1966**

1967*	1974*	1979**
1969**	1975**	1981**
1970*	1976**	1982*
1971**	1977*	
1973**	1978*	

The grape cluster is heavy for this little vintner.

CÔTES-DU-RHÔNE
Whites and rosés usually keep for only 2 to 3 years.

Reds:

1928**	1934**	1945**	1949**	1967**	1976**
1929***	1937*	1947**	1953*	1969**	1977*
			1955**	1970**	1978**
			1959*	1971**	1979**
			1961**	1972**	1980*
			1962**	1973*	1981*
			1964**	1974*	1982*
			1966**	1975*	

LOIRE
Dry whites usually keep for only 2 to 3 years. Whites and sweet rosés keep for several years.

Reds:

1928*	1934**	1945**	1948*	1967*	1978**
1929**	1937**	1947***	1949**	1969**	1979*
			1953**	1970*	1980*
			1955**	1971**	1981**
			1959**	1973**	1982*
			1961**	1974*	
			1962*	1975*	
			1964**	1976**	
			1966*	1977*	

How to Store Wine

In former times, the Greeks and Romans stored their wines in goatskins that still smelled of goat, or in amphorae that were oiled to make them less porous, and then stopped up with cloth steeped in tar. In both cases, the wine aged badly and took on a distinct (to put it mildly) flavor, which was disguised as much as possible with honey, spices, or resin (this was the origin of resinated wine). The wines of antiquity no doubt would have been undrinkable for a modern palate.

The Gauls' invention of the wine barrel changed everything as far as taste was concerned, but little in terms of aging. It was only when the industrial method of bottle-making was discovered (at the end of the eighteenth century) that the size of bottle necks and thus of corks could be standardized. It was thanks to these corks, which let the wine breathe without oxidizing too rapidly, that it was finally possible to conserve wine for long periods of time.

The Bottle

There are five classic French wine bottle types: Bordeaux, Burgundy, Champagne, Alsace, Jura. The capacity of the bottles must, by law, be indicated on their labels. The sizes commonly used are the bottle (750 ml) and the magnum (1.5 l). There are also smaller half-bottles and others with larger capacities, but they aren't often used for the best wines.

Whatever the size of the bottle, the form of the cork is always basically the same. The cork acts as the lungs of the wine; it must breathe just enough—but not too much. This means that in a half-bottle, the wine will breathe a great deal and consequently age quickly; in an oversize bottle, it won't breathe enough and will take many years to age properly.

For the same reason, screw tops or plastic stoppers prevent a wine from breathing and "strangle" it. On the other hand, a porous cork causes excessively rapid aging. That's why a bottle must always lie flat, so that the wine remains in contact with the cork and prevents it from drying out.

The Cellar

Its essential quality is a constant temperature, but not necessarily a very cold one (53 to 54 degrees F). It should be neither too humid nor too dry. It should be dark; avoid neon or strong lighting. No heating pipes should run through it. It should also not be shaken by vibrations (from a nearby street, a garage, a motor, etc.). Keep out of your cellar any foods with a strong odor, such as cheese, melons, mushrooms, or fruits.

The coldest spots (the lower shelves) should be reserved for the whites, which are more delicate. The bottles should lie flat, but so that you can read their labels without having to move them. If your bottles are covered with dust, don't wipe it off until just before serving. This dust protects the wine from light.

If you keep wines for several years, be sure to write out a "table of years" in which the number of bottles for each origin and year is recorded. In this way you can verify how much longer they can be kept or if they need to be consumed immediately.

If you hope to keep bottled wine longer than twenty years, you should ask your supplier to change the corks, which gradually weaken and become porous.

If you do not have space for a wine cellar, you can buy an "apartment cellar." These are storage devices that duplicate, within a small space, the characteristics of a wine cellar. In fact, any dark and thermally isolated space will do.

Average Time for Storing Wine

REGION	WHEN DRINKABLE	REGION	WHEN DRINKABLE
ALSACE	1-8 years Sometimes age remarkably well	CHAMPAGNE	3-5 years Rarely more than 10 years
BEAUJOLAIS		CÔTES-DU-RHÔNE	
Villages or Nouveau	November to April	Whites and rosés	2-6 years
Chiroubles, Juliénas, Morgon, etc.	2-6 years	Reds	2-10 years and up
		LOIRE	
BORDEAUX		Dry whites	1-3 years
Dry whites	1-3 years	Sweet whites	2-10 years
Sweet whites	2-50 years and up	Rosés	2-5 years
		Reds	2-8 years and up
Reds	3-50 years and up	PROVENCE	
		Whites and rosés	1-3 years
BURGUNDIES			
Whites	2-6 years Often age well	Reds	2-8 years Can age even longer
Reds	2-50 years and up		

How to Serve Wine

First of all, be careful to buy or transport your bottles of wine several days before opening them. You have in effect shaken them up, and you must allow time for the sediment to resettle. Cold can speed up the process, but a natural settling is preferable.

Bottle or Carafe?

Wine can be served in a carafe when there hasn't been time to open the bottle long enough beforehand and you want to let it breathe. (This applies to wines more than ten years old.) In most cases, a carafe is used when a wine with heavy sediment needs to be decanted. In such a case, the wine is poured gently from the bottle into the carafe, in front of a light source (a candle, traditionally) so that you can stop pouring the moment you detect any sediment.

When should the bottle be opened? For well-versed oenologists, that depends on the wine, the vintage, etc. To simplify, let's say that white wines should be opened just before serving—except for certain old, oxidized sweet wines which benefit from being opened three or four hours in advance.

For the reds: young wines should have time to breathe, and should thus be opened one or two hours in advance; older wines shouldn't be opened until thirty minutes to an hour before serving, while very old wines should be opened and decanted at the beginning of the meal.

In any case, you must always open a bottle and taste it before the meal, if only to check that the wine is not corked—i.e., infused with the taste and odor of the cork. If that happens, don't throw out the wine. Keep it for making a sauce or vinegar. If the wine tastes only slightly of cork, decant it. With a little luck, oxygenation will get rid of the taste.

The wine basket. When a wine has been lying flat for several years, you must not stand it up. It's prudent, therefore, to place it in a wine basket (in the same position it occupied in the wine cellar) and open it only at this inclined angle.

The corkscrew. Good wines have very long corks. The corkscrew should therefore have a long, wide, threaded screw, which should be driven in as far as possible. It should be extracted gently and gradually. Souvenir-type models should always be avoided. The best corkscrew is still the good old "sommelier" type, which allows you to open a bottle in an inclined position.

Whatever you do, don't hold the

Patrice Lopez, a young but talented **sommelier.**

The proper glass complements the wine.

bottle between your knees to open it—unless the wine is really very young and without sediment.

If you notice that a cork is leaking, open the bottle as soon as possible and drink the wine; otherwise it is in danger of oxygenating too quickly.

With Champagne, never pop the cork loudly. Hold the bottle at an angle, pull out the cork gently, and hold it when it is about to pop. No foam will overflow, as long as the Champagne is cold enough and has not been shaken beforehand.

Wine Glasses

The primary function of the glass is to bring out the best in the wine—not to ornament the table. As in many areas, simplicity is a virtue here, and elaborate glasses should generally be avoided.

Color. The first pleasure of wine drinking is to see the color of the wine; therefore, a wine glass should be transparent and colorless.

Fineness. Like its color, the glass itself should be forgotten in favor of the wine. The fineness of the edges and the

stem enhance the pleasure of wine drinking.

Shape. The second pleasure of wine drinking is to smell the wine. Thus the shape of the glass should be designed to augment the wine's bouquet. Its mouth should be more or less large depending on whether the wine is more or less heady. That is why Burgundy glasses are wider than Bordeaux glasses. The glass should be large enough—and filled only to a third of its capacity—for the wine to be swirled around in it in order to breathe. The stem is indispensable for the same reason.

The major shapes for glasses are:

The tulip glass. This is the traditional Bordeaux glass. However, it is suitable for all wines and is used more and more for Champagne, in which case it is given a more elongated form.

The thistle glass. With its tapering mouth, this glass is particularly suitable for red wines with a subtle bouquet.

The balloon glass. This is the traditional glass for Burgundy and, in general, for all heady wines.

The flute and the goblet glass. Both of these have been abandoned by connoisseurs. In the first, the bubbles rise so quickly that there is practically nothing left to drink; in the second, the Champagne goes flat too quickly.

The Alsatian wine glass. Undoubtedly of Hungarian origin, like the vines of this region, the Alsatian glass is generally tinted green.

The Serving Temperature of Wines

Below 41 degrees F, you might as well drink anything at all; above 65 degrees F, you might as well drink punch! Wine hates extremes of temperature. It also does not react well to sudden changes of temperature. To cool or warm it, you must act gently so as not to "break" the wine.

How to cool wine. The wine cellar is the ideal place, but the temperature there rarely goes below 50 degrees F. To obtain a lower temperature, it's best to use an ice bucket. First put in the bottle, then some water, and only then the ice cubes, so as to guarantee a gradual cooling. The refrigerator is not the ideal place to chill wine because it functions in fits and starts. You can, however, use the lowest (i.e., the least cold) shelf.

How to bring the wine to room temperature. Bringing a wine to room temperature means placing the bottle in the room where it will be drunk and leaving it there long enough for it to warm to the surrounding temperature. Because it is gradual, this is obviously the ideal method. Unfortunately, 60 degrees F is nowadays considered cold for a room, and bringing a wine up to a temperature higher than 68 degrees F would subject it to excessive heat. If you have no room with the ideal temperature for wine drinking or if you want to rapidly warm a wine that's too cold, wrap it in a cloth soaked in lukewarm water. In any event, be careful not to place a bottle near a source of heat such as a radiator or chimney.

A good Champagne should be served chilled but not ice cold.

Serving Temperatures for French Wines

ALSACE	chilled to 46° to 50°
BEAUJOLAIS	
Villages or Nouveau	chilled to 40° to 50° F
Chiroubles, Juliénas, Morgon, etc.	close to room temperature, 54° to 59° F
BORDEAUX	
Dry whites	very cold, 42° to 46° F
Sweet whites	iced, 41° to 42° F
Reds	room temperature, 62° to 65° F
BURGUNDIES	
Whites	fairly cold, 53° to 55° F
Reds	nearly at room temperature, 57° to 59° F

CHAMPAGNE	chilled, 46° to 50° F
CÔTES-DU-RHÔNE	
Whites and rosés	very cold, 42° to 46° F
Reds	room temperature, 61° to 63° F
LOIRE	
Dry whites and rosés	very cold, 42° to 46° F
Sweet whites	iced, 41° to 42° F
Reds	nearly room temperature, 54° to 59° F
PROVENCE	
Whites and rosés	very cold, 42° to 46° F
Reds	room temperature, 62° to 65° F

Which Wine to Drink with Which Dish

First of all, I would like to discuss what you should drink before the meal. For the menus in this book, I suggest wine-based apéritifs—or, more simply, wines and Champagnes—rather than cocktails and hard liquor. An apéritif should prepare your palate to appreciate the results of your culinary talents, not anaesthetize your taste buds.

As for which wine to serve with which dish, no subject is more controversial; tastes change, fashions come and go, and there are, in this domain, no absolute truths. To every rule there is a famous exception. Every hard-and-fast premise is debatable, and nowadays the greatest connoisseurs risk combinations that are odd, amusing, and often successful.

However, since some advice is called for, here are a few very general recommendations:

Preferably serve: white before red; light before robust; young before old. For dishes served in a sauce, drink the same wine that was used in the preparation of the sauce, or at least a wine of the same type.

Absolutely avoid: sweet white wines with red meat or game; fine red wines with shellfish or dishes rich in garlic; any wine with a vinaigrette recipe, with creamy cheeses, with chocolate, and with acidic cold fruits.

Soup. Traditionally no wine is served with soup, although a dry white wine can accompany a fish soup. With other soups, it's best to serve the wine that will accompany the following dish.

If you decide to follow the "*Chabrot*" method—a practice in country cooking that consists of adding a large glassful of red wine to your soup when you are half finished (on condition, naturally, that the soup contains no cream)—choose a solid red such as a Cahors.

Charcuterie. See "White meats."

Raw shellfish. Dry white wines such as Chablis, Muscadet, Pouilly-Fumé, Pouilly-Fuissé, Sancerre, St. Véran, Alsace, or a dry rosé.

Cooked shellfish, fish, crustaceans. In a sauce: the same wine as for the sauce. Cold or grilled: dry whites such as Graves, Chassagne-Montrachet, Puligny, Meursault, or Hermitage.

Pâtés. At the beginning of a meal: white Bordeaux (Graves), Alsace, dry Champagne. During a meal: relatively light red wines. The most refined hosts serve a Sauternes, a Barsac, or a white Vouvray with the foie gras of Landes; with Alsatian foie gras, a Gewürztraminer.

Mushrooms and truffles. Fine red wines or dry Champagne; rosé for chanterelles (girolles) and meadow mushrooms.

Poultry. In a sauce: the same wine as for the sauce—a dry white or a fairly rich red. Roast chicken: smooth red wines. Goose, turkey, guinea fowl: robust red wines.

White meats, charcuterie. In general, light red wines (Beaujolais, Mâcon, Côteaux-de-Provence, Côteaux d'Aix, Bourgeuil, etc.). With a brown sauce,

serve somewhat more robust reds (young Bordeaux, Côte-de-Beaune, young Côtes-du-Rhône, etc.).

Red meat and game. Robust reds—Burgundies, Côtes-du-Rhône, Bordeaux more than ten years old, Cahors, Madirant, Côtes-de-Buzet, etc.

Cheese. The best and simplest rule is not to choose the wine to go with the cheese, but on the contrary to select a cheese that suits the wine served with the preceding dish. You can thus avoid errors such as "white after red" and "young after old."

Cold cheeses: dry whites or rosés. Soft cheeses (Camembert, Brie, etc.): robust reds. Pressed cheeses (Port Salut, Cantal, etc.): light, fruity or dry wines. Sliced pressed cheeses (Comté, Gruyère, etc.): robust whites or reds. Goat cheeses and parslied cheeses (Roquefort, Bleu, etc.): dry whites or light reds.

But try these combinations as well: Roquefort and Sauternes; goat cheese and a fairly young white Burgundy.

Sweets and desserts. They rarely go well with wine. You can, however, drink sweet white wines, dry or semi-dry Champagne, or sparkling wines.

Pastry. Sweet white wines, naturally sweet wines.

Fruits. Never serve with wine—except for dried fruits, which actually bring out the qualities of a wine.

Cheese

France is privileged to produce some 300 to 400 varieties of cheese. And—an even greater privilege—it offers *farm* cheeses with a fresh milk base. These cheeses are living foods that evolve, mature, and ripen like fruit. To make them requires a great deal of knowledge and love on the part of both the farmer and the person who oversees the maturing process.

Dairy cheeses, on the other hand, are based on cooked or pasteurized milk, and their taste is determined once and for all the moment they leave the factory. These are inert cheeses whose quality can only go down.

A cheese should not be bought as if it were a package of salt or sugar. Only a qualified cheese merchant will be able to advise you and above all to sell you a perfectly mature cheese.

In my opinion, cheese should be served with bread (toasted country-style bread or bread with nuts or raisins) rather than with crackers or biscuits. It can be eaten with a salad (as long as it isn't too vinegary), as well as with certain fruits and nuts, such as apples, pears, grapes, and walnuts.

Above all, be sure that your friends' glasses are kept full, because nothing goes better with cheese than wine. It is a well-established tradition in France to say, "I think I'll have a little cheese to finish my wine." As a general rule, this leads to the opening of another bottle of wine, to finish the cheese.

Undeniably, cheese often reveals the quality of a wine. While a great wine has no need of such assistance, certain others, mediocre when paired with other foods, suddenly become marvelous with a cheese. For that matter, you should avoid eating cheese when tasting a wine you're interested in buying; you run the risk of being very disappointed when you drink it under other circumstances.

It's not necessary to serve cheese with each menu, nor to offer a large variety. You should rather prepare a platter of two or three cheeses chosen according to season and region. You can even select only one cheese: for example, a quarter of Brie, a Tomme, a slice of Roquefort (which is the only cheese served with butter), a Swiss Vacherin, a slice of Comté or Saint-Nec-

Selecting cheeses with my good friends Robert and Edouard Ceneri from La Ferme Savoyarde in Cannes.

taire. You can also offer a platter of small goat cheeses. Before arranging the cheeses on the platter, spread out a few fern branches, vine leaves, chestnut leaves, or fig leaves. Under the goat cheese you might also put some sprigs of savory, rosemary, or thyme.

You should also consider treating yourself and your friends to a meal consisting solely of cheeses. You can serve them with a crisp mixed green salad, dressed with wine vinegar and olive oil for goat cheeses and with walnut oil for somewhat stronger cheeses.

Serve the cheeses with large slices of toasted country-style bread and hot baked potatoes. You can also add a few walnuts, apples, pears, or grapes. Remember to have a block of fresh butter on hand, and above all don't forget to have a pepper mill nearby or even some strong Dijon mustard, which in my opinion goes very well with a Comté, a Gruyère, or an Emmenthal. Finally, there should be ample quantities of Beaujolais Villages, Bourgeuil, or Chinon.

There's no need for an elaborate table dressing. A corner by the fireside or the shade of an arbor will do nicely. You can also forget about dessert; it's good to leave the table with the taste of cheese still in your mouth.

Cheese Guide

CHEESE	BEST SEASON	WINES
Bleu d'Auvergne	All year	Hermitage
Bleu de Bresse	All year	Beaujolais
Boursault	All year	Clos Vougeot
Bouton de culotte	May–December	Chablis
Brie de Meaux	June–December	Médoc, Pomerol
Brillat-Savarin	All year	Slightly fruity wine
Camembert fermier	May–November	Burgundy, Bordeaux
Camembert normand	All year	Côtes-du-Rhône
Cantal	All year	Côtes-d'Auvergne
Chabichou	May–November	Bourgeuil
Fresh chèvre	May–October	White Saumur
Comté	All year	Arbois jaune
Coulommiers	June–March	Côte-de-Beaune
Crottin de Chavignol	May–October	White Sancerre, Sauvignon Blanc
Emmanthal	All year	Beaune, Volnay
Forme d'Ambert	June–December	Cotes-d'Auvergne
Livarot	May–December	Morgon
Maroilles	June–March	Corton
Mimolette	All year	Madeira, Port, Banyuls
Munster	All year	Gewürztraminer
Olivet cendré	June–March	Chinon
Pont-l'Evêque	June–March	Bouzy, Pommerol

CHEESE	BEST SEASON	WINES
Reblochon	June-December	Crépy-Mondeuse
Rigotte de Condrieu	All year	Côtes-du-Lyonnais
Rocamadour	March-November	Cahors
Roquefort	March-December	Cháteauneuf-du-Pape
Sainte-Maure	June-December	Dry Vouvray
Saint-Marcellin	All year	Côtes-du-Rhône
Saint-Nectaire	June-December	Côtes-d'Auvergne
Selles-sur-Chèr	May-December	Chinon, Bourgeuil
Tomme de Savoie	May-December	Mondeuse
Vacherin	November-March	Moussette
Valençay	May-December	Quincy

Coffee

The moment for drinking coffee represents the pleasant prolongation of a successful dinner. Never neglect it, and always offer it along with its natural companions: brandy, liqueurs, cigars, and chocolate.

It's a good idea to arrange everything on platters in advance: cups, saucers, spoons, coffeepot, cream, small napkins, sugar bowl. On another platter, arrange the liqueur glasses and the bottles. Always keep the white liquors and their glasses in the refrigerator until the last moment. (When you open a bottle of spirits for the first time, it should be allowed to air for several hours before drinking, in order to dissipate the ethers that can make the eyes sting.) Also prepare the cigar box, the cigar cutter, and the matches.

Everything will thus be ready in advance. But never the coffee! That absolutely must be left until the last moment, in order to preserve its

Coffee and chocolate, a pleasant blending of flavors after dinner.

aroma. And don't forget to rinse the coffeepot with boiling water before filling it with coffee.

Now let me give you a few recipes:

Café Brûlot

Servings: 6

2 cups very strong coffee
½ cinnamon stick
6 cloves
 Zest of 1 orange cut into thin strips

 Zest of 1 lemon cut into thin strips
3 sugar cubes
½ cup fine Cognac
2 tablespoons Curaçao

Make the coffee very black and very strong.

In a small saucepan (or a *plat brûlot*), crush with a ladle the cinnamon, the cloves, the orange and lemon zests, and the sugar cubes. Add the Cognac and the Curaçao and mix everything together.

Flambé the mixture. Stir the ingredients while they are afire, until the sugar is completely dissolved. Add the coffee gradually, while continuing to stir until the flame subsides.

This café brûlot was made famous by Brennan's Restaurant in New Orleans, and it was from the founder's grandson (who spent three months in my kitchens at Moulin de Mougins) that I learned the secret of this preparation.

Café Royal

Servings: *1*

 Superfine sugar
3 strips of lemon zest
½ cup coffee

½ cinnamon stick
4 good tablespoons of Cognac

Spread a layer of superfine sugar over a dessert plate. Rub the inner side of a strip of lemon zest over the rim of a thick-stemmed glass. Turn the glass upside down in the sugar; the sugar will adhere to the moisture left by the lemon.

Squeeze the other strips of lemon zest into the glass and drop the strips in the bottom of the glass.

Place a spoon in the glass to prevent it from cracking because of heat.

Carefully heat the Cognac in a small ladle placed over a flame, then pour it into the glass. Ignite it and flambé.

When the flame subsides, pour in the hot coffee and serve.

All the ingredients for Café Brûlot, a mixture of bitter and sweet. (The cup was designed by Raoul Dufy in 1921.)

Irish Coffee

Servings: *1*

1 cup strong coffee
2 sugar cubes

2 to 3 tablespoons Irish whiskey
Heavy cream

Make the coffee very black and very strong.

Put the sugar cubes in the bottom of a thick-stemmed glass. Fill the glass with hot coffee, leaving ½ inch between the coffee and the rim of the glass.

Add the Irish whiskey and stir. (Do not confuse whiskey and whisky. The first is Irish, the second Scottish.)

Top it with lightly whipped cream, poured delicately over the back of a spoon so that it remains on top of the coffee without blending in.

Café Bistouille

Servings: *1*

1 sugar cube
  Pinch of ground cinnamon
2 tablespoons Marc, Grappa, or

  Calvados
1 cup coffee

Make the coffee.

Put the sugar cube and cinnamon in a coffee cup. Add the Marc and fill with hot coffee. Serve very hot.

To conclude the topic of coffee, liquor, and chocolate, I would like to undertake a small defense of private pleasure.

I sometimes indulge in a small, intimate ceremony, which I have no desire to share with anyone. At birthdays and at year's end I often receive a few very special bottles, some succulent chocolates, and some lovely *marrons glacés*. I choose an evening when I know I won't be busy the next morning....

Now, follow me closely. The first thing to do is to change into comfortable clothes: pajamas, dressing gown, or some other night wear.

Act Two: Settle by the fire with a bottle of Armagnac that is at least fifteen years old and a box of chocolates—but not those chocolates that contain more sugar than cocoa, nor chocolates with liquor or fruit or, in general, anything at all. No! Just good, true, pure chocolate, black and bitter.

To go with the Armagnac and the chocolate, you can also open a box of *marrons glacés*—the ones that are covered in candy sugar as if frosted. And above all, don't be stingy about the size of the box!

Perfect. So there you are: the fire is burning, your attire is comfortable, the armchair is deep. . . .

Without further delay, let the celebration begin. First, a chocolate in the mouth, then a *marron glacé*, then a generous glassful of Armagnac. Let's close our eyes and chew slowly, slowly, slowly. . . .

At that point, if you don't have utterly insensitive taste buds, only one thing in the world will matter to you: to begin again as quickly as possible, and again and again . . . until the amount of Armagnac in the bottle has seriously decreased.

And afterwards? Taste for a moment more the sweet sense of well-being that has overtaken you . . . and prudently take yourself off to bed. There, once again, you will realize how good it is (for a while at least) to be alone. For on this evening you are surely not the ideal bed companion, and you won't be able to share with anyone the sweet dreams you're already having.

But don't repeat the ceremony until next Christmas. It's unforgettable—but wearing.

Flowers

How sad life would be without flowers! What scents and beauty we would lack. To sit at a table decorated with flowers is one of the first pleasures of a

My wife, Denise, arranges flowers for our two restaurants in Mougins.

good meal, in addition to the quality of the dishes, the delicacy of the glasses, the texture of the silverware, the crispness of the table linen.

Flower arrangement is a very personal form of expression—similar to cooking. Don't both arts have the same supplier—the sun? And the same products as well? Because a floral decoration is not necessarily made only of flowers. My wife, Denise, who so beautifully arranges the decoration of our two restaurants, the Moulin de Mougins and l'Amandier, sometimes blends together fruits, plants, and vegetables. Even the harmony of a leafless branch can provide the basis for a table arrangement.

Sprigs of aromatic plants like pink-flowering thyme, blue rosemary, and white savory, together or separately, not only make a pretty bouquet but perfume the table. You can also use bay laurel for its glossy leaves, velvety sage, mint, basil with its warm aroma, tarragon with its creeping leafage, as well as olive branches, branches of fruit trees (with, if possible, their flowers or their fruit), verbena, creeping ivy, oak with its acorns, chestnut with its burrs, and so many others.

As in cooking, let your imagination and your feelings guide you. Give the bouquet something of yourself.

Here is some advice that may help to guide you:

Avoid flowers with too heady an aroma, such as tuberoses, unless the ta-

ble is large enough so that the bouquet isn't right under the noses of your guests.

The bouquet should not overshadow the food. Flowers are only a decorative element. Your guests are there to enjoy a meal, not to admire a floral display.

Avoid bouquets that are too large and too high; they can transform conversations into games of hide-and-seek and give people a stiff neck.

On the other hand, tall narrow fluted vases will allow your guests to see each other across the table, even if the bouquets themselves are large.

Try to harmonize the colors of the flowers with those of the tablecloth and the plates, as well as with the theme of your dinner. If you want a springlike atmosphere, choose wildflowers over a bouquet of roses.

The bouquet should be easy to move, in case you want, for example, to place a spectacular dish or the dessert in the center of the table.

It isn't always necessary to place the flowers directly on the table. If the table is too small, you can put the bouquet on a sideboard or a nearby piece of furniture. You can also place a single flower on the tablecloth in front of each guest, or on the napkin.

Complete your floral decoration with candles of the same color. Their illumination gives the softest possible light and makes glances softer as well.

Children in the Kitchen

Don't chase your children out of the kitchen when you set to work on your recipes. They can often give you excellent advice.

My little Cordelia, who is six, loves to make pastry. She's already told me that she wants to be a pastry chef. One

day when she was making some little sugared pastry tarts, the pastry having been shaped beforehand in little molds, I noticed her spreading honey on the bottom of each mold and then sprinkling it with sugar. When I asked her why she had put the honey in beforehand, she replied very simply, as if astonished at my ignorance: "It's to hold the sugar." Logical, isn't it?

In the old days, when family traditions and recipes were passed from generation to generation, every young girl grew up knowing how to make a soup, an omelette, a tarte, and so many other wonderful things. Although I never was a young girl, I owe my vocation as chef to this same tradition, and to my Aunt Celestine. She bought me, for my fifth birthday, a little wooden bench on which I hoisted myself up to see what was simmering in the saucepans. I didn't help her much, of course, and I probably even got in her way a bit, but she knew that in this way she would open my mind and lead me to discover the marvelous world of cooking.

So give your children small tasks in the kitchen that will make them proud to help you today, and will make them happy adults tomorrow.

Cordelia has already developed a sure hand with pastry.

Menu for 6 People

Les Herbes de Provence

The Herbs of Provence

Difficulty:
Moderately easy
Cost: *Moderate*

La Soupe à la Farigoulette
Artichoke Soup with Wild Thyme

La Fricassée de Moules au Fenouil
Mussels and Fennel in Saffron Cream Sauce

Les Côtes de Veau à l'Anis et aux Pions d'Ail
Veal Medallions with Anise and Garlic

La Glace à la Lavande avec les Petits Pains d'Anis
Lavender-Scented Ice Cream with Anise Cookies

Although my wife, Denise, has a veritable passion for flowers, I personally am more attracted to aromatic plants: thyme, savory, rosemary, sage, mint, marjoram, oregano, laurel, basil, coriander, fennel. . . . In fact, when I stroll through the countryside of Provence, I often cut a few sprigs of herbs—rosemary, wild thyme, or lavender—and put them in my pocket. When I take my hand out of my pocket, it is steeped in the smells of my beautiful countryside.

I also love to use the herbs of Provence in my cooking, of course, as well as the leaves of the olive tree and the young leaves of the fig tree. I'm not about to disclose all of my chef's secrets, but the next time you roast a beautiful chicken in a heavy iron pot, first let it brown well as usual, then cover it with tender fig leaves. Close the lid to finish the roasting . . . and you'll see the difference.

Doing the Marketing

Order the veal in advance, asking for 3 double-thick chops, weighing about 1 pound each. Ask the butcher to remove the bones and trim off the fat. The mussels can be purchased a day ahead and stored in the vegetable bin of your refrigerator. (If they're stored higher, the cold will kill them.) Be sure to choose mussels that have not opened.

What to Drink

For an apéritif, you can serve a sweet white wine (Sauternes-type) flavored with 1½ tablespoons of Campari per glass and garnished with an almond. In Provence I might serve a *vin d'orange*, an apéritif made with wine infused with orange. Here is the recipe:

In a large glass jar, place 3 bitter oranges, washed and cut into quarters. Add 10 peppercorns, 1 stick of vanilla, half a stick of cinnamon, 1 bottle of red or rosé wine, and 1 cup of Cognac. Steep for 20 days in a cool, dark place (but not in the refrigerator). After that

An apéritif in Roquefort-les-Pins.

time, add ½ pound of sugar in cubes and let stand another 10 days. You can now filter the wine and bottle it. It will keep for a long time, and should be served at room temperature.

For the wines, choose a Provençal white such as a Cassis or an Hermitage to serve with the mussels. With the veal, serve a well-structured red such as a Côteau d'Aix or a Côtes-du-Rhône.

Table Linens and Decoration

There's nothing more typical of Provence or prettier than the table linens of Soleïado, which would be ideal for this menu. Fold the napkins into cone shapes and lean the menus against them.

For the menus, use sturdy, bright paper that picks up the dominant color of your table and embellish them, if you choose, by cutting a small slit in the corner of each to hold a sprig of lavender.

The centerpiece should remain simple since the dishes and linens are very colorful. A bunch of lavender would be perfect. You can also arrange candles in small handkerchiefs filled with sand, coarse salt, or gravel and tie them with ribbons.

Tableware

To carry out the Provençal theme, choose brightly decorated plates in the style of Moustiers, the colorful faience of the South of France:

overleaf: *At the home of my friend César, the famous sculptor.*

1	large soup tureen			shells
1	large, deep serving platter for the mussels		6	dinner plates for the veal
12	soup plates for the soup and the mussels		6	small bowls for the ice cream
3	large bowls for the mussel		6	dessert plates
			6	paper doilies
			1	glass plate for the anise cookies

Silverware

12	soup spoons		6	dessert or ice cream spoons
6	dinner knives and forks		2	serving ladles
6	finger bowls for the mussels			

Glassware

18 goblets for water, white wine, and red wine

Getting Organized

Many things in this menu can be prepared in advance. They are indicated in each recipe with the symbol ✳✳✳. The symbol ✳✳ indicates those tasks that must be done just before serving.

Put the white wine in the refrigerator to chill several hours in advance.

About 20 minutes before serving, remove the ice cream from the freezer, scoop into the serving bowls, and place in the refrigerator until time to serve.

Fifteen minutes before sitting down to eat, preheat the oven to 400 degrees F. Warm 12 soup bowls and 6 dinner plates over a casserole of warm water or on the back of the stove.

Five minutes before serving, reheat the soup and place the mussels, covered with aluminum foil, and the veal in the oven to warm.

After serving the soup, you will need 10 minutes to prepare the sauce for the mussels. Just before serving them, remove the veal from the oven and keep it warm while eating the mussels.

Finishing the sauce for the veal will take about 5 minutes. As for the dessert, just remove it from the refrigerator and serve with the anise cookies.

La Soupe à la Farigoulette

ARTICHOKE SOUP WITH WILD THYME

Time required: *1 hour*
advance preparation
10 minutes reheating just before serving
Difficulty: *Very easy*
Cost: *Inexpensive*

Ingredients

2	large artichokes or 5 small purple artichokes		¼	cup plus 1 tablespoon virgin olive oil
	Salt		4	cups water
1	large onion		¼	cup short-grain rice

1 bunch flat-leaf or Italian parsley, tied together with a string
1 small bunch *farigoulette* (see
Note), or fresh thyme, tied together with a string
1 cup crème fraîche (see Appen-

dix), or heavy cream
Freshly ground pepper
½ of a 30-inch baguette
6 sprigs *farigoulette*, or fresh
thyme, for garnish

Utensils

2 large saucepans
Food processor
2 large mixing bowls
Chef's knife

Small knife
Whisk
Measuring cups and spoons

Preparation

✳✳✳To cook the artichokes, bring a
large saucepan of well-salted water to a
boil. Add the artichokes and cook, uncovered, until the leaves pull away
easily from the base. This should take
about 45 minutes, but start testing the
leaves after 30 minutes of cooking.

Meanwhile, peel and chop the
onion.

Heat the olive oil in a large saucepan. Add the onion and sauté over medium heat until softened. Just before
the onions begin to brown, add 4 cups
water, season with salt, and bring to a
boil. Add the rice and the bundles of
parsley and *farigoulette*. Simmer over
medium heat until the rice is thoroughly cooked, about 30 minutes.

While this cooks, drain the artichokes and strip off the leaves. If
you're using large artichokes, use a
spoon to scrape the pulp from the base
of the larger leaves and add it to the
soup. (If you're using small artichokes,
the tender meat at the base of the leaves
is the cook's bonus: nibble on it while
you remove the chokes!) Use a small

knife to remove the hairy chokes and
discard them. Coarsely chop the hearts
and add to the soup.

Bring the soup to a boil. Then remove from the heat and remove the
parsley and *farigoulette* bundles. Pour
the soup into a food processor and
process until creamy and well blended.

Place the crème fraîche in a large
mixing bowl and whisk until it's just
thick enough to adhere to the whisk.

Cut the baguette half into thin slices.

If preparing in advance, place the
soup and the whipped crème in separate bowls in the refrigerator and set
the bread aside.

✳✳Before serving, bring the soup to a
boil over low heat. Meanwhile, toast
the baguette slices.

Season the soup with salt and pepper. Pour into a serving tureen and
float the whipped crème on top. Take

the tureen to the table and stir the
crème into it just before ladling it into
individual soup bowls. Garnish each
bowl with a sprig of *farigoulette*.

Pass the toasted baguette slices
separately.

Note: *Farigoulette,* or *farigoule,* is the name for the wild thyme from the rocky foothills of Provence. When you smell it, you can almost hear the cicadas singing. If you're not lucky enough to have farigoulette growing close to you, use the freshest, most fragrant thyme you can find.

La Fricassée de Moules au Fenouil

MUSSELS AND FENNEL IN SAFFRON
CREAM SAUCE

Time required: *30 minutes
advance preparation
15 minutes just before serving*
Difficulty: *Moderately easy*
Cost: *Moderate*

Ingredients

4½	pounds small mussels
9	tablespoons virgin olive oil
18	cloves
1	bouquet garni composed of 1 sprig fresh thyme, 1 bay leaf, and several sprigs parsley, tied together with string
3	small carrots
1	sweet red pepper
1	bulb fresh fennel

6	tablespoons water
	Salt
6	egg yolks, at room temperature
1¼	cup crème fraîche (see Appendix), or heavy cream
	Pinch of saffron threads
	Freshly ground pepper
3	tablespoons coarsely chopped parsley

Utensils

	Large stockpot with cover
2	large skillets
	Mixing bowl
	Fine sieve
	Whisk
	Wooden spoon
	Chef's knife

Skimmer
Cheesecloth
Measuring cups and spoons
Deep serving platter
Aluminum foil
Stiff brush for mussels
Vegetable peeler

Preparation

***Scrub the mussels with a stiff brush and rinse in 3 or 4 changes of cold water to remove any grit; pull off their "beards."

Mussels steamed with fresh herbs are served with vegetable strips in a saffron-flavored sauce.

In a large stockpot, heat 6 tablespoons of the oil. Add the mussels, cloves, and bouquet garni. Cover and simmer over high heat for about 5 minutes, stirring occasionally, so that all the mussels cook and open. Remove from the heat.

Scrape the carrots. Split and core the

pepper, and remove the seeds. Trim the fennel. Cut all the vegetables into julienne strips.

Place the remaining 3 tablespoons oil in a large skillet. Add the carrots, peppers, fennel, and 6 tablespoons water, and season with salt. Simmer over high heat for about 10 minutes, until all of the water has evaporated.

Meanwhile, remove the mussels from the pot with a skimmer. (Don't discard the cooking broth—it will be used in the sauce.) Open the mussels, retaining the shell to which the meat is attached and discarding the other half.

Arrange the mussels on a deep serving platter, spread the sautéed vegetables over the top, cover with aluminum foil, and set aside in a cool place.

In a large mixing bowl, combine the egg yolks, crème fraîche, and saffron, and whisk until blended.

Strain the mussel broth through a fine sieve lined with cheesecloth, being careful not to pour the sandy residue into the bottom of the pot. Set aside.

If preparing in advance, place the egg-cream mixture in the refrigerator.

**Fifteen minutes before serving, preheat the oven to 400 degrees F.

About 5 minutes before serving, place the platter of mussels in the oven and reheat.

Pour the mussel broth into a large skillet and bring to a boil. Remove from the heat and pour the broth in a thin steady stream into the egg-cream mixture, whisking constantly. Return the mixture to the skillet and simmer over low heat, whisking constantly until the sauce thickens; do not let it boil. Season if necessary with salt and pepper.

Pour the sauce over the mussels, sprinkle with the parsley, and serve.

Les Côtes de Veau à l'Anis et aux Pions d'Ail

VEAL MEDALLIONS WITH ANISE AND GARLIC

Time required: *45 minutes*
advance preparation
5 minutes reheating just before serving
Difficulty: *Moderately easy*
Cost: *Very expensive*

Ingredients

3 double-thick veal chops (about 1 pound each)
2 heads of garlic
Salt
Freshly ground pepper
⅓ cup flour
1½ teaspoons sweet paprika

8 tablespoons unsalted butter
⅓ cup dry white wine
1½ teaspoons Pernod or other anise-flavored liquor
Parsley sprigs

A gathering of aromatic herbs that flavor the food of Provence.

Utensils

Large ovenproof skillet
Medium saucepan
Small bowl
Ovenproof plate
Paring knife

Cutting board
Wooden spoon
Spatula
Measuring cups and spoons
Colander

Preparation

***Trim all excess fat from the chops and remove the bones, or ask your butcher to do it for you.

Separate each head of garlic into cloves, peel, and cut into matchstick-size strips. Remember to remove the pale green sprout often found at the center of the cloves of garlic; it's very bitter.

Place the garlic in a medium saucepan with a quart of cold water. Bring to a boil over high heat, drain immediately, and set aside.

Season the veal chops with salt and pepper on both sides.

Combine the flour and paprika on a plate and dredge the veal chops in it, turning them several times and pressing down firmly so that the flour is absorbed into the meat.

In a large ovenproof skillet, melt 4 tablespoons of the butter over medium heat. When the butter begins to sizzle, add the chops, pressing them down flat with a spatula. Let them brown over

medium heat for 5 minutes, then turn, sprinkle with the garlic pieces, and let cook for 5 minutes longer. Remove the chops from the skillet and set them aside on a plate.

Add the wine to the skillet and bring to a boil, scraping up with a wooden spoon the brown bits that cling to the bottom of the pan.

If preparing in advance, remove the skillet from the heat and set aside. Cover the veal chops and set aside in a cool place.

**Fifteen minutes before serving, preheat the oven to 400 degrees F. About five minutes before serving, add the remaining 4 tablespoons butter to the juices in the skillet, swirling it gently into the cooking liquid to create a creamy, well-bound sauce that's not greasy. Stir in the Pernod, along with any juices that the veal chops have rendered. Pour the sauce into a bowl and

keep it warm.

Cut each veal chop in half, place on an ovenproof plate, and put in the hot oven to warm for 2 to 3 minutes.

Arrange the chops on 6 warmed serving plates. Spoon generous amounts of the sauce and garlic over the chops. Sprinkle with sprigs of fresh parsley and serve.

La Glace à la Lavande

LAVENDER-SCENTED ICE CREAM

Time required: *30 to 40 minutes*
preparation
(at least 3 hours in advance)
Difficulty: *Easy*
Cost: *Moderate*

Ingredients

1½ teaspoons lavender flowers (see Note)
1¼ cups granulated sugar
1 cup milk

8 egg yolks at room temperature
1 cup crème fraîche (see Appendix), or heavy cream
6 sprigs fresh lavender

Utensils

Sorbet or ice cream machine
Food processor or mortar and pestle
2 mixing bowls

Wooden spoon
Measuring cups and spoons
Plate
Ice cream scoop

Preparation

***Begin by preparing the lavender sugar. Combine the lavender and 1 cup of the sugar in the container of a food processor and process until the lavender is reduced to a powder and thoroughly blended with the sugar. (Or use a mortar and pestle to crush the flowers to a fine powder, then mix with the sugar.)

In a large mixing bowl, combine the lavender sugar and milk and stir until the sugar dissolves. In a second bowl, combine the egg yolks and crème fraîche and blend thoroughly. Pour the milk mixture into the egg-crème mixture and blend well.

Pour into the container of an ice cream or sorbet machine and freeze according to the manufacturer's instructions. Place in the freezer for at least 3 hours.

Sprinkle the remaining ¼ cup sugar over a plate. Dip the lavender sprigs in water, then roll in the sugar until lightly coated. Leave on the plate with any excess sugar to dry.

**About 20 minutes before serving, scoop out 12 balls or ovals of ice cream with an ice cream scoop or two soup spoons dipped in hot water. Place 2 scoops in each of 6 ice cream bowls. Return the bowls to the refrigerator (not the freezer) until serving so that the ice cream will not be too cold and hard.

At serving time, place the ice cream bowls on dessert plates covered with paper doilies. Garnish each plate with a frosted lavender sprig and serve with Petits Pains d'Anis (recipe follows).

Note: For this ice cream, lavender flowers, fresh or dried lavender, or lavender sugar can be used. But, by all means, do not use the lavender flowers

put in sachets meant for scenting cupboards and linens. The lavender used in these sachets contains perfume and is not to be eaten.

Les Petits Pains d'Anis

ANISE COOKIES

Time required: *1 hour*
advance preparation
Difficulty: *Moderately easy*
Cost: *Inexpensive*
Servings: *Makes about 3 dozen*

Ingredients

4	cups flour	Salt
2½	cups granulated sugar	4 egg whites, at room
¼	cup anise seeds	temperature

Utensils

2 large mixing bowls	Wooden spoon
Baking sheet	Small knife
Rolling pin	Brush
Small oval cookie cutter	Measuring cups and spoons
Egg beater	

Preparation

***In a large mixing bowl, combine the flour, sugar, anise seeds, and a pinch of salt.

Place the egg whites in a separate bowl and beat until stiff. Fold the egg whites into the dry ingredients. Knead the dough until it is thoroughly blended. Wrap the dough in a damp cloth and refrigerate for at least 1 hour.

Preheat the oven to 350 degrees F.

Quickly roll out the dough on a lightly floured work surface to a thickness of slightly more than ¼ inch. Using an oval cookie cutter dipped in flour, cut out the dough and place on a generously buttered baking sheet.

Make a herringbone pattern on the top of each cookie with the point of a sharp knife. Remove any excess flour from the cookies with a brush.

Place in the hot oven and bake for 15 minutes, or until golden. Remove from the oven and let cool.

**Arrange on a small serving plate and pass with the lavender-scented ice cream.

(These cookies will keep well for several days if stored in a cookie jar or tin with a tight-fitting lid.)

The sugar in the ice cream recipe can be replaced with two spoonfuls of lavender honey.

Menu for 6 People

Les Copains d'Abord

A Dinner with Pals

Difficulty:
Moderately easy
Cost: *Moderate*

I have a number of pals with moustaches who, like myself, wear them thick and somewhat bushy. Our philosophy is that you shouldn't disguise your moustache as a decorative garland, but rather make it the guardian of your memories. In it you can savor the warm bouquet of a liqueur, a cigar, a peppery sauce, or the sweet aroma of a woman. . . .

But let's not confuse friends and pals. A dinner with friends, that's fine. But a dinner with pals! . . .

There, no problems of rank or fortune. With your napkin barely unfolded, you are already immersed in the sheer pleasure of being together. You drink a first toast, you click your tongue, you look at each other already laughing at the jokes to come, and then, as dish follows dish and the wine flows freely, the faces light up, the talk gets warmer, and you feel the happiness of being alive.

Oh, sure, the jokes become a bit low and refinement is no longer so evident.

Le Gratin d'Escargots en Persillade
Baked Escargots with Parsley Butter

Le Pavé de Boeuf à la Moëlle, Sauce Bordelaise
Tenderloin Steaks with Marrow and Bordelaise Sauce

Le Pâté de Pommes de Terre Bourbonnais
Bourbonnais Potato Pie

La Tartine de Fondue des Copains
Goat Cheese Fondue on Country-Style Bread

Le Clafoutis aux Fruits Divers
Mixed Fruit Clafoutis

La Confiture de Vieux Garçon
Bachelor's Jam

But what is more sincere, simple, and true than a meal with pals like this summer luncheon under an immense linden tree in Mougins?

Doing the Marketing

You can buy canned snails, but don't forget to buy the shells to put them in, as well as the special plates with indentations in them for the snails. Or, if you prefer, use small individual earthenware pots to serve the snails in.

Order 6 thick tenderloin steaks or 3 boneless strip steaks, to be cut in half when serving.

What to Drink

For an apéritif "des copains," make a Kir with 1½ teaspoons of cassis in a glass of well-chilled dry vermouth. Serve with rillettes or with sausage. Or, make any number of variations on the Kir by starting with a base of 4 ounces dry white wine (Sancerre, Mâcon, or even Champagne) and adding 1 large teaspoon of fruit liqueur—strawberry or raspberry brandy, for example, or Campari. A chilled, light red wine (a Rully, perhaps) would be just as agreeable with the same addition of fruit liqueur. (This is called a Cardinal.)

For the wines, serve a dry white Burgundy with the escargots and a Bordeaux with the beef (maybe a Côte-de-Bourg or a Blaye).

Table Linens and Decoration

Choose a tablecloth of unbleached linen. For napkins, use some good cotton dishtowels with blue or red patterns.

Stand some large candles in metal dishes or in promotional ashtrays. Don't forget a large basket for the country bread. Decorate the table with wildflowers.

The menu could be written on a page from a student's composition notebook, carefully torn out.

Tableware

For good friends, no affectations are necessary. Choose rustic and sturdy tableware, such as the large white bistro-style plates with colored border:

- 6 escargot plates
- 6 plates for under the escargot plates
- 6 large serving plates for the beef
- 6 dessert plates for the potato pie
- 1 large plate or large round cutting board for the beef
- 1 large round serving platter for the potato pie
- 6 dessert plates for the goat cheese fondue and tartines
- 6 dessert plates for the clafoutis
- 1 large round plate for the clafoutis

Silverware

- 6 escargot forks and clamps (if you serve them in the shells)
- 12 dinner forks
- 12 dinner knives
- 6 dessert forks
- 2 pie servers (for the potato pie and the clafoutis)

Glassware

- 18 goblets for water, white wine, and red wine

overleaf: Les copains: *José Albertini, Roger Muhl, César, Roger Vergé, Bernard Chevry, and Patrick D'Humieres.*

*Getting
Organized*

Many things in this menu can be prepared in advance. They are indicated in each recipe by the symbol ***. The symbol ** indicates those tasks that must be done just before serving.

Put the white wine in the refrigerator several hours in advance.

Thirty minutes before sitting down to eat, warm 6 dinner plates and 18 dessert plates over a pan of hot water or on the back of the stove.

Preheat the oven to 400 degrees F.

When the oven is hot, place the escargots in it to bake for 8 to 10 minutes.

Meanwhile, prepare the fondue and keep it warm in a bain-marie.

Cook the steaks, keep them warm (see recipe), and deglaze the pan.

When the escargots have finished cooking, turn the oven to 300 degrees F and place the potato pie and the steaks in it to warm, leaving the door ajar.

After serving the escargots, return to the kitchen to finish the steaks; reheat the sauce and finish it with the remaining butter. Warm and drain the marrow, cut the steaks (if serving strip steaks), and place on the warm plates. After removing the steaks and potatoes from the oven, preheat the broiler.

When you've finished eating the steaks, toast the bread for the tartines in the broiler, then spread the fondue over them and serve. Turn off the oven and place the clafoutis in it to warm.

Le Gratin d'Escargots en Persillade

BAKED ESCARGOTS WITH PARSLEY BUTTER

Time required: *45 minutes*
advance preparation
8 to 10 minutes cooking just before serving
Difficulty: *Moderately easy*
Cost: *Moderate*

Ingredients

2	cans Burgundy snails (7 ounces each) and 48 snail shells
2	tablespoons unsalted butter
1½	tablespoon chopped shallots

PARSLEY BUTTER
1⅔	cups unsalted butter
1	bunch parsley, chopped
1½	tablespoons minced garlic
2½	tablespoons minced shallots

1½	cup dry white wine
	Salt
	Freshly ground pepper
5	slices white bread

½	cup hazelnut powder, or ½ cup hazelnuts, ground to a fine powder in a food processor
1	tablespoon salt
	Freshly ground pepper

Utensils

	Food processor
	Medium saucepan
	Sieve

	Chef's knife
6	escargot plates

Whether cooked in their shells or in small terrines, the snails are just as savory.

Preparation

*** Place the snails in a sieve and drain well.

Melt the butter in a medium saucepan. Add the shallots and sauté until softened. Add the snails and wine, season with salt and pepper, and simmer over medium-low heat for 15 minutes to tenderize the snails. Set aside.

Remove the crusts from the bread, place in a food processor, and process until finely chopped. (The bread will be white and moist, unlike prepared breadcrumbs, which are dry and lightly browned.)

To make the snail butter, place the butter in a food processor and process to a creamy consistency. Add the parsley, garlic, shallots, hazelnut powder, salt, and a pinch of pepper, and process until finely chopped and well blended.

Drain the snails and place one in each snail shell. Place the shells, open ends facing up, in the cavities of the snail plates. Spoon a little of the snail cooking liquid into each shell. Then press about 1 tablespoon of the snail butter into each snail shell. Sprinkle a little of the chopped bread over the top of each snail.

If preparing in advance, place snails in the refrigerator until ready to cook.

** About 25 minutes before serving, preheat the oven to 400 degrees F. After 15 minutes, place the snails in the oven and bake for 8 to 10 minutes.

Serve immediately. (If you burn your fingers a little taking the snails from the oven, just lick them. It may not be very elegant, but it will taste good!)

Le Pavé de Boeuf à la Moëlle, Sauce Bordelaise

TENDERLOIN STEAKS WITH MARROW AND
BORDELAISE SAUCE

Time required: *10 minutes
advance preparation
25 to 35 minutes preparation
and cooking just before serving*
Difficulty: *Moderately difficult*
Cost: *Expensive*

Ingredients

2   pounds beef marrow bones, sawed into 2-inch pieces
6   beef tenderloin steaks, cut 1½ inches thick (6 to 7 ounces each), or 3 boneless strip steaks
    Salt
    Freshly ground pepper
2   tablespoons unsalted butter

BORDELAISE SAUCE
5   tablespoons unsalted butter
2   tablespoons chopped shallots
1¼ cups Bordeaux or other dry red wine
2   beef bouillon cubes
10 peppercorns, cracked
1   bay leaf
2   sprigs fresh thyme
3   cups water, salted
    Coarse salt

Utensils

Large skillet
Large saucepan
Mixing bowl
Large plate
Small plate
Sieve
Knife
Skimmer
Wooden spoon
Aluminum foil
Measuring cups and spoons

Preparation

***Several hours in advance or the day before, carefully remove the marrow from the bones and place it in a mixing bowl filled with cold water. Set aside to soak to remove any blood from the marrow and make it white.

**Shortly before beginning the meal, season the meat on both sides with salt and pepper.

Place the butter in a large skillet and let it melt and brown lightly. Add the meat and sauté over medium-high heat for 2 to 3 minutes per side, depending on the texture of the meat and the degree of doneness preferred. Two to 3 minutes per side will produce rare steaks.

Remove the steaks from the pan and place them on a small plate turned upside down on a large ovenproof plate so that the meat doesn't sit in its juices. Place in the oven with the potato pie to keep warm until serving. Discard the butter the steaks cooked in, but do not rinse the skillet.

To make the Bordelaise sauce, melt 2 tablespoons of the butter in the skillet, add the shallots, and sauté until lightly browned. Add the wine and deglaze the pan, scraping up the bits of meat that stick to the bottom. Add the bouillon cubes, peppercorns, bay leaf, and thyme, and let the sauce reduce to one-fourth of its original volume.

Meanwhile, drain the marrow and cut into ¼-inch slices.

Just before serving the steaks, bring 3 cups salted water to a boil in a large saucepan. Add the marrow and allow the water to return to a boil. Immedi-

ately remove from the heat.

Strain the sauce through a fine sieve and return it to the skillet. Add the remaining 3 tablespoons butter to the sauce, one at a time, swirling the pan in a circular motion until the butter is incorporated. Adjust the seasonings if necessary.

Place the steaks on the plates (if you're using strip steaks, cut each in half first). Remove the marrow slices from the water with a slotted spoon, gently shaking off excess water, and place 1 slice on each steak. Spoon the sauce over the meat and sprinkle the marrow with a few grains of coarse salt.

Le Pâté de Pommes de Terre Bourbonnais

BOURBONNAIS POTATO PIE

Time required: *45 minutes*
advance preparation
1½ hours cooking
and 30 minutes "resting"
before serving
Difficulty: *Moderately difficult*
Cost: *Inexpensive*

The potato pie in this menu is a dish of my mother's, a very simple dish that comes from Bourbonnais, where I was born. The recipe that I am presenting here is given without embellishment or embroidery, just as my mother used to make it. You can of course substitute a puff pastry for my mother's pastry—it might even be better—but for me it would surely be less authentic.

In my home we also ate the leftovers

of this cold pie the following day. The cream by then would have just a hint of acidity—very agreeable for a 10 A.M. snack.

With what was left of the pastry, I remember that my mother would make a flat *galette*. Using a goose feather, she brushed the top with egg wash and sprinkled powdered sugar over it before baking it in a hot oven. We ate this little pie as soon as it came out of the oven; it wasn't particularly light, but what could be better than something one's mother makes?

Ingredients

DOUGH
1½ cups unsalted butter
4½ cups flour

POTATOES
2 pounds potatoes
1 tablespoon chopped shallots
2 tablespoons chopped parsley
Salt
Freshly ground pepper

Salt
½ cup plus 2 tablespoons cold water

4 tablespoons unsalted butter
1 egg
1 tablespoon cold water
1½ cups crème fraîche (see Appendix), or heavy cream

Utensils

Baking sheet
Chef's knife
Large mixing bowl
Small bowl
Rolling pin

Colander
Brush
Measuring cups and spoons
Dish towel or plastic wrap

Preparation

***The dough for this recipe can be prepared the day before your dinner. Finish preparing and assembling the tart several hours before eating.

To make the dough, cut the butter into small pieces, and work with your fingers until softened. Mound the flour onto a marble slab or cool work surface. Make a well in the center of the mound, add the butter, a pinch of salt, and ½ cup plus 2 tablespoons cold water. Gradually incorporate the flour into the wet ingredients, working with your fingers. Knead thoroughly but *quickly* so that all ingredients are well blended. Form the dough into a ball and wrap in a damp dish towel or plastic wrap. Refrigerate for at least 30 minutes.

Wash and peel the potatoes. Slice them into ⅛-inch rounds and place in a large mixing bowl with the shallots and parsley. Season with salt and pepper and toss together. Let sit for 15 minutes. (The salt will draw out the excess water.) Drain in a colander.

Preheat the oven to 400 degrees F.

Divide the dough in half. Roll half of it out on a lightly floured work surface to form a very thin (1/16-inch) round, a little larger than 10 inches in diameter. Use a sharp knife to trim to a neat 10-inch round. Place the dough on a well-buttered baking sheet. Roll out the remaining dough in the same manner and trim to a 10-inch circle. Set aside.

Mound the potatoes on top of the first dough round, leaving a 1-inch border around the edge. Cut the butter into small pieces and sprinkle them over the top of the potatoes.

In a small bowl, beat the egg with 1 tablespoon of cold water. Brush the border of the dough round with the egg wash. Place the second round of dough on top of the potatoes. Press the edges of the two dough rounds together firmly. Roll the edges up to form a rim.

Prick the top of the tart with the tip of a knife and make a criss-cross pattern on the top with the tines of a fork.

Brush with the remaining egg wash and place in the hot oven. Bake for 1½ hours.

When 1½ hours have elapsed, remove the tart from the oven and cut off the top of the pastry. Pierce the potatoes with a fork to test for doneness. (If they're not tender, replace the pastry top and return the tart to the oven to bake longer.)

**You can keep this warm in an open oven until serving or reheat in a

When the potatoes are cooked, remove the pastry top and pour the crème fraîche over the potatoes, lifting them with a fork so that the crème seeps through to the potatoes on the bottom. Replace the pastry top. Let stand for at least 30 minutes before serving so that the potatoes are well saturated with the crème.

300 degree F oven with the door ajar for 15 minutes before serving.

La Tartine de Fondue des Copains

GOAT CHEESE FONDUE ON COUNTRY-STYLE BREAD

Time required: *20 minutes*
advance preparation
5 minutes just before serving
Difficulty: *Very easy*
Cost: *Moderate*

This recipe is adapted from a concoction that used to be made in the south of Bourbonnais, in which all the leftover pieces of cheese, both cow and goat, were used.

We ate these little cheese pies with baked potatoes cooked in the embers, after a good vegetable soup. It may not have been a gala menu, but with a glass of good wine, it brought a smile to everyone's face.

Ingredients

3	small crottins de Chavignol, or about 7 ounces Montrachet cheese
3½	ounces Gruyère or Swiss cheese
¼	cup plus 1 tablespoon dry white wine, such as Chablis or Mâcon
1	clove garlic
1½	tablespoons unsalted butter

1½	teaspoons strong Dijon mustard
2	tablespoons Marc de Bourgogne, Grappa, or Cognac
6	thick slices country-style bread
6	sprigs fresh savory or thyme, or 1 teaspoon dried savory or thyme
	Freshly ground pepper

Utensils

Small heavy saucepan
Wooden spoon
Paring knife

Baking sheet
Grater

Preparation

***This dish can be made almost entirely in advance.

Use a paring knife to trim away any mold from the goat cheese; coarsely chop the cheese. Shred the Gruyère.

Place the wine and garlic in a small heavy saucepan. Bring to a boil over low heat and let reduce by half. Add the goat cheese and let melt over low heat, stirring with a wooden spoon. Remove the garlic. Add the Gruyère

**Preheat the broiler.

A few minutes before serving, place the bread slices on a baking sheet and toast under the broiler. Remove from the oven and immediately spread each

and butter and stir over low heat until the cheeses are melted and well blended.

Remove from the heat and stir in the mustard and Marc.

If preparing just a short while in advance, place the saucepan in a bain-marie (or a roasting pan half-filled with water and placed over low heat) to keep warm until served.

slice of bread with the warm fondue. Garnish each with a sprig of fresh savory or thyme, and top with a grind of fresh pepper. Serve at once.

Le Clafoutis aux Fruits Divers

MIXED FRUIT CLAFOUTIS

Time required: *30 minutes*
advance preparation
40 minutes cooking
Difficulty: *Very easy*
Cost: *Inexpensive*

This clafoutis can be made with any fruit, but especially the fruits with pits, starting of course with cherries— black, Morello, or any other variety. Apricots, damsons, cherry plums, or greengages will all do magnificently well, but be careful with fruits that yield a great deal of water; for them, reduce the quantity of milk by 20 percent.

The great question is whether or not

to remove the pits. For large fruits, it's necessary to cut them in several pieces, thus pitting them. But with cherries and small plums, the pits add a subtle and incomparable almond taste.

Traditionally, clafoutis is a rustic dessert that has been made with unpitted fruit. In the Auvergne countryside of my childhood, it was made with tiny wild black cherries that tasted of honey, but there were so many pits that each diner was transformed into a machine gun.

This clafoutis can be made equally well with raspberries, blueberries, or blackberries. If you are using these fruits, coat the cold clafoutis lightly with a glaze of the same fruit. Other fruits, such as apples or pears, can also be used. Even fruits in syrup are suitable as long as they are well drained.

How many resources are available for a single dessert!

Ingredients

1⅓	pounds black cherries, apricots, plums, or other fruit with pits
¼	cup plus 3 tablespoons unsalted butter
¾	cup granualted sugar, or 1 cup if using apricots or prunes
⅔	cup flour
1¼	cups almond powder (see Appendix), or 1½ cups almonds, ground to a fine powder in a food processor
	Salt
2	eggs
⅔	cup milk, or ½ cup if using apricots or prunes

Utensils

8-inch round gratin or baking dish
Mixing bowl

Small saucepan
Whisk
Brush

Preparation

***This dessert can be prepared several hours in advance or even the day before.

Preheat the oven to 400 degrees F.

Remove the stems, wash, and drain the fruit. Cut the large fruit into quarters.

Melt the butter in a small saucepan over low heat. Remove from the heat and brush enough of the melted butter over the sides and bottom of an 8-inch round gratin dish to coat it well. Set the saucepan with the remaining butter aside.

Pour the sugar into the buttered dish, turning it to coat thoroughly with sugar. Empty the excess sugar into a mixing bowl. Add the flour, almond powder, and a pinch of salt to the mixing bowl and blend well. Add the eggs and beat into the dry ingredients with a whisk. Stir in the milk.

Warm the saucepan containing the remaining butter over low heat until it turns light brown. Pour it into the batter and blend thoroughly.

Arrange the fruit in the bottom of the prepared gratin dish. Pour the batter evenly over the fruit. Bake in the preheated oven for 40 minutes.

To test for doneness, insert the tip of a knife in the clafoutis. If it comes out clean, the clafoutis is cooked.

If preparing in advance, remove the clafoutis from the oven and set aside in a cool place.

**Clafoutis is best served warm, not hot. Place in a low oven for about 10 minutes just before serving so that it is just slightly warm when served.

La Confiture de Vieux Garçon

BACHELOR'S JAM

Time required: *20 minutes
preparation (at least
15 days in advance)*
Difficulty: *Easy*
Cost: *Moderately expensive*

One day I ate this bachelor's jam at the house of a friend who served it on slices of slightly stale country-style bread. Obviously I wouldn't recommend doing that for breakfast, unless you want to start the day on a particularly euphoric note. I will, however, advise you never to empty the jam jar completely, but to replace the fruits, sugar, and liqueur each time the level seriously diminishes. Remember that winter is long and not a good time of year for finding all these fruits.

Now, if you want to discuss this

delicacy in terms of calories, let's close the conversation. Or else don't dip into the jar with anything larger than a demitasse spoon.

Ingredients

½	pint fresh strawberries
½	pint fresh raspberries
½	pint red currants
½	pint black currants
1¾	pounds sugar cubes
1	cinnamon stick
1	vanilla bean
2	cups Armagnac, Cognac, eau de vie, or whisky

Utensils

Large glazed earthenware crock or wide-mouthed jar
Large mixing bowl

Wooden spoon
Saucer

Preparation

***This recipe must be prepared at least 15 days before serving. The longer it sits, the better it becomes. It keeps for several months.

Wash the strawberries and remove their stems. (Never wash them after hulling, since sand from the berry might wash into the stem cavity.) Hull the raspberries, but do not wash them or the currants. (They are very fragile and become soggy if rinsed. Just sort through to remove dirt and damaged berries.)

In a large mixing bowl, combine all of the fruit and mix gently with a wooden spoon.

Alternately spoon the fruit and sugar cubes into a large earthenware crock or wide-mouthed jar, starting with a layer of fruit, then adding a layer of sugar cubes, then another layer of fruit, and continuing in this manner until all the fruit and sugar have been used. Finish with a layer of sugar.

Insert the cinnamon stick and vanilla bean into the center of the fruit. Pour the alcohol over; there should be enough to completely cover the fruit. If necessary, place a small saucer on top of the fruit to keep it submerged in the alcohol. Cover tightly and place in a cool place (but do not refrigerate) for 5 to 7 days.

At the end of this time, uncover the fruit and stir with a wooden spoon. Cover and let sit for at least 10 more days before serving.

Coffee is served in the studio of Roger Muhl, where he has hung his recent painting Mediterranean Gardens.

Menu for 6 People

Un Déjeuner au Soleil

Lunch in the Sun

Difficulty:
Moderately difficult
Cost: *Expensive*

Le Rendez-vous des Sportifs in Nice is not one of those well-known restaurants where you bump into famous gourmets from all over the world, nor is it a temple devoted to sensationalist cuisine. Marinette serves a simple, healthy cuisine, rich in aromas, delicious—and of Rabelaisian robustness.

Now, obtaining a recipe from Marinette is considerably more complicated than eating one of her dishes. It isn't that she tries to protect her secrets—it's that her cooking seems so simple to her that she figures anyone ought to be able to do it. Here, for instance, is how she explained to me her recipe for *pissaladière*:

"Oh, you know, it's very easy. You take a little lukewarm water, some olive oil, some salt, pepper, and some little packets of bakers' yeast—you know, the kind that comes in cubes. And you take some flour. You crush up the yeast, mix, and there you are! You see how easy it is."

"But, Marinette, what are the quantities for all that?"

She looked at me as if beginning to suspect that I wasn't really a chef.

La Salade de Langoustes au Beurre d'Orange
Warm Lobster Salad with Orange Butter Sauce

Le Filet de Turbot aux Poivrons Doux
Turbot Fillets with Sweet Red Peppers

La Fondue de Gigot aux Aubergines
Lamb and Eggplant Timbales

La Compote Niçoise
Niçoise Vegetable Compote

Les Crêpes au Miel et aux Pignons de Provence
Crêpes in Honey Sauce with Provençal Pine Nuts

Quantities? What an absurd question! She has never weighed or measured anything at all. She does cooking, not mathematics. Those "great chefs" really have some strange ideas!

And that is why I, who may be able to make a fricassee of lobster, still don't know how to make *pissaladière* Marinette style. And I regret it deeply.

Doing the Marketing

Order the lobsters, the turbot, and the lamb in advance. Ask your fishmonger to fillet the turbot for you.

What to Drink	For an apéritif, you can serve Champagne or a dry white wine cocktail flavored with orange. To make this cocktail, combine ½ cup orange juice, ¼ cup plus 1 tablespoon orange-flavored liqueur, ¼ cup plus 1 tablespoon sugar syrup, and a few drops of Angostura bitters in a large glass pitcher. Pour in one bottle of dry white wine.

Serve from the pitcher with orange slices floating in it.

For the wines, serve a dry white wine such as an Hermitage from the Côtes-du-Rhône or a Pouilly-Fuissé for the lobster and the turbot. To accompany the lamb, choose a full-bodied red such as a Châteauneuf-du-Pape or a Côte-Rôtie.

Table Linens and Decoration

If you can't serve this meal outdoors in the sun, try to re-create the atmosphere with plates, a tablecloth, and napkins all of light, sunny colors; yellow or orange flowers (sunflowers preferably, or else nasturtiums, chrysanthemums, jonquils, or marigolds); and menus written on yellow paper.

Tableware

18 large serving plates for the lobster, the turbot, and the lamb
6 dessert plates for the crêpes

overleaf: *This tablesetting brings sunshine to the plates even before the meal is served.*

Silverware	6 forks and 6 knives for the lobster and 6 dessert spoons for the sauce	6 dessert forks and 6 dessert spoons for the crêpes
	6 fish forks and 6 fish knives for the turbot	1 serving spoon
		1 serving fork

Glassware   18   goblets for water, white wine, and red wine

*Getting
Organized*

Many things in this menu can be prepared in advance. They are indicated in each recipe by the symbol ⁕⁕⁕. The symbol ⁕⁕ indicates those tasks that must be done just before serving.

Put the white wine in the refrigerator to chill several hours in advance.

Thirty minutes before serving, preheat the oven to 400 degrees F. Warm 18 large dinner plates and 6 dessert plates over a pan of hot water or on the back of the stove.

Arrange the lobster salad on the plates.

Place the lamb timbales in a bain-marie or large roasting pan half-filled with water over low heat.

Sauté the turbot and keep warm. Place the pepper sauce and the sauce for the lamb in the bain-marie.

Just before sitting down to eat, finish the orange butter. Place the lobster salads in the oven for 2 to 3 minutes; spoon the sauce over them. Put the lamb and the vegetable compote in the oven to warm. Serve the lobster salad.

After serving the lobster, place the fish in the oven for 2 to 3 minutes while you whisk the red pepper sauce and spoon it onto the plates. Place the fish on top and serve.

When you've finished the turbot, unmold the lamb timbales on hot plates, whisk the sauce, and spoon it over the lamb. Serve with the vegetable compote and turn the oven to its highest setting (for the crêpes).

Just before serving, place the crêpes in the oven for several minutes, until lightly golden.

La Salade de Langoustes
au Beurre d'Orange

WARM LOBSTER SALAD WITH
ORANGE BUTTER SAUCE

Time required: *1½ hours*
Difficulty: *Moderately difficult*
Cost: *Expensive*

Ingredients

6 artichokes (about 5 ounces each; see Note)
3 medium very ripe tomatoes
1 large onion
1 bouquet garni composed of 1

bay leaf, 1 sprig of thyme, a few sprigs of chervil, and 2

Serve this warm lobster salad on a bed of mixed salad greens.

sprigs of parsley, all tied together with string

3 small lobsters or 1 large lobster (about 2¼ pounds total weight)

3 oranges (about 5 ounces each)

3 cups salad greens (see Note)

Salt

Freshly ground pepper

¾ cup unsalted butter

Chervil leaves

Utensils

Stockpot or large, heavy casserole

2 small saucepans

Chef's knife

Paring knife

Colander

Kitchen scissors

Juicer

Whisk

Plate

Measuring cups and spoons

Nutcracker

Preparation

❋❋❋ Everything but the final assembly and saucing of this dish can be prepared several hours in advance.

In a stockpot or large, heavy casserole, bring 4 quarts of salted water to a boil.

Break the stems from the artichokes close to the bulbs. (If the artichokes are fresh, the break will be clean. If necessary, trim evenly with a knife.) Rinse the artichokes in cold water. Place in the boiling water to cook over high heat for 20 minutes.

Meanwhile, fill a small saucepan

I prefer the Royal Red spiny lobster for this dish because of the firmness of its flesh.

with water and bring to a boil. Plunge the tomatoes into the water for a few seconds. Rinse under cold water and peel. Cut each tomato in half and gently squeeze out the seeds and juice. Cut the tomatoes into small cubes and set aside on a plate.

After 20 minutes of cooking, check the artichokes for doneness by pulling out a center leaf. If it detaches easily, the flesh is cooked. If not, continue to cook for 5 to 10 more minutes. When they're ready, remove the artichokes from the pot and rinse in cold water. Turn upside down to drain. When cooled, remove the leaves and the fibrous chokes. You'll be left with only the hearts, which should be finely sliced. Set the sliced artichoke hearts aside on the plate with the tomatoes.

Peel and quarter the onion.

Rinse out the stockpot, fill with about 4 quarts of well-salted water, and bring to a boil. Add the bouquet garni and the onion. When the water boils, add the live lobsters. Let the water return to a boil, cover, and cook over high heat for 10 to 12 minutes.

Meanwhile, peel the skin and white membrane from 1 of the oranges. Working over a small saucepan to catch the juice, cut the orange into 12 segments and remove the membrane around the segments. Set aside on the plate with the tomatoes and artichoke hearts.

Extract the juice from the remaining 2 oranges and add it to the saucepan. Place over medium heat and simmer until the juice is reduced to about 2 tablespoons. Set aside.

Wash and thoroughly dry the salad greens. Refrigerate until just before serving.

Drain the lobsters and let cool slightly. Separate the tails from the rest of the body. Using kitchen scissors or a sharp paring knife, cut through the thin undershell on the bottom side of the tail. Carefully lift out the tail meat in one piece. Cut into ¼-inch-thick slices. Carefully crack the claws with a nutcracker and remove the meat without damaging it. Set aside in a cool place, but do not refrigerate.

** Fifteen minutes before serving, preheat the oven to 300 degrees F. Place the salad greens on 6 warmed serving plates. Fan out the artichoke heart slices in the center of the greens. Place the tomato cubes and orange slices on top of the artichoke hearts. Divide the lobster slices among the 6 plates, overlapping them attractively in the center of each plate. Decorate each plate with a lobster claw (or part of one, if you've used one large lobster). Season each

salad lightly with salt and pepper.

Place the plates in the oven for 2 minutes to warm.

Meanwhile, place the saucepan of reduced orange juice over very low heat and, a small piece at a time, quickly whisk in the butter until thoroughly incorporated.

Remove the salads from the oven, divide the orange butter among the plates, and sprinkle the chervil leaves over the top of each. Serve at once.

Note: Choose purple artichokes if you can get them. If not, use green globes.

For the salad greens, mix lettuces such as lamb's lettuce, curly endive, romaine, escarole, and radicchio. In Provence, I use mesclun de paysan, a mixture of wild field lettuces.

Le Filet de Turbot aux Poivrons Doux

TURBOT FILLETS WITH
SWEET RED PEPPERS

Time required: *45 minutes advance
preparation and cooking
15 minutes just before serving*
Difficulty: *Moderately easy*
Cost: *Expensive*

Ingredients

3	small turbots (about 2 pounds each), or other white-fleshed salt-water fish such as sea bass
2	medium-size white onions
3	sweet red peppers
3	very ripe tomatoes
3	cloves garlic
¾	cup virgin olive oil

3	sprigs fresh thyme, or 1 teaspoon dried thyme
	Salt
	Freshly ground pepper
¾	cup flour
1	tablespoon paprika
2	tablespoons unsalted butter

Utensils

2	large skillets
	Small saucepan
	Chef's knife
	Paring knife
	Wooden spoon

Blender or food processor
Roasting pan to serve as bain-marie
Waxed paper
Whisk

Preparation

✳✳✳ The majority of this dish can be prepared several hours in advance.

Ask your fishmonger to clean and fillet the turbots, so that you're left with 6 skinless, boneless fillets.

Peel the onions and thinly slice. Cut the peppers in half, remove the cores and seeds, and cut into thin julienne.

In a small saucepan, bring 2 cups of salted water to a boil. Plunge the tomatoes into the water for a few seconds. Rinse under cold water and peel. Cut each tomato in half and gently squeeze out the seeds and juice. Chop coarsely.

Peel and chop the garlic.

Heat ½ cup of the olive oil in a large skillet, add the onions, and sauté over low heat until softened. Add the peppers and sauté for 5 minutes. Stir in the tomatoes, garlic, and thyme; season with salt and pepper. Simmer over low heat for 7 to 8 minutes.

Remove the thyme sprigs and turn the sautéed vegetables into a blender or food processor. Process briefly, until reduced to a purée and return to the saucepan. Adjust the seasonings if necessary.

Combine the flour and paprika on a sheet of waxed paper. Dredge the fillets in the flour and season with salt.

Combine the remaining ¼ cup oil and the butter in a large skillet. Warm slightly, add the fillets, and let them brown for about 3 minutes on each side.

Prepare to this point in advance, and

** Fifteen minutes before serving, preheat the oven to 300 degrees F. Place the saucepan of sauce in a bain-marie (or a roasting pan half-filled with water) over low heat and warm for 15 minutes. Just before serving, place the

set the sauce and fillets aside until just before serving.

fillets in the oven to warm for 2 to 3 minutes.

Whisk the sauce to blend well and spoon onto 6 warmed serving plates. Place a fillet on each plate and serve immediately.

La Fondue de Gigot aux Aubergines

LAMB AND EGGPLANT TIMBALES

Time required: *3 hours*
advance preparation
25 minutes cooking
just before serving
Difficulty: *Moderately difficult*
Cost: *Moderately expensive*

Ingredients

1	leg of lamb (4½ pounds)
⅔	cup crème fraîche (see Appendix), or heavy cream
1	medium onion
1	celery rib
2	medium carrots
3	or 4 cloves garlic
3	or 4 medium tomatoes (about 1 pound)
2	tablespoons peanut oil
1	bouquet garni composed of 4 or 5 sprigs parsley, 2 sprigs

	fresh thyme, and 2 bay leaves, all tied together with string
	Salt
	Freshly ground pepper
2	cups strong red wine
1	tablespoon cornstarch
	Fresh basil leaves (optional)
	Freshly grated nutmeg
2	large, firm eggplants
4	tablespoons olive oil
	Cherry tomatoes (optional)
6	bay leaves (optional)

Utensils

2	large roasting pans
2	medium saucepans
	Large, fine sieve
2	rimmed baking sheets
	Food processor or meat grinder with fine disc
	Boning knife

	Paring knife
	Cutting board
6	individual soufflé molds or timbales, about 3 inches in diameter and 1½–2 inches deep
	Measuring cups and spoons

Preparation

❊❊❊ Most of this dish can be prepared the day before or several hours in advance.

Remove and discard the fat from the leg of lamb or ask your butcher to prepare the lamb as follows: Using a sharp boning knife, remove the bones, following the membranes covering the muscles so that you do not cut the three distinct pieces of meat, or the *noix*, as we call them, that make up the leg. Remove these three pieces and set the largest two aside to be sliced later. Place the third *noix* and any remaining smaller pieces of meat on a plate, and refrigerate. These will be used to make the stuffing. Reserve the bones and trimmings.

Place the crème fraîche in the coldest part of your refrigerator. It should be very cold when added to the stuffing.

Peel the onion. Trim and wash the celery. Scrape the carrots. Coarsely chop the onions, celery, and carrots. Peel and crush 2 cloves of the garlic. Coarsely chop 1 of the tomatoes.

Place the peanut oil in a large roasting pan, add the onion, celery, carrots, lamb bones and trimmings, and sauté over medium heat until lightly browned. Add the two larger pieces of lamb, the garlic, and the chopped tomato. Add the bouquet garni and season with salt and pepper. Add the wine and enough water to cover, about 1½ cups.

Bring to a boil and simmer, uncovered, over low heat for 1¼ hours. (If you prefer, the meat can be baked in a 350 degree F oven for the same length of time.) While it cooks, you can start to prepare the Niçoise Compote that accompanies this dish.

When the lamb is cooked, remove the 2 pieces of meat from the roasting pan and set aside to cool.

Strain the cooking liquid through a fine sieve into a medium saucepan. Place over medium heat and let reduce, if necessary, until only 3 cups remain. Skim off the fat from the surface of the sauce.

Mix the cornstarch with a little cold water. Slowly stir the cornstarch mixture into the sauce, adding a small amount at a time, until the sauce reaches the consistency of a light syrup. Do not thicken too much. Add the basil leaves, if using, and if you like garlic, crush the remaining garlic and add to the sauce. Set aside.

Remove the remaining, raw pieces of lamb from the refrigerator and season them with salt, pepper, and a few gratings of fresh nutmeg. Place in the container of a food processor and process until finely chopped. Add the chilled crème fraîche in a slow stream, with the processor still running. Stop the processor immediately when all of the crème has been added so that it doesn't turn to butter.

If using a meat grinder instead of a food processor, grind the meat twice. Place it in a mixing bowl and stir in the crème. Place the stuffing mixture in the refrigerator until ready to assemble the dish.

Preheat the oven to 400 degrees F.

Cut the eggplants crosswise into ½-inch rounds.

Brush 2 rimmed baking sheets with about 2 tablespoons of the olive oil. Arrange the eggplant slices on the sheet and salt them lightly. Place in the oven and bake for 10 to 15 minutes, until the eggplant is softened. Remove from the oven and let cool.

Fill a medium saucepan with water, bring it to a boil, plunge the remaining tomatoes in the water for a few seconds, and remove. Rinse under cold

All the delicious ingredients for Lamb and Eggplant Timbales.

water and peel. Cut each tomato in half, squeeze out the seeds and juice, and coarsely chop.

Empty the water from the saucepan the tomatoes blanched in, add the remaining 2 tablespoons oil and the tomatoes. Season with salt and pepper. Place over high heat and simmer until the liquid from the tomatoes has evaporated completely, about 10 minutes. Set aside to cool.

To assemble, slice the baked lamb pieces crosswise into ¼-inch thick rounds, trimming them, if necessary, so that they are slightly smaller than the diameter of the soufflé molds.

Place a round of eggplant on the bottom of each of the 6 lightly oiled soufflé molds. Spread a light layer of the stuffing over each eggplant slice. Place a slice of lamb on top and spread with a layer of the tomatoes. Add another layer of eggplant, a layer of stuffing, and another slice of lamb to each mold and finish by topping each with a layer of stuffing.

If you're working in advance, place the soufflé molds in the refrigerator.

❖

** Thirty-five minutes before serving, preheat the oven to 350 degrees F.

Fifteen minutes later, arrange the soufflé molds in a roasting pan and add warm water to reach halfway up the sides of the molds. Place in the oven to bake for 20 minutes.

Meanwhile, reheat the sauce over low heat.

Just before serving, unmold the

soufflés onto the plates and generously spoon the warm sauce over them.

If you wish, decorate each with a cherry tomato and a bay leaf. Serve immediately.

La Compote Niçoise

NIÇOISE VEGETABLE COMPOTE

Time required: *1¾ hours*
advance preparation
and cooking
30 minutes just before serving
Difficulty: *Very easy*
Cost: *Moderate*

Ingredients				
1	large onion		12	leaves fresh basil
1	sweet red pepper		2	tablespoons fresh thyme flowers or fresh thyme, or 2 teaspoons dried thyme
½	cup plus 3 tablespoons virgin olive oil			Salt
4	medium eggplants			Freshly ground pepper
3	medium zucchini			
3	cloves garlic			

Utensils

Shallow oval baking dish (about 12 inches long)
Large skillet
Mixing bowl

Chef's knife
Cutting board
Vegetable peeler
Measuring cups and spoons

Preparation

*** This recipe can be prepared the day before or several hours in advance.

Peel the onion and thinly slice. Cut the pepper in half, remove the core and seeds, and cut into fine julienne.

Heat 3 tablespoons of the olive oil in a large skillet. Add the onions and sauté over low heat until softened. Add the peppers and continue to cook for 20 minutes.

Meanwhile, peel the eggplants. Peel the zucchini zebra-style, using a vegetable peeler or a small knife to peel off even lengthwise bands separated by equal widths of skin, to give a striped effect. Holding the knife at a slight angle, cut the eggplant and zucchini into ⅛-inch rounds.

Arrange the sautéed peppers and onions in the bottom of a shallow baking dish. Arrange a layer of eggplant slices on top, followed by a layer of zucchini slices. Continue to arrange eggplant and zucchini in alternating layers until all of the vegetables have been used.

Preheat the oven to 400 degrees F.

Peel and chop the garlic; finely chop the basil. Combine in a mixing bowl and add the remaining ½ cup olive oil and the thyme flowers, and season with salt and pepper. Mix well.

Drizzle the seasoning mixture over the vegetables. Place in the preheated oven and bake for 1 hour. The vegetables will soften to a compote consistency and brown lightly. Watch to make

sure the compote doesn't brown too much. If necessary, cover with a sheet of foil.

If preparing in advance, remove the vegetables from the oven and set aside.

** Forty-five minutes before serving, preheat the oven to 400 degrees F. After 15 minutes, place the vegetables

in the oven and reheat for about 30 minutes.

Les Crêpes au Miel et aux Pignons de Provence

CRÊPES IN HONEY SAUCE WITH PROVENÇAL
PINE NUTS

Time required: *1 hour*
advance preparation
10 minutes just before serving
Difficulty: *Moderately difficult*
Cost: *Inexpensive*

Ingredients

¾ cup flour
2 eggs
2 tablespoons sugar
3 tablespoons orange juice

Salt
¾ cup milk
6 tablespoons unsalted butter, melted

HONEY SAUCE
1 cup heavy cream
4 egg yolks, at room temperature
⅓ cup honey

Few drops Pernod or other anise-flavored liqueur
¼ cup plus 2 tablespoons pine nuts

Utensils

Food processor or electric mixer
2 mixing bowls
2 6- to 7-inch crêpe pans
Small ladle
Spatula

Whisk
Baking sheet
Measuring cups and spoons
Brush
Waxed paper
Plate

Preparation

*** Both the batter and the sauce for this recipe can be prepared in advance.

Combine the flour, eggs, sugar, orange juice, and a pinch of salt in an

electric mixer, food processor, or mixing bowl and blend until smooth. Gradually mix in the milk and 2 tablespoons of the butter. Place the batter in the refrigerator to chill for at least 30 minutes.

Meanwhile, make the sauce. Beat the cream until stiff. Carefully stir in the egg yolks, honey, and a few drops of Pernod.

Brush two 7-inch crêpe pans with some of the remaining butter and place over medium heat. When the pans are

hot, ladle about ¼ cup of the batter into the center of each pan, swirling in a rapid circular motion to distribute the batter evenly over the bottom of each pan. Let the crêpes brown for about 1 minute. Turn with a spatula and let brown for 1 minute on the other side. Continue making crêpes in this manner, stacking the crêpes between sheets of waxed paper, until you have made 12 crêpes.

If preparing in advance, cover and refrigerate the crêpes and the sauce.

**Ten minutes before serving, preheat the oven to its highest temperature. Scatter the pine nuts over a baking sheet and place in the oven until lightly browned.

Meanwhile, spoon some of the sauce over the bottom of 6 dessert plates.

Fold the crêpes in quarters and arrange 2 on each plate. Spoon another layer of the sauce over the crêpes and sprinkle each serving with toasted pine nuts.

Place in the oven for 2 to 3 minutes, or until lightly browned on top, and serve.

A dessert that I would have liked to share with the writer Jean Giono, who lived in and wrote about Provence.

Tutti Frutti

Menu for 6 people

Difficulty:
Moderately difficult
Cost: *Moderate*

Anyone who has had the experience of biting into a freshly picked red pepper, green bean, or carrot knows that these vegetables have a sweetness, a crispness, and a bouquet comparable to the best fruit. And fruit—just as well as vegetables—can be used in savory dishes with delicious results. It's simply a matter of getting the proportions right.

In this chapter I present some of the ways I use fruits in my own cooking. After that, it's up to you to create your own combinations.

La Petite Soupe de Melon Glacée aux Fraises des Bois
Chilled Melon Balls and Wild Strawberries

La Daurade Royale Rôtie à la Sarriette avec le Beurre de Gingembre à l'Orange
Royal Daurade Baked with Savory in Orange-Ginger Butter

La Fricassée de Poulet aux Figues Fraîches
Fricassee of Chicken with Figs and Port Sauce

La Terrine de Fruits à la Crème d'Amande
Terrine of Assorted Fruits in Almond Cream Sauce

Doing the Marketing

One or two days in advance, order the daurade (or other white salt-water fish such as red snapper or sea trout), the chicken (free-range if you can get them), and, to be safe, the ginger. Buy the figs the day before, so that they can marinate. All the other ingredients can be bought the same day.

What to Drink

For an apéritif, you can serve a raspberry-flavored wine cocktail prepared as follows: Combine 1 bottle of dry white wine with ½ cup strained raspberry purée, 2 tablespoons Cognac, and ¼ cup raspberry liqueur. Serve well chilled in frosted glasses, with a few fresh raspberries in the bottom of each glass, and garnished with fresh mint leaves.

For the wines, choose a fruity white wine for the fish—a Loire wine, such as Pouilly-Fumé, or an Hermitage. With the chicken, serve a good red wine, such as a Châteauneuf-du-Pape or a Côtes-de-Nuits.

Table Linens and Decoration

For this menu, use a tablecloth and napkins with fruit motifs. Instead of the traditional bouquet in the middle

Not even a meal of fruit is complete without flowers.

of the table, why not substitute a lovely basket of fruits mixed with garden flowers? You could make candle holders composed of three fruits (apples, pears, etc.) joined by wooden matches or toothpicks, and placed on large fig leaves. Put brightly colored candles in them.

If you wish, write the menu on fruit-shaped silhouettes, about 4 to 6 inches across, cut out of thick colored paper.

Tableware

Plates with a fruit motif would be a good choice:
- 6 small bowls and 6 dessert plates for the melon
- 6 large plates for the daurade
- 6 large plates for the chicken
- 6 dessert plates for the fruit terrine
- 2 serving platters for the daurade and the chicken
- 1 large sauce boat for the orange butter

Silverware

- 6 dessert spoons for the melon
- 6 fish forks and knives for the daurade
- 6 dinner forks and knives for the chicken
- 6 dessert forks for the terrine
- 3 serving forks
- 3 serving spoons
- 1 ladle for the sauce boat
- 1 knife for cutting the fish

A raspberry-flavored wine apéritif makes a colorful and refreshing opener to this meal.

Glassware	18 goblets for water, white wine, and red wine

Getting Organized

Many things in this menu can be done in advance. They are indicated in each recipe by the symbol ***. The symbol ** indicates those tasks that must be done just before serving.

The day before your dinner, place the figs in the port to marinate and prepare the Terrine of Assorted Fruits.

Put the white wine in the refrigerator to chill several hours in advance.

One hour before serving, preheat the oven to 475 degrees F. Warm 12 plates, 1 sauce boat, and 2 large platters over a pan of hot water or on the back of the stove. Place 6 glasses for the apéritifs and 6 dessert plates in the refrigerator to chill. Prepare the daurade and grate the ginger and orange. Fifteen minutes before sitting down to eat, place the daurade in the oven for 35 to 40 minutes.

After serving and eating the first course, return to the kitchen and put the water on to boil for the rice. Finish the sauce for the daurade. Just before serving, put the rice in the water to cook for about 20 minutes, and place the chicken in a low oven to reheat.

When you've finished serving the daurade, finish the sauce for the chicken, arrange the chicken, sauce, and figs on a platter, and serve.

All that needs to be done before serving the dessert is to cut the terrine in slices and serve them on the strawberry coulis.

La Petite Soupe de Melon Glacée aux Fraises des Bois

CHILLED MELON BALLS AND
WILD STRAWBERRIES

Time required: *30 minutes*
Difficulty: *Easy*
Cost: *Inexpensive*

Ingredients

2	ripe Charente melons or cantaloupes (1¼ to 1½ pounds each; see Note)	½	teaspoon freshly ground pepper
¾	cup dry white wine	½	pint wild strawberries, fresh raspberries, or fresh strawberries (see Note)
⅓	cup superfine sugar	6	sprigs fresh mint

Utensils

Food processor or food mill with fine disc	Chef's knife
Large mixing bowl	Measuring cups and spoons
Melon baller	Plastic wrap
	Small bowl

Preparation

***This recipe should be prepared at least 1½ hours before serving. If you wish, most of the preparation can be done several hours in advance.

Place 6 small serving bowls in the refrigerator to chill.

Cut each melon in half; scoop out and discard the seeds.

Using a melon baller, scoop out the flesh of each melon half and place in a large mixing bowl. Cover with plastic wrap and place in the refrigerator. (Don't forget to cover the bowl or your whole refrigerator will smell like melons.)

Cut up the remaining bits of melon and place in a food processor with the wine, sugar, and pepper. Process to obtain a syrup. (If you don't have a food processor, pass the melon through a food mill and mix with the other ingredients.) Place in a small bowl and refrigerate.

Hull the strawberries and refrigerate. (If substituting fresh strawberries for wild strawberries or raspberries, wash, drain, hull, and slice them thinly. Don't wash the wild strawberries or raspberries; they are very fragile and become soggy if rinsed. Just sort through to remove dirt and damaged berries.)

An hour before serving, divide the melon balls among the chilled bowls and spoon the syrup over them. Divide the berries among the bowls and refrigerate, covered, until serving time.

❧

**When ready to serve, garnish the plates with crushed ice or decorate with paper doilies and strawberry leaves. Place the bowls of chilled melon and berries on the plates. Place a sprig of fresh mint in each bowl and serve.

❧

Note: For this recipe, choose melons that are wrinkled and marked with rough spots. Don't avoid melons that are slightly split; they will certainly have more juice than the others. A good melon must be soft to the touch on the end opposite the stalk. This recipe makes a good first course for a summer or winter meal, since you can use any kind of melon, even a watermelon.

Raspberries substitute well for tiny French fraises des bois (wild strawberries). If neither are available, use fresh strawberries but slice them thinly.

Small, honey-flavored melons from the Charentais region are ideal for this recipe.

La Daurade Royale Rôtie à la Sarriette avec le Beurre de Gingembre à l'Orange

ROYAL DAURADE BAKED WITH SAVORY IN
ORANGE-GINGER BUTTER

Time required: *20 minutes
advance preparation
45 minutes cooking*
Difficulty: *Moderately difficult*
Cost: *Expensive*

Ingredients

1	daurade royale or other whole fish such as red snapper (4½ to 5½ pounds; see Note)
	Salt
	Freshly ground pepper
1	large bunch fresh savory
½	cup virgin olive oil
3	ounces fresh gingerroot
3	large seedless oranges, Thompson if possible
½	cup water
10	tablespoons unsalted butter

Utensils

Shallow baking pan large
enough to hold the fish
Grater
Small saucepan
Whisk
Paring knife
Measuring cups
Small bowl

Orange, sarriette *(wild savory), and ginger—a marvelous combination of flavors for a summer dish.*

Preparation

Ask your fishmonger to clean and scale the fish, leaving the head and tail on.

***The first steps in the preparation of this recipe can be done 2 hours in advance.

Generously season the fish inside and out with salt and pepper. Stuff the cavity with several sprigs of savory.

Spread the remaining savory evenly over the bottom of a shallow baking pan large enough to hold the whole fish. Place the fish on the bed of savory and drizzle the olive oil evenly over the top of it. Pour 3 to 4 tablespoons of

water in the bottom of the pan. The fish should sit above the water, so that it is cooked by steam. Set aside in a cool place until ready to cook. Do not refrigerate.

Peel the gingerroot and grate. Grate the skin of half an orange and set aside

**Forty-five minutes before sitting down to eat, preheat the oven to 475 degrees F.

After 15 minutes, place the daurade in the hot oven and bake for 30 minutes. Watch the fish during the cooking so that the water does not evaporate completely. If it does, add a tablespoon or 2 more water to the pan.

Just before serving, place the water and a pinch of salt in a small saucepan and bring to a boil. Cut the butter into

with the ginger.

Working over a small bowl so that you don't lose any of the juice, peel the oranges, removing all of the white membrane underneath the skin. Separate each orange into segments and remove the dividing membranes.

small pieces and vigorously whisk into the water, a little at a time over medium-high heat, until the butter and water are entirely emulsified. Add the ginger, orange zest, and orange juice; do not let the sauce boil.

Place the orange segments in a sauce boat and pour the butter sauce over them.

Place the daurade on a large platter and serve. Pass the ginger and orange butter separately.

Note: The daurade royale is one of the most noble Mediterranean fish. It's distinguished by a steel-gray color and a snub-nosed head with a small gold bump on it. Other fish that can be used in this recipe include red snapper, striped bass, sea bass, and sea trout.

La Fricassée de Poulet aux Figues Fraîches

FRICASSEE OF CHICKEN WITH
FIGS AND PORT SAUCE

Time required: *2 hours*
Difficulty: *Moderately difficult*
Cost: *Moderate*

Ingredients

12	large ripe purple figs
1¼	cups port wine
3	bay leaves
2	teaspoons coriander seed
1	large ripe tomato
1	celery rib
3	cloves garlic
2	chickens (3½ pounds each; see

	Note)
	Salt
	Freshly ground pepper
1	cup unsalted butter
3	tablespoons minced shallots
2	cubes chicken bouillon
1¼	cups white rice

Utensils

Large ovenproof casserole with cover
Medium saucepan
2 small saucepans
Small skillet
Fine sieve
Large jar with lid

Rolling pin
Wooden spoon
Paring knife
Chef's knife
Plate
Cheesecloth

Preparation

***Twenty-four hours before you plan to serve this dish, place the figs in a large jar. Pour the port over them, add 1 of the bay leaves, and cover tightly with a lid. Set aside to marinate outside of the refrigerator. (If you are short of time, the figs can be marinated more quickly by combining them with the port and bay leaf in a saucepan and simmering over very low heat while you're preparing the chicken.)

The preparation of the chicken can be started several hours in advance. Place the coriander seeds in a small skillet and toast to dry over high heat. Tie the seeds in a square of cheesecloth and crush to a fine powder with a rolling pin.

Cut the tomato in half and gently

The fricassée can be served on a bed of fresh fig leaves.

squeeze out the seeds and juice. Trim the celery. Dice the tomato and celery. Crush the garlic cloves.

Cut each chicken into 6 pieces: 2 breasts with wings, 2 thighs, and 2 drumsticks. Season with salt and pepper. Break up the wing ends, necks, and carcasses and reserve for the sauce.

Melt 4 tablespoons of the butter in a large ovenproof casserole over medium heat. Add the chicken pieces and sauté over medium-high heat until lightly browned on all sides. Remove the chicken pieces to a plate. Add the carcasses, necks, and wing ends to the casserole and sauté over medium heat until browned. Add the shallots and sauté briefly.

Pour off the excess butter and return the casserole to the heat. Add the crushed coriander seeds, 2 bay leaves, the garlic, celery, and tomatoes.

Pour half of the port in which the figs have been marinating (about ⅔ cup) into the casserole. Return the chicken to the casserole, arranging the pieces so that they are not completely covered with the port. Cover the casserole and let simmer over very low heat for 30 minutes.

Meanwhile, pour the remaining port into a small saucepan and reduce over medium heat until only about 2 tablespoons of thick syrup remains. Set aside.

After the chicken has simmered for half an hour, add ⅔ cup water and the bouillon cubes to the casserole. Simmer, uncovered, for 10 minutes, stirring with a wooden spoon to loosen

The silverware and tablecloth contribute to the atmosphere of the menu.

the bits of meat that stick to the bottom of the casserole.

Drain the cooking liquid from the casserole and strain though a fine sieve. (There should be about ⅔ cup.) Re-

**Twenty-five minutes before serving, bring 1 quart of salted water to a boil in a medium saucepan. Add the rice and cook over medium-high heat for about 20 minutes, until all the water is absorbed.

Place the casserole with the chicken over very low heat to warm. (Don't let the liquid reduce.)

Meanwhile, place the marinated figs in the saucepan with the reduced port syrup. Warm over low heat, rolling the figs gently in the syrup to give them a glistening coat.

move the wing ends, necks, and carcasses. Pour the strained cooking liquid back over the chicken in the casserole and set aside.

Arrange the chicken on a large, warmed serving platter and keep warm. Pour the sauce into a small saucepan and place over low heat. Cut 9 tablespoons butter into small pieces and add to the sauce one piece at a time, whisking vigorously over medium-low heat until the sauce is just below boiling.

Spoon the sauce over the chicken, and place the glistening figs on top.

Stir the remaining 3 tablespoons butter into the rice, transfer to a serving dish, and serve with the chicken.

La Terrine de Fruits à la Crème d'Amande

TERRINE OF ASSORTED FRUITS
IN ALMOND CREAM SAUCE

Time required: *30 minutes*
preparation
(24 hours in advance)
Difficulty: *Moderately difficult*
Cost: *Expensive*

Ingredients

1⅓	cups unsalted butter
1	ripe pear
1	kiwi fruit
1½	oranges
1⅓	cups sugar
1¾	cups almond powder (see Appendix), or 2 cups almonds ground to a fine powder in a food processor
4	eggs
⅔	cup green grapes
⅔	cup black grapes
1	tablespoon chopped pistachios
1	tablespoon chopped candied orange peel
1	pint fresh strawberries, or 1 package (10 ounces) frozen whole strawberries

Utensils

Food processor
Electric mixer
Rectangular terrine, about 6
inches long
Mixing bowl
Whisk

Spatula
Small bowl
Large, sharp knife
Paring knife
Measuring cups

❧

Preparation

*** This recipe should be prepared at least a day in advance and kept in the refrigerator until serving time.

Remove the butter from the refrigerator to allow it to soften.

Peel and core the pear. Peel the kiwi. Cut both into thin slices. Peel the oranges, removing all the white membrane underneath the skin. Separate into segments and remove the dividing membrane. Cut each segment in half lengthwise.

Place the butter in a food processor or mixing bowl and process until creamy. Add 1 cup of the sugar, processing constantly. Add the almond powder and eggs and process until creamy, smooth, and very firm.

Using a spatula, spread the almond

cream over the sides and bottom of the terrine. Arrange the kiwi, pears, oranges, and the green and black grapes in successive layers, alternating colors and separating each layer with a layer of almond cream and a sprinkling of pistachios and candied orange peel. Finish with a layer of almond cream. Cover and place the terrine in the refrigerator to chill for at least 1½ hours, or overnight, if possible.

Wash, drain, and hull the strawberries. (Never remove the stems before washing the berries or sand may wash into the stem cavity.) Place the berries in a food processor with the remaining ⅓ cup sugar and process to a smooth purée. Refrigerate until just before serving.

❧

**Just before serving, spoon the strawberry coulis over the bottom of 6 dessert plates. Unmold the terrine. Using a very sharp knife dipped in hot

water, cut the terrine into 6 equal slices. Place one slice on top of the coulis on each plate and serve.

❧

Note: Select the most succulent, beautiful fruit you can find for this terrine.

A collage of fruits in almond cream—a dessert terrine that must be quickly consumed.

Menu for 6 People

Un Petit Air de Vacances

A Holiday Mood

Difficulty: *Moderate*
Cost: *Expensive*

Le Gaspacho de Thon et de Saumon Frais
Gazpacho of Fresh Tuna and Salmon

La Salade d'Écrevisses en Nage Froide
Chilled Crayfish Salad

Les Cailles en Tourte de Pommes, aux Baies de Genièvre
Quail in a Potato Tourte with Juniper Berries

Le Cocktail de Fruits Rouges au Champagne
Red Fruit Cocktail with Champagne

A vacation is a time when you abandon a cozy house or apartment and exchange it for another, generally less comfortable one, located hundreds of miles away. But above all, it's an occasion for abandoning obligations, proprieties, and depressing daily habits, to rediscover—well, what you rediscover depends on you. Some people merely rediscover other obligations, proprieties, and depressing daily habits. But for some people, like myself, a real vacation is a sort of return to childhood. I try to put my dignity and seriousness in mothballs for a few weeks and to rediscover the freedom of movement, of attitude, and of feeling I had as a child. I also rediscover those innocent and pointless pleasures—like casually crumbling my bread into my gazpa-cho. I would never do that at home in front of my guests—and that's exactly what vacations are for.

Doing the Marketing

Be sure that the fish for the gazpacho are very fresh. If tuna or salmon is not available, many other fresh salt-water fish can be used. I have even used fresh shrimp or scallops.
Order the crayfish and the quail in advance.

What to Drink

For the apéritif, since you've opened a bottle of Champagne for the dessert, finish it. (To prevent Champagne from going flat if you don't drink it all shortly after opening, you can place the handle of a silver spoon into the neck of the bottle. Yes. This prevents the bubbles from escaping.)
For the wine, serve a dry white wine, such as a Cassis or Graves, with the gazpacho and the crayfish. With the quail, choose a light red wine (a young red Graves or a chilled Bourgueil).

Table Linens and Decoration

Choose light, colorful table linens that evoke a holiday feeling. If you cannot eat outdoors, try to re-create the open-air atmosphere with garden chairs and table, green plants, leafy branches, and large bunches of wildfowers. And why not add the chirping of birds or cicadas for background music? (They exist on cassette.)

Write the menu on the back of old vacation postcards.

Tableware

Choose country-style dishes, or even those with vacation motifs (like little boats):

- 6   shallow soup bowls for the gazpacho
- 6   small bowls or 6 large glasses for the crayfish
- 6   large dinner plates
- 6   dessert plates
- 6   paper doilies
- 1   large round platter for the quail tourte

Silverware

- 6   spoons and 6 dessert forks for the gazpacho
- 6   spoons and 6 dessert forks for the crayfish
- 6   dinner forks and knives for the quail
- 6   dessert spoons
- 1   serving spoon and 1 serving fork
- 1   pie server

Glassware

- 18   Bordeaux glasses for water, white wine, and red wine

Getting Organized

Even the preparation of this menu is in keeping with the vacation spirit, because the majority of the recipes can be prepared in advance. You will have almost nothing to do during the meal.

In the recipes the symbol *** indicates all that can be prepared the day before or several hours in advance. The symbol ** indicates those tasks that must be done just before serving.

Put the white wine in the refrigerator to chill several hours in advance.

Thirty minutes before serving, warm 6 large plates over a saucepan filled with warm water or on the back of the stove.

Ten minutes before serving, finish preparing the gazpacho, and preheat the oven to 400 degrees F.

After serving the gazpacho, place the quail tourte in the oven and serve the crayfish.

To serve the other dishes, all you'll need to do is put them on the table.

Try to find old menus with common themes for this luncheon. Even the ashtrays are part of the décor.

Menu

- Gaspacho de thon et de saumon frais.
- Salade d'écrevisses en nage froide.
- Cailles en croûte de pommes aux baies de genièvre.
- Cocktail de fruits rouges au champagne.
- Café.

Le Gaspacho de Thon et de Saumon Frais

GAZPACHO OF FRESH TUNA AND SALMON

Time required: *35 minutes*
advance preparation
15 minutes just before serving
Difficulty: *Very easy*
Cost: *Expensive*

Ingredients

2½ pounds ripe Italian plum tomatoes, or 2 cans (28 ounces each) Italian plum tomatoes, drained
1 sweet red pepper
1 cucumber
1 clove garlic
Salt
¼ cup virgin olive oil
2 tablespoons wine vinegar

Tabasco sauce
1 medium-size white onion
1 tablespoon chopped fresh tarragon
1 tablespoon chopped fresh parsley
½ pound fresh tuna fillets
½ pound fresh salmon fillets
Juice of 1 lemon

Utensils

Food processor or food mill with fine disc
Mixing bowl
Colander
Sieve

Chef's knife
Spoon
Large plate
Whisk
Measuring cups and spoons

Preparation

***It's best to prepare the gazpacho 2 to 3 hours in advance so that it can chill before serving. Or, if you wish, prepare everything except the fish a day in advance. Cut and season the fish just before serving.

Place a medium saucepan filled with water over high heat and bring to a boil. Plunge the tomatoes into the water and boil for 30 seconds. Drain, rinse in cold water, and peel. Cut the tomatoes in half and gently squeeze out the seeds and juice.

Served by the pool, this **pique-nique** *becomes a more formal event with the addition of quails in a hot tourte preparation.*

Cut the pepper in half and remove the core and seeds. Peel the cucumber, cut in half lengthwise, and scoop out the seeds with a small spoon. Peel the garlic clove.

In a food processor or a food mill with a fine disc, combine the tomatoes, half of the pepper, half of the cucumber, and the garlic, and purée. Season with salt. Add the oil, vinegar, and 2 or 3 drops Tabasco and purée until the mixture is reduced to the consistency of light cream. Adjust the seasonings, if necessary.

Peel the onion and cut into small dice. Place in a fine sieve and rinse under cold water. Cut the remaining cucumber and pepper into small dice the size of the onion. Finely chop the tarragon or parsley leaves. Combine the onions, cucumber, pepper, and tarragon in a mixing bowl and toss well. Chill.

Place a large plate in the refrigerator to chill.

**About 15 minutes before serving, cut the tuna and salmon fillets into thin julienne about 2 inches long. Place the fish on the chilled plate and season lightly with salt. Sprinkle with the lemon juice. Place in the refrigerator to chill for 12 minutes. (The fish should not sit for longer than this as the lemon juice will dry it out. If you prefer to slice the fish in advance, wait until 10 or 12 minutes before serving to add the lemon juice.)

Just before serving, divide the fish among 6 chilled large, shallow bowls, arranging the pieces attractively in the center of each bowl. Pour the vegetable purée over the fish. Sprinkle each portion with the diced vegetables and chopped herbs and serve.

Note: You'll need very fresh fish for this dish. Use Norwegian or Scotch salmon, if possible. Ask your fishmonger to give you tuna from the midsection; pieces cut from close to the head or tail can be coarse. If tuna and salmon are not available, many other fresh salt-water fish, such as sea bass and monkfish, can be substituted.

La Salade d'Ecrevisses en Nage Froide

CHILLED CRAYFISH SALAD

Time required: *1 hour*
Difficulty: *Moderately easy*
Cost: *Expensive*

Ingredients

¾ to 1 pound cucumbers (about 2 medium)
Salt
1 egg
1 bouquet garni composed of 3 or 4 sprigs parsley, 1 bay leaf, 2 sprigs fresh thyme, and 1 small bunch fresh mint or tarragon, all tied together with string
4½ pounds live crayfish
1 carrot

1 small onion
2 tablespoons chopped shallots
2 tablespoons chopped celery
½ cup dry white wine
½ cup water
¾ cup plain yogurt
1 tablespoon crème fraîche (see Appendix), or heavy cream

The sauce for the crayfish salad is made of vegetables, herbs, yogurt, and a little crème fraîche.

Freshly ground pepper
1½ teaspoon chopped fresh mint or tarragon

1½ teaspoons chopped fresh chervil

❧

Utensils

Stockpot
Food processor
2 small saucepans
Colander
Chef's knife

Paring knife
Large mixing bowl
Small bowl
Measuring cups and spoons

❧

Preparation

***This salad can be almost entirely prepared 3 to 4 hours in advance.

Peel the cucumbers, cut them in half lengthwise, and scoop out the seeds with a small spoon. Slice thinly, place in a colander, sprinkle with 1 tablespoon salt, and toss. Let drain.

In small saucepan of boiling water, cook the egg for 10 minutes.

Fill a stockpot with 6 quarts water. Season with 3 tablespoons salt, and add the bouquet garni. Bring to boil over high heat. Add the crayfish and boil for 5 minutes. Remove from the heat and drain the crayfish immediately; let cool.

Scrape the carrot and coarsely chop. Peel the onion and coarsely chop.

Place the carrot, onion, shallot, and celery in a small saucepan. Add the wine and water. Bring to a boil and cook for 2 minutes.

Pour the vegetables and their liquid into a food processor and purée. Pour into a small bowl and refrigerate until chilled.

Rinse the cucumber in cold water and let drain.

Remove the heads from the crayfish, reserving 6 heads to decorate the plates and discarding the rest. Remove the shells from the crayfish tails, being careful to pull out the meat all in one piece.

Place 2 cups of the well-chilled vegetable purée in the food processor along with the yogurt and crème fraîche. Season with salt and pepper and process until smooth and creamy.

In a large mixing bowl, combine the crayfish tails, cucumbers, mint or tarragon, chervil, and the vegetable cream mixture. Adjust the seasoning and mix well.

❧

**Just before serving, chop the egg.

Divide the crayfish salad among 6 chilled bowls. Sprinkle each portion

with chopped egg and decorate with a crayfish head.

❧

Note: It is important that the crayfish be alive. A dead crayfish—like all crustaceans—loses its fluids very quickly and becomes inedible. You will find commercially raised crayfish that have been gutted. But, if you are lucky enough to find wild crayfish, it is necessary to take out their intestinal tract just before cooking them. To do this,

hold the crayfish's head with one hand; with the other, seize the body between your thumb and index finger and pull backwards quickly, giving a quarter turn. This operation has to be done just before cooking, otherwise the crayfish will drain very rapidly. For commercially raised crayfish this procedure is of less importance because they have generally been without food for 2 or 3 days and their intestines are quite empty.

Les Cailles en Tourte de Pommes, aux Baies de Genièvre

QUAIL IN A POTATO TOURTE WITH JUNIPER BERRIES

Time required: *1¼ hours*
advance preparation
20 minutes cooking just before serving
Difficulty: *Moderately easy*
Cost: *Moderate*

Ingredients

6	fresh quail
24	juniper berries
	Salt
7	tablespoons unsalted butter
2¾	pounds potatoes
	Freshly ground pepper
1	small bunch parsley or watercress

Utensils

Round tart pan, 9 or 10 inches in diameter, or a baking sheet
Large heavy skillet, 9 or 10 inches in diameter
Food processor with a julienne attachment
Chef's knife
Tablespoon
Large metal spatula

Preparation

Ask your butcher to clean the quail, removing the head and neck.

***Crush the juniper berries with the blade of a chef's knife held flat.

Place 4 juniper berries in the cavity of each quail. Season generously with salt, inside and out.

Melt 1 tablespoon of the butter in a large skillet. Add the quail and cook over medium-high heat until lightly browned on all sides, about 10 minutes. Remove the skillet from the heat and set the quail aside on a plate.

Wash and peel the potatoes. Using a food processor with a julienne attachment, or a knife, cut the potatoes into fine julienne.

Melt 3 tablespoons butter in the skillet. Add half of the potatoes, spreading them out evenly over the bottom of the skillet and pressing down gently with a spatula to form a potato cake. Season with salt and pepper and sauté over high heat until the bottom is golden, about 5 minutes. Turn the potato cake with a large metal spatula, being careful not to break it. Season with salt and pepper and cook over high heat until the second side is golden.

Transfer the potato cake to a buttered tart pan that is the same diameter as the skillet, or a buttered baking

sheet.

Melt the remaining 3 tablespoons butter in the skillet, add the remaining potatoes, and cook as you did the first potato cake.

Meanwhile, cut each quail in half through the breastbones and distribute them evenly over the first potato cake.

**Forty minutes before serving, preheat the oven to 400 degrees F.

Trim the stems from the parsley or watercress.

After 20 minutes, place the quail pie in the oven and bake for 20 minutes.

Press the quail halves down gently so that they stay in position.

Remove the second potato cake from the skillet and position it over the quail and the first potato cake. Gently press the edges of the potato cakes together.

Carefully invert the pie onto a large round serving platter. The bottom should be well browned. Place the parsley or watercress in the center the pie and cut into wedges to serve.

Le Cocktail de Fruits Rouges au Champagne

RED FRUIT COCKTAIL WITH CHAMPAGNE

Time required: *40 minutes*
Difficulty: *Very easy*
Cost: *Expensive*

Ingredients

½	pint fresh strawberries
½	pint fresh wild strawberries
½	pint fresh raspberries
½	pint fresh red currants

¾	cup sugar
2	tablespoons water
½	bottle chilled Champagne (about 1½ cups)

Utensils

Small saucepan
Small mixing bowl
Cheesecloth

Plates
Wooden spoon
6 paper doilies

Preparation

***Prepare the fruits several hours in advance.

Wash, drain, and hull the strawberries. (Never remove the stem before washing the fruit or sand may wash into the stem cavity. Don't wash the wild strawberries or raspberries; they

are very fragile and become soggy if rinsed. Just sort through to remove dirt and any damaged berries.) Remove the currants from their stems, rinse, and drain.

Place half of the currants in a small saucepan. Add ¼ cup of the sugar and the water. Bring to a boil over medium heat. Remove from the heat and let cool slightly.

preceding overleaf: A taste of sea and holiday in this Charles Atamian painting.

Line a small mixing bowl with cheesecloth. Pour the currants and their juice into it. Draw up the corners of the cheesecloth and wring out, squeezing the juice into the mixing bowl. (If you're not using currants, replace them with raspberries and add the juice of ½ lemon.)

Pour the remaining ½ cup sugar onto a large plate. Dip the rims of 6 goblets or glass dessert bowls into the currant syrup. Shake off the excess syrup, then dip each goblet into the sugar to frost the edges with sugar.

Spoon the fruit into the goblets, being careful not to disturb the sugar frosting and filling each dish only two-thirds full. Divide the remaining currant syrup among the 6 portions.

If preparing in advance, chill until serving time.

❀

**At serving time, line 6 dessert plates with paper doilies. If you wish, make a small slit in each doily and slip a fresh flower into each. Place the fruit-filled goblets on the plates and take them to the table.

At the table, pour the chilled Champagne into the goblets, filling each to the rim. A pink mousse will form on top of each.

❀

Note: The combination of fruits can be varied in this recipe according to what's available. The wild strawberries (fraises des bois) are often difficult to find: substitute blackberries or blueberries, or increase the quantity of fresh strawberries in their place. Or, if you wish, use only one type of fruit (except for the currants, which are too acid to be used alone). If you have to eliminate the currants, add a little lemon juice to the syrup to give it a pleasant acidity.

Black currants and blackberries may be added to the red fruit in this dessert cocktail.

Menu for 6 People

Sous la Tonnelle

Under the Arbor

Difficulty: *Moderate*
Cost: *Inexpensive*

I don't know if the French word for arbor, *tonnelle*, has the same origin as the word "tunnel," but it is exactly the image that the long, arched walkway in our garden evokes from my childhood. It was covered with raspberry vines and intertwined with wisteria; in springtime, bees hummed around its flowers and birds nested in its foliage. We used to have our summer meals under its shady arch, a covering so thick that not even the autumn rains could penetrate it.

I don't know whether the passage of time makes places and events from childhood seem more beautiful, but one thing I am certain of is that no other place has given me more pleasant recollections than this one.

La Compote de Poivrons Doux aux Anchois
Roasted Sweet Pepper and Anchovy Compote

La Croûte de Volaille de Grand-Mère Catherine
Grandmother Catherine's Chicken Pie

Salade de Chicorée Frisée à l'Huile de Noix et à l'Estragon
Salad of Chicory with Hazelnut Oil and Tarragon Dressing

Le Dôme de Fromage Frais aux Herbes Vertes
Dome of Fresh Cheese with Green Herbs

Les Tartelettes aux Fruits du Temps
Seasonal Fruit Tartlets

Doing the Marketing

Order the chicken in advance to make sure that you get the finest quality.

Buy the ingredients for the dome of fresh cheeses the day before so that you can make it the night before serving. The remaining ingredients can be purchased the day of the dinner.

What to Drink

For an apéritif, serve the same dry white wine you plan to serve with the Roasted Sweet Pepper and Anchovy Compote (a Chablis or Mâcon, for example), adding 1 large tablespoon of crème de cassis or framboise to each glass.

For the wines, after the white wine, serve a light, slightly chilled (53 to 55 degrees F) red such as a Chinon, a Beaujolais Villages, or a Côte-de-Bourg.

Lunch under the arbor of Bernard Chevry, a celebrated organizer of many civic functions in Cannes.

Table Linens and Decoration

If you have an arbor, think first of your guests' comfort: make sure there are cushions on the chairs and a few straw hats available for those whom the sun might bother. And above all, make sure there's a tub full of ice to keep the bottles of wine cold.

If you don't have a garden, you can still capture the right atmosphere with a tablecloth and napkins of unbleached linen, earthenware or stoneware pitchers, wicker baskets, branches, and even—why not—boater hats for your guests.

Write out the menu on little ribboned chopping boards or on cards. Wrap the rolled-up napkins in an ivy branch.

Tableware

Choose a rustic faïence tableware, or terra cotta:

- 6 salad plates for the roasted pepper compote
- 6 dinner plates for the chicken pie
- 6 dessert plates for the salad
- 6 dessert plates for the fresh cheese
- 6 dessert plates for the tartlets
- 1 crock or earthenware bowl for serving the roasted pepper compote
- 1 round platter for the chicken pie
- 1 salad bowl
- 1 round plate for the fresh cheese

Silverware

- 6 forks and knives for the peppers
- 6 forks and knives for the chicken
- 6 dessert forks and knives for the cheese
- 6 dessert forks and knives for the tartlets
- 2 serving forks and 2 serving spoons
- 1 pie server
- 1 knife for cutting the chicken
- 2 salad servers

Glassware

18 rustic glasses, with or without stems

Getting Organized

Many items in this menu can be prepared well in advance. They are indicated in each recipe with the symbol ***. The symbol ** indicates those tasks that must be done just before serving.

Put the white wine in the refrigerator to chill several hours in advance.

Forty-five minutes before the meal, set the oven to 400 degrees F. Warm 6 serving plates and 1 round platter on the back of the stove or over a saucepan filled with warm water.

Fifteen or 20 minutes later, when the oven is hot, place the chicken pie in the oven. After 20 minutes of cooking, reduce the oven temperature to 300 degrees and cook for another 10 minutes.

Toast the bread slices for the Roasted Sweet Pepper and Anchovy Compote in the hot oven.

Just before sitting down to eat, turn

off the oven, open the oven door slightly, and let the chicken pie rest un-til serving time.

La Compote de Poivrons Doux aux Anchois

ROASTED SWEET PEPPER AND ANCHOVY
COMPOTE

Time required: *40 minutes
advance preparation
5 minutes just before serving*
Difficulty: *Easy*
Cost: *Inexpensive*

Ingredients

30 flat anchovy fillets, drained (about three 2-ounce cans)
    Milk
6   large, fleshy sweet red or yel-low peppers
3   cloves garlic
18 fresh basil leaves
6   fresh mint leaves
⅔   cup virgin olive oil
¾   teaspoon thyme flowers, fresh thyme, or ¼ teaspoon dried thyme
    Freshly ground pepper
12 thick slices country-style bread

Utensils

Heavy medium skillet
Large mixing bowl or earthen-ware crock
Cutting board
Chef's knife
Wooden spoon
Small bowl
Measuring cups and spoons

Preparation

***This recipe can be prepared a day in advance or on the morning of the din-ner. If you store it in the refrigerator, remember to take it out at least 1 hour before serving.

Preheat the broiler.

Place the anchovy fillets in a small bowl. Add enough milk to cover and let soak.

Place the peppers under the broiler

and let them roast, turning frequently until the skin is blackened on all sides. (This can also be done by piercing the pepper with a wood-handled fork and holding over the flame of a gas burner or over a grill.) When the peppers are charred, hold them under cold water and peel off the black skin with your fingers. Remove the stems, cut the peppers open, and remove the core and seeds. Slice the peppers into long, thin strips.

Peel and chop the garlic. Chop the basil and mint.

Heat the oil in a heavy medium skillet. Add the peppers and thyme flowers and simmer over very low heat for 15 minutes.

Meanwhile, drain the anchovy fillets and pat dry. Add to the skillet with the peppers and stir with a wooden spoon until the anchovies have "melted."

Remove the skillet from the heat and stir in the garlic, basil, and mint. Season with pepper. Turn the mixture into a large mixing bowl or earthenware crock.

**Just before serving, toast 12 slices of country-style bread and serve on a platter with the pepper compote and knives for spreading the compote on

the bread. Hard-cooked eggs, black Niçoise olives, and flaked white tuna can be served along with this compote.

La Croûte de Volaille de Grand-Mère Catherine

GRANDMOTHER CATHERINE'S CHICKEN PIE

Time required: *1 hour and 10 minutes*
advance preparation
30 minutes cooking
just before serving
Difficulty: *Moderately difficult*
Cost: *Inexpensive*

Ingredients

DOUGH
4   cups flour
¾   cup lard or unsalted butter

1   tablespoon salt
½   cup water

CHICKEN FILLING
6   chicken quarters (3 wing sections and 3 thigh sections)
    Salt
13 tablespoons unsalted butter
¾   to 1 pound slab bacon
3   medium white onions

4   cloves garlic
2   leeks
    Freshly ground pepper
6   small bay leaves, fresh if possible
6   small sprigs fresh thyme
1   egg

Utensils

Food processor or large mixing
bowl and wooden spoon
Large skillet with cover
Small skillet
Small saucepan
Baking sheet
Chef's knife
Cutting board

Cleaver
Rolling pin
Small sharp knife
Small bowl
Brush
Dishcloth
Measuring cups and spoons
Colander

Preparation

✳✳✳The dough can be made a day in advance, and the chicken and vegetables can be prepared several hours in advance.

To make the dough, place the flour in a food processor or in a large mixing bowl. Place the lard, salt, and ½ cup water in a small saucepan and bring to a boil. Pour this mixture into the flour and process or blend with a wooden spoon until a ball forms. Wrap the dough in a damp dishcloth and chill for at least 1 hour.

To prepare the chicken filling, make a cut in the joint between the drumstick and thigh. Insert the tip of a sharp knife under the skin at the end of the drumstick and cut to detach the skin and flesh from the bone. Push the drumstick meat up toward the thigh, and, using a cleaver or large knife, cut away half of the drumstick bone. Pull the meat and skin back down over the cut bone. To prepare the wing quarters, remove the wing ends and the breastbones. Season the chicken pieces with salt.

Melt 4 tablespoons of the butter in a large skillet. Add the chicken pieces, skin sides down, and sauté over medium-high heat until just lightly browned, about 4 minutes per side.

While the chicken cooks, cut the slab bacon into thin julienne about 1 inch long. Melt 1 tablespoon butter in a small skillet. Add the bacon and sauté for about 5 minutes. Drain.

Remove the chicken pieces from the skillet and let cool. Rinse the skillet.

Peel the onion and garlic. Trim and thoroughly wash the leeks, discarding all but the white portions. Mince the onion, garlic, and leeks and set aside separately.

Melt 7 tablespoons butter in the skillet. Add the onions and leeks, cover, and sauté slowly over low heat until tender. Season lightly with salt and add the garlic. Add the bacon, toss with the vegetables, and set aside to cool.

Remove the dough from the refrigerator and divide into two equal parts. Sprinkle a flat work surface with flour and roll out half of the dough into a 13-inch circle. Place on a well-buttered baking sheet.

Spread the vegetable and bacon mixture evenly over the round of dough, leaving a 1-inch border all around the edge. Place the chicken on the bed of vegetables, intertwining the wings and thighs. Season with a grind of fresh pepper. Place a bay leaf and a sprig of fresh thyme on each piece of chicken.

Roll out the remaining dough into a circle slightly larger than the first round.

In a small bowl, beat the egg with 1 tablespoon water. Using a brush, coat the edge of the bottom half of the pastry dough with the egg wash. Place the second round of dough on top of the chicken so that it covers the chicken and lines up with the bottom round of dough. Press the edges of the two pieces of dough together carefully with

your fingers, flattening the borders slightly. Trim the edge of the dough to 1 inch. Brush with the egg wash, then fold the dough edge back over itself to form a neatly crimped edge. Brush the border and the top of the dough with the egg wash.

Roll out the dough trimmings and cut into diamonds. Form into petals and make a flower for the center of the pie. Brush with the egg wash. Pierce the dough in 10 or 12 places with the point of a knife to prevent it from bursting during cooking.

✳✳An hour before serving, preheat the oven to 400 degrees F. Twenty minutes later, place the pie in the oven and bake for 20 minutes.

After 20 minutes, reduce the oven temperature to 300 degrees F and continue to cook for 10 minutes longer.

Turn off the oven and let the pie rest for 10 minutes with the oven door ajar. Melt the remaining 1 tablespoon butter and brush it over the top of the pie just before serving to give the pie a glistening crust.

La Salade de Chicorée Frisée à l'Huile de Noix et à l'Estragon

CHICORY SALAD WITH HAZELNUT OIL AND
TARRAGON DRESSING

Time required: *15 minutes*
Difficulty: *Easy*
Cost: *Moderate*

Ingredients				
1	tablespoon strong Dijon mustard		2	tablespoons wine vinegar
	Salt		1½	teaspoons finely chopped tarragon
	Freshly ground pepper		¼	cup plus 2 tablespoons hazelnut oil
1	egg yolk			
1	tablespoon Cognac (see Note)		2	heads chicory or curly endive

Utensils		
	Large salad bowl	Measuring spoons
	Whisk	

Preparation

***In a large salad bowl, combine the mustard, salt, pepper, and egg yolk and beat with a whisk. Add the Cognac, vinegar, and tarragon and whisk until blended.

Pour in the oil in a thin, steady stream, whisking continuously until thoroughly incorporated. Adjust the seasoning, if necessary.

Wash and dry the endive, removing any bad leaves.

**Just before serving, place in the salad bowl and toss with the dressing. (You can toss with your hands: it's the easiest way, and your guests won't be any the wiser!) Bring the salad to the table when you serve the chicken and serve the salad on separate plates.

Note: I have substituted Cognac for the white fruit liqueur that my grandmother used to use when making this salad. This white liqueur, extracted from a variety of garden fruits, was distilled at home and had a slight taste of almonds. There was nothing remarkable about it, but it was special to us because it was our own little dram.

Le Dôme de Fromage Frais aux Herbes Vertes

DOME OF FRESH CHEESE WITH GREEN HERBS

Time required: *25 minutes*
preparation (at least 12 hours in advance)
5 minutes preparation just before serving
Difficulty: *Easy*
Cost: *Inexpensive*

Ingredients

1   small white onion
1   clove garlic
1   pound chilled fresh fromage blanc, drained, or 1½ cups small-curd cottage cheese and ½ cup plain yogurt, at room temperature
1   tablespoon strong Dijon mustard

1   teaspoon freshly ground pepper
    Salt
1   cup crème fraîche (see Appendix), or heavy cream
3   small heads Bibb lettuce, or other soft lettuce
1   bunch parsley
1   bunch chives
    Bread slices

Utensils

Large mixing bowl
Medium mixing bowl
Fine sieve, about 8 inches in diameter
Garlic press

Grater
Whisk
Chef's knife
Cutting board
Plastic wrap

Large, round serving platter   Measuring cups and spoons

Preparation   ***This fresh cheese should be prepared at least 12 hours before serving.

Peel the onion and garlic. Grate the onion as finely as possible into a large mixing bowl. Crush the garlic through a press into the bowl. Add the cheese, mustard, pepper, and salt. Beat the mixture with a whisk until well blended.

In a medium mixing bowl, beat ½ cup of the crème fraîche until thick. Do not overwhip. Add the crème to the cheese and blend thoroughly.

Turn the mixture into a fine sieve placed over a medium mixing bowl. Cover with plastic wrap and let drain in the refrigerator for at least 12 hours.

**Fifteen minutes before serving, preheat the broiler. Wash and drain the lettuce and separate the leaves. Finely chop the parsley and chives.

Remove the cheese from the refrigerator and sprinkle with some of the herbs. Invert the dome of cheese onto a chilled serving platter. Sprinkle the dome with the remaining herbs, gently

pressing them into the cheese.

Toast the bread slices under the broiler.

Surround the cheese with the lettuce leaves. Drizzle the remaining crème fraîche over the top of the cheese and place the toasted bread in a basket. Serve the dome of cheese with the warm bread.

Les Tartelettes aux Fruits du Temps

SEASONAL FRUIT TARTLETS

Time required: *1 hour*
advance preparation
2 minutes preparation just before serving
Difficulty: *Moderate*
Cost: *Moderate*

Ingredients

½ cup unsalted butter
1 orange
1 apple
1 pear
1 peach
1 large lemon
1 cup almond powder (see

Fresh fromage blanc will be served on lettuce leaves with lightly toasted bread.

Appendix)
3½ cups sugar
3 eggs
1 pint fresh raspberries
½ cup apple or quince jelly
6 fresh, unblemished strawberries
½ ripe banana
½ cup fresh red currants or blueberries
Mint leaves

Utensils

6 individual tartlet molds, each 4 inches in diameter
Small saucepan
Food processor, blender, or food mill
2 large mixing bowls
Baking sheet

Paring knife
Chef's knife
Small spatula
Whisk
Wooden spoon
Measuring cups and spoons

Preparation

***Most of this recipe should be prepared in advance, on the morning of the dinner, if possible.

Remove the butter from the refrigerator and let soften to room temperature.

Peel the orange, pear, apple, and peach. Core, if appropriate, and chop into ½-inch cubes. Place the fruit in a mixing bowl and sprinkle with the juice of the lemon to prevent darkening.

Preheat the oven to 425 degrees F.

In a large mixing bowl, combine the softened butter with the almond powder and mix well. Add ½ cup of the sugar and blend thoroughly. Add the eggs, one at a time, and beat with a whisk until the eggs are thoroughly incorporated and a smooth dough has formed.

Divide the almond dough into 6 equal parts. Press the dough firmly and evenly into the bottom and sides of 6 well-buttered individual tartlet molds. Place the molds on a baking sheet and bake for 15 minutes.

Meanwhile, set aside 12 unblemished raspberries for decorating the tarts. Purée the remaining raspberries in a food processor or food mill fitted with a fine disc. Drain through a fine sieve to separate the juice from the

pulp. If using a food mill, scrape the pulp off the disc of the mill and reserve. Add 1 cup sugar to the juice, blend well, and set aside.

Scrape the raspberry pulp into a small saucepan. Add the remaining 2 cups sugar and heat over low heat, stirring with a wooden spoon, for about 15 minutes, until the mixture thickens.

Remove the almond tart shells from the oven, let cool slightly, and unmold them. Spread each tart shell with a layer of the raspberry pulp mixture. Arrange the mixed chopped fruit attractively on each tart. (If you have used large fruit, you may have more filling than needed. Do not overfill the tarts.)

Melt the jelly in a small saucepan placed in a larger saucepan of boiling water. Spoon about 1 tablespoon of the jelly over each tart. When it dries, this glaze will hold the fruit in place.

To decorate the tarts, rinse the strawberries and cut each in half. Cut the banana in rounds. Arrange the strawberry halves, bananas, currants, and the reserved raspberries attractively over the top of each tartlet. Place a few mint leaves on each to complete the harmony of colors.

**Before serving, spoon a pool of the raspberry sauce onto each of 6 plates and place a tartlet in the middle of each plate.

If you wish, serve the tarts with vanilla ice cream. (See recipe on page 281.)

Menu for 6 People

Le Déjeuner de Fleurs

A Luncheon of Flowers

Difficulty: *Moderate*
Cost: *Expensive*

When I lived in Var, I inhabited an agricultural development where vegetables, fruits, and grapes were cultivated. One evening, after several weeks away, I came home on a moonless night. Out of habit I walked in the darkness toward what I thought was a patch of musclun salad, as it had been when I left, and I picked several leaves which seemed particularly tender. Seasoned and with a dash of garlic, the salad surprised me by its unfamiliar, but far from disagreeable, taste.

The next morning, my friend Felix, the farmer, said to me: "Somebody destroyed my marigold bed last night. Look at this massacre! I'd like to get my hands on the guy!"

I burst out laughing and confessed that I was the guilty party, but that I had been misled by the darkness.

Felix declared that in Provence people ate a fair variety of plants in salads, but that up until now no one had been crazy enough to try marigolds. "You have to be a Parisian to ingest something like that." (For Felix, a Parisian is anyone born north of Aix.) Despite my "foreign" origins, I was finally forgiven after drinking innumerable quantities of pastis with him.

The preparation of this menu will unfortunately keep you away from

Les Fleurs de Courgettes aux Truffes
Stuffed Zucchini Flowers with Truffles

**Le Blanc de Turbot et de Poireaux
aux Fleurs de Capucine**
*Turbot Fillets and Leeks with
Nasturtium Flowers*

**Le Carré d'Agneau Rôti à la Fleur
de Thym**
Roast Rack of Lamb with Thyme Flowers

**Les Tartelettes d'Oranges Meringuées
aux Fleurs de Lavande**
*Orange Meringue Tartlets with
Lavender Flowers*

**Les Grappes de Fleurs d'Acacia
en Beignets**
Acacia Flower Beignets with Powdered Sugar

Le Liqueur de Coquelicot
Poppy Liqueur

your guests, because it includes a number of recipes that must absolutely be made just before serving. Such is the hard lot of the chef. But this menu also gives you a good opportunity to act like a real chef, that is, a cook who thinks above all of the happiness of his or her guests.

I can think of no better example to illustrate this attitude than my friend Danny Kaye. This famous commedian (who is also a great cook) never sits down with his guests until he has served the dinner to each of them. His

happiness stems solely from the pleasure he gives.

Doing the Marketing

Order the zucchini flowers, nasturtiums, turbot, and the lamb in advance. Ask your fishmonger to fillet the turbot for you. If you wish, have

the butcher "french" the racks of lamb, asking him to reserve the trimmings and bones for you.

What to Drink

For an apéritif, stick with the flower theme, but don't get carried away. Don't go as far, for example, as a restaurateur who once served Paul Bocuse and me a lemon sorbet flavored with Chanel No. 5. After tasting this, even the taste of an *aïoli* was difficult to recognize.

I suggest serving simply a bottle of Champagne to which you've added 5 tablespoons of Cointreau and 1½ teaspoons orange flower water. Serve very cold, and float a few orange flowers in each glass.

For the wine, begin with a dry white wine, such as a Condrieux, which has

overleaf: *Rather than putting flowers on the table, set up the table among the flowers.*

the scent of violets. With the lamb, serve a red wine with a full bouquet, such as a Volnay, a Fleury, a Santenay, or a red Sancerre.

Table Linens and Decoration

Choose flower-patterned tablecloth and napkins. Put flowers everywhere. You could also change the centerpiece bouquet with each course, harmonizing it with the ingredients of each recipe: bouquets of zucchini flowers, nasturtiums, thyme, lavender. . . . For the acacia flower fritters, simply put the platter in the middle of the table.

For the menu, take some heavy colored paper and write with a different-colored felt-tip pen for each dish. Cut two slits in the paper and insert a tiny bouquet.

Tableware

Choose faïence or porcelain plates decorated with flowers:

- 18 plates for the zucchini flowers, the turbot, and the rack of lamb
- 12 dessert plates for the tartlets and the beignets
- 2 platters for the turbot and the lamb
- 1 platter with a folded white napkin for serving the beignets
- 1 sauce boat for the sauce for the rack of lamb

Silverware

- 6 forks, 6 knives, and 6 sauce spoons for the zucchini flowers
- 6 fish forks, 6 fish knives, and 6 sauce spoons for the turbot
- 6 forks and 6 knives for the rack of lamb
- 6 dessert forks and knives for the tartlets
- 1 spoon for the sauce boat

Glassware

- 18 goblets for the water, white wine, and red wine (for this flower-filled lunch, you might want to use decorated stemware)
- 6 port glasses for the liqueur

Getting Organized

Many things in this menu can be prepared in advance. They are indicated in each recipe with the symbol ✳✳✳. the symbol ✳✳ indicates those tasks that must be done just before serving.

The Liqueur de Coquelicot should be made at least 10 days in advance.

Begin preparing the tartlets the day before or the morning of the dinner. Prepare the zucchini flowers several hours in advance.

Two hours before the meal, preheat the oven to 400 degrees F. Put the white wine in the refrigerator to chill and begin preparing the turbot and leeks. Make the meringue for the tartlets.

Twenty minutes later, bake the tartlets for 10 minutes.

One hour before serving, set the oven to its highest temperature. Place the racks of lamb in the roasting pan and soak the garlic cloves.

Warm 18 dinner plates, 2 platters, and 1 sauce boat on the back of the stove or over a saucepan filled with hot water.

Put the lamb in the oven to cook for 30 minutes. Remove from the oven and keep warm; reduce the oven temperature to 400 degrees F.

Finish preparing the turbot and put it in the oven to cook. Meanwhile, steam the zucchini flowers and heat the sauce in a bain-marie.

When the turbot has cooked, keep it warm while you finish its sauce.

After serving the zucchini flowers, arrange the turbot on a platter and serve.

Before serving the lamb, warm in the oven while you sauté the garlic cloves. Carve the lamb and serve it.

Ten minutes before serving the tartlets, place them in the oven to finish baking.

Prepare the acadia flower beignets at the last moment.

Les Fleurs de Courgettes aux Truffes

STUFFED ZUCCHINI FLOWERS WITH TRUFFLES

Time required: *1 hour*
advance preparation
15 minutes steaming just before serving
Difficulty: *Moderate*
Cost: *Very expensive*

Ingredients

1 pound fresh mushrooms
Juice of 1 lemon
1 shallot
1 cup plus 1 tablespoon unsalted butter
Salt
5 tablespoons crème fraîche (see Appendix), or heavy cream
2 egg yolks
6 small black truffles (about ½ ounce each), canned or fresh
6 zucchini flowers with zucchini attached (see Note)
1 pound fresh young spinach leaves, or several bunches mâche
Freshly ground pepper
Several sprigs fresh chervil (optional)

Utensils

Food processor
Large saucepan
Medium skillet
Small saucepan
Couscousière, or wire rack set over a deep baking dish, or a bamboo steamer over a wok
Stainless-steel sieve
Paring knife
Cutting board
Small mixing bowl
Whisk
Bowl
Large plate
Aluminum foil
Wooden spoon
Measuring cups and spoons

Preparation

***The preparation and assembling of these zucchini flowers can be done several hours in advance. Only the final steaming will need to be done just before serving.

Trim the stems of the mushrooms

and wipe them clean of any dirt. Rinse quickly in cold water, without letting them soak; drain. Place the mushrooms in a food processor and finely chop, without reducing them to a purée. Place in a bowl and sprinkle with the lemon juice to prevent the mushrooms from discoloring.

Peel the shallot and finely chop.

Melt 1 tablespoon butter in a medium skillet. Add the shallot and sauté over medium heat until the butter begins to sizzle. Add the mushrooms, season with salt, and cook for 3 to 4 minutes, stirring with a wooden spoon.

Drain the mushrooms in a stainless-steel sieve placed over a small saucepan. (It's necessary to use stainless steel to prevent the mushrooms from turning dark. If you don't have a stainless-steel sieve, drain the mushrooms in a piece of cheesecloth stretched over a small saucepan.)

Place the mushrooms in a large saucepan and cook over high heat, stirring with a wooden spoon, until all of the excess moisture has evaporated.

Combine the crème fraîche and egg yolks in a small mixing bowl and whisk until blended. Whisk this mixture into the mushrooms and let cook over high heat for about 2 minutes. Adjust the seasoning, if necessary. Mound the

**About 20 minutes before serving, fill the bottom of the couscousière with water and place the top part with the squash blossoms over the water. (If you're steaming the flowers on a rack or in a bamboo steamer, fill a small baking dish or a wok with a little water and place the rack or steamer over it.)

Squash blossoms are best picked at sunrise, before they start to wilt.

mushrooms on a large plate and let cool.

Drain the truffles in a sieve set over the saucepan containing the mushroom juice.

Gently pat any moisture from the petals of the zucchini flowers. (They should not be rinsed unless it is absolutely necessary.) Gently open out the petals of each blossom and fill the center of each with ½ tablespoon of the mushroom mixture. Nestle a truffle in the center of each blossom and carefully close the petals up around the truffle and stuffing. Place the flowers in the top of a couscousière, on a wire rack, or in a bamboo steamer. Cover with a sheet of aluminum foil.

Remove the stems from the spinach, wash the leaves thoroughly, and drain. (If you're using mâche, cut off the sandy roots, wash the leaves, and drain.)

Place the saucepan containing the mushroom and truffle juice over medium heat and let simmer and reduce until only 3 tablespoons of liquid remain.

Cut the remaining 1 cup butter into small pieces and add it, a little at a time, whisking over high heat after each addition until the butter is thoroughly incorporated. Season with salt and pepper and remove from the heat.

Place over high heat and steam for about 15 minutes. The flowers will be perfectly cooked when a knife can be inserted easily into the zucchini that are attached to them.

While the flowers steam, reheat the sauce, if necessary, in a bain-marie.

To serve, spread the spinach leaves or mâche over 6 warmed serving plates. Place a zucchini blossom on each plate. Season with salt and pepper, and spoon a little of the sauce over

each. Sprinkle each portion with chervil, if using, and serve.

Note: Zucchini flowers should be very fresh when you buy them because they wilt quickly. They can be replaced by pumpkin flowers (but first remove the

pistils), by beet leaves blanched in boiling water, or by young cabbage leaves blanched briefly in boiling water.

Le Blanc de Turbot en de Poireaux aux Fleurs de Capucine

TURBOT FILLETS AND LEEKS WITH
NASTURTIUM FLOWERS

Time required: *30 minutes*
preparation (at least 2 hours in advance)
30 minutes cooking just before serving
Difficulty: *Moderate*
Cost: *Moderate*

Ingredients

6 turbot fillets (6 to 7 ounces each), or 1 whole turbot (about 4½ pounds; see Note)
4 cups milk
6 young leeks
8 tablespoons unsalted butter
Salt
6 small bay leaves, fresh if possible
3 cups crème fraîche (see Appendix), or heavy cream

2 egg yolks
¼ cup plus 1 tablespoon chopped fresh parsley
¼ cup plus 1 tablespoon chopped fresh chervil
10 fresh tarragon leaves
¼ cup chopped fresh chives
12 nasturtium flowers and 24 leaves, divided into 6 small bouquets with short stems (see Note)

Utensils

Large skillet with cover
Small saucepan
Large baking dish
Food processor, blender, or mixer
Mixing bowl
Colander
Cutting board
Filleting knife
Chef's knife

Whisk
Brush
Bowl
Spatula
Aluminum foil
Measuring cups and spoons

The nasturtium flower adds a distinctive peppery taste.

Preparation

***Start the advance preparation of this recipe at least 2 hours ahead of time.

If you're starting with a whole turbot, ask your fishmonger to fillet it and remove the skin. If the fishmonger is insensitive to your charms and you're forced to fillet the fish yourself, don't panic. Proceed in the following manner: Cut off the head. With a very sharp filleting knife, make a deep cut from head to tail, following the line of the fins. Then cut from head to tail along the central bone. Then carefully slide the knife between the flesh and bones and lift off the fillet. Repeat the operation for the other side. In the end you will have 4 fillets: 2 thick and 2 thin.

To remove the skin, lay the fillets, one at a time, skin side down, on a cutting board. Holding the tail firmly, slide the sharp knife between the flesh and the skin, cutting in a slight back and forth movement and keeping the knife close to and parallel with the skin. Discard the skin.

Finally, slice each of the 2 thick fillets into 2 thin fillets, cutting crosswise through the thickness. You will now

**About 30 minutes before serving, preheat the oven to 400 degrees F.

On either side of the central vein, trim each bay leaf into the shape of a palm leaf.

Drain the turbot fillets and arrange them in a single layer in a large baking dish. Season with salt and place 1 bay leaf on each fillet.

Pour 2⅔ cups of the crème fraîche over the fish, place in the hot oven, and bake for 8 minutes. To test for doneness, press your finger lightly into the thickest portion of the fish fillets—the fish should give way to pressure but re-

have a total of 6 thin fillets.

Place the fish fillets in a shallow bowl with the milk and several ice cubes. If necessary, add enough water to cover the fillets completely. Set aside to soak for at least 2 hours. (If you're pressed for time, this procedure is not absolutely necessary, but it will make the fish fillets very white.)

Remove the root ends of the leeks, and trim off the green parts. (Save these for a soup.) Thoroughly wash the leeks, drain in a colander, and slice the white parts crosswise into 2-inch lengths.

Melt 2 tablespoons butter in a large skillet. Add the leeks and enough water to cover. Season lightly with salt. Simmer over low heat for 15 to 20 minutes, until the leeks are tender to the bite. Cook longer if necessary, adding a little more water to keep them from burning. When the leeks have finished cooking, only a light, buttery sauce should remain in the bottom of the skillet. If the sauce is too thin, reduce it gently until the desired consistency is reached. Remove from the heat, cover, and set aside.

main slightly firm to the touch.

Place the remaining ⅓ cup crème fraîche in a small mixing bowl with the egg yolks and beat with a whisk until blended.

Remove the fish from the oven and carefully spoon its cooking cream into a saucepan, leaving a small amount in the bottom of the baking dish to keep the fish from drying out. Cover the baking dish with foil and keep warm while making the sauce. Place the skillet with the leeks over very low heat to warm.

Bring the cream in the saucepan to a

boil. Quickly whisk in the crème/egg mixture and remove from the heat immediately. Pour into the bowl of an electric mixer, food processor, or blender, add the parsley, chervil, tarragon, and chives, season with salt, and blend or process for 1 minute or so. The sauce should be a light green and have a velvety smooth consistency. Return the sauce to the saucepan and keep warm in a bain-marie if not serving immediately.

To serve, form six rectangles of well-flattened leeks on a platter. Spoon the warm herb sauce over the leeks and on the bottom of the platter. Using a large spatula, carefully transfer the turbot fillets to the platter and arrange on top of the leeks. Dip a brush in the butter sauce remaining from the leeks and brush over the top of the fish fillets to get rid of any remaining traces of cream and to add a sheen. The fish should be very white, clean, and bright.

Place the bouquets of nasturtium flowers around the fish on the platter and take to the table. Serve each guest a fish fillet with leeks and a bouquet of nasturtium flowers. Spoon the sauce onto the plates or over the fish.

Note: If turbot is not available where you live, any number of white-fleshed salt-water fish, including sea bass, John Dory, or even very fresh cod, can be used in this recipe.

Nasturtium flowers and leaves have a taste similar to watercress that adds a punch to this dish. They are not absolutely indispensable for this recipe; if you don't have them, use watercress leaves instead.

Le Carré d'Agneau Rôti à la Fleur de Thym

ROAST RACK OF LAMB WITH THYME
FLOWERS

Time required: *35 minutes*
advance preparation
40 minutes cooking just before serving
Difficulty: *Easy*
Cost: *Expensive*

The best thyme comes from scrubland, not far from the ocean. This is the thyme that grows only on stony, arid, sun-burnt hills, the thyme that survives the terrible Mistral and the no less fearful assaults of grazing sheep.

These little shriveled plants are rarely more than 4 inches high. They spring up after the last rains of winter, which somewhat refresh the barren hills. Then, in May, the thyme adorns itself in blue and pink flowers, which color all the hills of Provence.

Their splendor lasts only two weeks, and this is the only time when one can obtain the flowers of scrubland thyme.

Ingredients

2	large heads garlic (about 20 large cloves)
3	racks of lamb (about 2½ pounds each)
	Salt

3	tablespoons fresh thyme flowers (optional)
1	large sprig fresh thyme
5	tablespoons unsalted butter
	Freshly ground pepper

Utensils

Roasting pan large enough for 3 racks of lamb
Small sharp knife
Small saucepan with cover
Large sieve

Medium skillet
Large plate
Small plate
Aluminum foil

Preparation

***Begin preparing this recipe about 1 hour before the meal.

Separate the garlic heads into cloves. Place in a bowl of cold water to soak (unpeeled) for 15 or 20 minutes.

Preheat the oven to its highest setting.

To prepare the racks of lamb for cooking, carefully trim them of any skin and most of their fat, leaving only a thin layer of fat over the back of each rack. Using a small sharp knife, trim away the meat and connective tissue between the rib ends of each rack, cleaning the bones well and reserving all the trimmings. When you're finished, about 2 inches of the rib bones will be exposed by this method of trimming, which is known as "frenching."

(If you wish, ask your butcher to trim and french the racks, but be sure to tell him to reserve all the trimmings for you.)

Score the fat on the back of each rack in a crisscross pattern with a sharp knife, being very careful not to cut into the meat. Season the meat on all sides with salt and sprinkle with the thyme flowers, if using.

Place the lamb trimmings on the bottom of a large roasting pan. Place the racks of lamb, fat side up, on the

**Twenty minutes before serving, pre-

bed of trimmings.

Place in the preheated oven and roast for 10 minutes.

Meanwhile, drain the garlic cloves.

Add the garlic cloves (still unpeeled) to the roasting pan and roast for 10 minutes longer. Turn the racks of lamb and roast for 10 minutes longer.

Remove the lamb from the pan and place on a small plate inverted on a larger plate. Cover with a sheet of aluminum foil and keep warm by placing the plate over a saucepan of water on low heat. Letting the meat rest in this fashion keeps it from bathing in its juices while resting.

Remove the garlic from the roasting pan and set aside.

Skim off the grease on the surface of the cooking juices in the roasting pan and discard. Add ½ cup water to the pan and stir over medium heat to scrape up the bits that cling to the bottom and sides of the pan.

Strain the liquid through a fine sieve into a small saucepan. Bring to a boil over high heat and let the liquid reduce by half. Add the sprig of thyme and remove the saucepan from the heat. Cover and let steep for 10 minutes.

Meanwhile, peel the garlic cloves.

heat the oven to 300 degrees.

Five minutes before serving, return the lamb to the roasting pan and place in the hot oven to warm.

Meanwhile, melt the butter in a medium skillet, add the garlic and sauté until lightly browned. Reheat the sauce, remove the thyme, season with salt and pepper, and pour into a warmed sauce boat. Turn the garlic cloves into the sauce boat, along with any juices from the plate the lamb rested on.

Remove the lamb from the oven, add a twist of pepper, and serve immediately.

Les Tartelettes d'Oranges Meringuées aux Fleurs de Lavande

ORANGE MERINGUE TARTLETS WITH
LAVENDER FLOWERS

Time required: *1 hour
advance preparation and cooking
20 minutes cooking just before serving*
Difficulty: *Moderate*
Cost: *Inexpensive*

Ingredients

DOUGH

2	cups flour
¾	cup sugar

	Pinch of salt
¾	cup unsalted butter
4	egg yolks

FILLING

1	lemon
1	orange
½	cup sugar

3	whole eggs
4	tablespoons unsalted butter, softened

MERINGUE

3	egg whites
1	cup powdered sugar

1	teaspoon lavender flowers (see Note)

Utensils

Food processor
Baking sheet
Mixing bowl
Whisk
Spatula
Rolling pin

4-inch round pastry cutter
Plastic wrap
Sugar sifter
6 4-inch round flan rings, or 6 3-inch round tartlet pans
Measuring cups and spoons

Preparation

***Most of this recipe can be prepared well in advance—the day before or several hours ahead. It must be begun at least 1½ hours before the meal.

If using the tart pans, place them in the refrigerator to chill.

To make the dough, combine the flour, sugar, and salt in a mixing bowl, the bowl of an electric mixer, or a food processor. Add the butter and egg yolks and beat slowly until the dough forms into a ball. Wrap in a damp cloth or plastic wrap and chill for at least 1 hour.

Meanwhile, make the filling. Wash, quarter, and remove the seeds from the orange and lemon. Place them in a food processor with the sugar, whole eggs, and butter and process to a purée. Place in a bowl and chill.

On a lightly floured work surface, roll out the chilled dough $\frac{1}{16}$ inch thick. Cut out six 4-inch rounds of dough with a pastry cutter or use a sharp knife to cut around an inverted 4-inch bowl.

✤✤Thirty minutes before serving, preheat the oven to 300 degrees F.

Meanwhile, place the egg whites in a very clean mixing bowl. (The bowl cannot have any trace of grease or the whites will not stiffen well. It's best to rub the sides and bottom of the bowl with a lemon half, rinse in water, and dry thoroughly before beating the egg whites.)

Beat the egg whites until firm.

Note: Do not use the lavender flowers sold at the drugstore or perfume counter. These flowers are made to scent closets and drawers and are usually augmented by powerful oils and extracts that will ruin this dessert. If you can't find fresh lavender flowers, omit them. The tarts will be very good without them.

If you're using flan rings, place the dough rounds on a baking sheet, place the rings over them, and chill for 30 minutes. If using individual tart pans, drape the dough rounds over them and carefully press the dough into the bottom and sides, trimming off any excess dough from the edges and pricking the bottom of each with a fork. Chill for 30 minutes.

When the dough has chilled, preheat the oven to 400 degrees F.

Place the pastry in the hot oven and bake for 10 minutes. Remove from the oven and spread each tart with the filling mixture. Return to the oven and bake for 20 minutes longer.

Remove from the oven and let cool for 10 minutes. Remove the rings, or carefully remove the tarts from the pans and set the tartlets aside on the baking sheet until just before serving.

Gradually sift in the powdered sugar and continue to beat for about 2 minutes, until stiff.

Top each tart with a generous tablespoon of the meringue mixture, smoothing it into a dome with a metal spatula. Sprinkle the lavender flowers over the top of each tartlet and bake for 20 minutes. Place on dessert plates and serve warm.

The quantities specified here will make more than 6 tartlets, but it's often difficult in cooking to make less than a minimum quantity. These tarts will, however, keep perfectly well in the refrigerator for several days.

If fresh lavender flowers are not available, they may be easily omitted from this recipe.

Les Grappes de Fleurs d'Acacia en Beignets

ACACIA FLOWER BEIGNETS WITH
POWDERED SUGAR

Time required: *5 minutes*
advance preparation
20 minutes cooking just before serving
Difficulty: *Easy*
Cost: *Moderately expensive*

Ingredients

1¾ cups flour
1 cup beer
2 quarts peanut oil, for frying

12 clusters of acacia flowers or rose petals
½ cup powdered sugar

Utensils

Large mixing bowl
Deep fryer or large, heavy saucepan
Whisk
Slotted spoon or skimmer

Wooden spoon
Wire rack
Paper towels
Sugar sifter

Preparation

***The acacia flowers must be fried just before serving, but the batter can be made in advance.

Place the flour in a large mixing bowl. Add the beer, little by little, whisking vigorously to obtain a batter about the consistency of a slightly thick crêpe batter. Chill.

**About 20 minutes before serving, place the oil in a large saucepan or deep fryer and heat until it begins to smoke. (The oil should reach 350 degrees F before you start to fry the acacia flowers.)

Carefully dry the acacia blossoms if they are damp and remove any blemished petals.

One by one, dip the clusters into the batter, letting them soak for a second. Slide each cluster carefully into the hot oil. Don't fry more than 5 clusters at once or they will stick together.

Turn the beignets in the oil with a wooden spoon until lightly browned on all sides. Remove carefully with a slotted spoon or skimmer and place on a wire baking rack covered with paper towels to drain. Continue to dip and fry the flowers until all 12 clusters are fried.

Just before serving, sprinkle the powdered sugar through a sifter or fine sieve over the beignets. Place them in a folded linen napkin on a plate and serve immediately.

La Liqueur de Coquelicot

POPPY LIQUEUR

Time required: *20 minutes preparation (at least 10 days in advance)*
Difficulty: *Easy*
Cost: *Moderately expensive*

This poppy liqueur is a pure marvel, like the wild, red poppies scattered in the wheat fields of Provence at the beginning of summer. It is said to have certain miraculous qualities, but I've forgotten which ones. However, think of all the life-giving sunlight trapped in these beautiful flowers. Moreover, it is delicious, original, and inexpensive—all of which already are miracles in a liqueur.

Ingredients

Fresh poppies
Eau de vie

Zest of 1 lemon
Sugar

Utensils

Mortar and pestle
Mixing bowl
Saucepan

Fine sieve
Bottle with tight seal
Cheesecloth

Preparation

***At least ten days in advance, gather a full basket of poppies and place in the sun so that they will not be too damp or humid.

Remove the stems and crush the flowers in a mortar.

In a mixing bowl, combine this purée with an equal quantity of eau de vie. Decant this mixture into a bottle, add the lemon zest, seal tightly, and let infuse for 10 days at room temperature in a shaded place.

When it has aged for at least 10 days, pass the mixture though a fine sieve lined with cheesecloth.

In a saucepan, prepare a syrup composed of the same quantity of water and sugar to obtain a volume equal to half the volume of the liqueur. Bring the syrup to a boil. Let cool.

When it has cooled, add to the liqueur and blend well.

That's all.

Note: This liqueur will keep well if you seal it and store it away from light.

Menu for 6 People

Un Dîner à Mougins

A Dinner in Mougins

Difficulty:
Moderately easy
Cost: *Moderate*

Ocb One day an old man from Mougins said to me: "You know, Vergé, on the spot where your restaurant is, there used to be a wonderful oil mill. When we were working near there or in winter when there wasn't much to do, we used to go see the miller from time to time. You'd always have a few cloves of garlic and a knife in your pocket. And then you'd pick a few dandelions, with the roots—because, of course, the best thing about a dandelion is the root.

"You'd wash them in the stream as you went by, and when you got to the millstone, you'd always find a bit of stale, week-old bread. The miller would give you a crock of olive oil that had just flowed off the presses. Then you'd rub the bread with the garlic, dip it in the olive oil, and eat it with the dandelions and some coarse salt.

"Add to that a bit of our wine from

La Tourte d'Olives Mouginoise
Mougins-Style Olive Tart

Les Cuisses de Poulet en Court Bouillon de Citron
Chicken Legs with Lemon and Aromatic Vegetables

L'Anchoïade de Salade de Légumes
Fresh Raw Vegetables with Provençal Anchovy Dressing

Le Biscuit au Chocolat Fourré de Marmelade d'Oranges Amères
Chocolate Sponge Cake Filled with Orange Marmalade

the hills! Well, you see, Vergé, I'm not sure your customers feast as well on all your complicated creations as we did on that simple food.

"Anyway, to your health!"

Doing the Marketing

This menu requires many fresh vegetables, so it's best to shop the day you plan to cook, whether it's the day before or the morning of the dinner. The vegetables can be varied according to what's available. Make your choices first according to the freshness of the vegetables, then for their color. When it comes to taste, they all are good. The ideal bread for this meal is fougassettes, a distinctive, Provençal-style bread. But any fresh, crusty, country-style bread will be good with the meal.

What to Drink

For an apéritif, Pastis, the anise-flavored apéritif of the south of France, is ideal with this meal. Or serve a glass of Provençal rosé or dry white wine.

A painting by Lennart Jirlow, a Swedish artist living in Provence.

For the wine, the same rosé or dry white served as apéritif can be served with the dinner. Or choose a light red wine that can be served chilled. And why not Champagne? Sometimes it's good to play the snob!

Table Linens and Decoration

Rustic table linens, such as burlap or a coarse linen cloth in olive green, for example, would be a good choice for this meal. Hand-letter the menus on good paper, rolled around the napkins and tied with ribbons to match the color of the table linens.

For the centerpiece, fill a basket with fresh, colorful vegetables and surround it with leaves or bouquets of wild flow-

ers. Use accessories in keeping with the fresh vegetable theme, such as salt and pepper shakers in the shape of tomatoes.

Place candles in the center of small purple artichokes that have been trimmed at the bottom to prevent them from tipping over. In other words, let your imagination go.

Tableware

Choose a colorful, rustic style of dishes, such as faience plates with bright vegetable motifs:
1   large, round raffia or wicker platter for the olive tart

1   large earthenware casserole for the chicken
1   round platter for the chocolate cake
1   small bowl or crock for the

anchoïade

1	small wicker basket for the vegetables

18	dinner plates
6	dessert plates

Silverware

18	dinner forks and knives
6	dessert forks
2	pie servers

2	serving spoons
1	serving fork

Glassware

12	goblets for water and wine

Getting Organized

All the dishes in this menu are served cold, so you can prepare everything either the day before or the morning of the dinner. Just cover with plastic wrap and set aside in a cool place—it's best not to refrigerate them. Don't forget to chill the wine in the refrigerator several hours in advance.

La Tourte d'Olives Mouginoise

MOUGINS-STYLE OLIVE TART

Time required: *1¼ hours*
advance preparation
Difficulty: *Moderately easy*
Cost: *Moderate*

Don't look for this recipe among the traditions of Mougins. It came directly from my imagination, but it could very well be the product of this region, with all the local ingredients.

Whether you serve this pie hot or cold, drink a good bottle of chilled rosé with it.

Ingredients

2¼	cups flour
¾	cup virgin olive oil
	Salt
½	cup lukewarm water (90 to 110 degrees F)
2	medium onions
1½	pounds Swiss chard, or 1 pound fresh spinach
3	cloves garlic

¾	pound small black Niçoise olives, or other oil-cured olives
½	teaspoon wild thyme flowers, or 1 teaspoon fresh thyme, or ½ teaspoon dried thyme
2	eggs
2	tablespoons crème fraîche (see Appendix), or heavy cream
	Fresh ground pepper

Utensils

Large mixing bowl
Small mixing bowl
12-inch skillet
Baking sheet, or 12-inch tart pan

opposite: Little black olives from Nice are preferable for this tart.
overleaf: On the terrace of my friends the Polverinos, where from two stories up you can look out over the main square of Mougins.

Cutting board
Chef's knife

Whisk
Measuring cups and spoons

Preparation

***This recipe can be prepared entirely in advance.

Start by preparing the pastry dough, working it as quickly as possible. In a large mixing bowl, combine the flour, ½ cup of the oil, a pinch of salt, and the lukewarm water. Blend the ingredients with quick, light finger movements until the dough holds together. Form into a ball, flatten slightly, and wrap in a damp cloth or plastic wrap. Chill for at least 30 minutes.

Meanwhile, peel and chop the onions.

Separate the green leaves from the chard stems, discarding stems. (You should have about a pound of chard leaves.) Wash and drain the leaves thoroughly. Cut into small pieces.

Peel and finely chop the garlic.

Remove the pits from the olives. If you're using large olives, quarter them. Set aside.

Place the remaining ¼ cup oil in a large skillet, add the onions, and sauté over low heat until softened, about 10 minutes. Add the chard, garlic, and thyme flowers and cook over low heat until all the liquid has evaporated, 8 to 10 minutes. Set aside to cool slightly.

Preheat the oven to 400 degrees F.

In a small mixing bowl, combine the eggs and crème fraîche and beat well. Stir the egg mixture into the chard and onions, season with pepper, and blend. (If you're using the small tasty black olives of Provence, the egg mixture shouldn't need salt. However, if using other varieties, you may wish to add a little salt.)

With your fingertips, spread the chilled dough into a 12-inch circle over a baking sheet or into a 12-inch tart pan. Crimp the edges of the circle, forming a ¼-inch border all around.

Pour the chard and egg mixture into the tart shell, distributing and flattening it with a fork. Sprinkle the olives evenly over the tart and bake for 25 to 30 minutes, or until golden.

**Serve hot or cold.

Les Cuisses de Poulet en Court Bouillon de Citron

CHICKEN LEGS WITH LEMON AND
AROMATIC VEGETABLES

Time required: *1¾ hours*
Difficulty: *Moderately easy*
Cost: *Inexpensive*

Ingredients

6   large chicken legs with thighs (about ½ pound each), or 6 chicken quarters
Salt

2   ripe tomatoes
3   organic lemons (see Note)
¾   cup virgin olive oil
4   or 5 medium carrots

1 leek, white part only
1 large white onion
1 rib celery
½ sweet red bell pepper
1½ teaspoons coriander seed
1½ teaspoons black peppercorns
2 cups dry white wine
1 bouquet garni, composed of 1 large sprig fresh thyme, 1 bay leaf, and a few sprigs parsley, all tied together with string
2 cubes chicken bouillon
2 cloves garlic
1 small bunch fresh parsley
1 small bunch fresh chervil, or 1 tablespoon dried chervil
12 to 15 leaves fresh tarragon, or 2 teaspoons dried tarragon

Utensils

Ovenproof baking dish large enough for 6 chicken legs with thighs or 6 chicken quarters
Medium saucepan
Boning knife
Chef's knife
Cutting board
Wooden spoon
Aluminum foil
Skimmer
Measuring cups and spoons
Cheesecloth

Preparation

***To prepare the chicken legs for cooking, make a shallow cut through the drumstick-thigh joint. Using a small sharp knife, detach the meat from the bone at the bottom end of the drumstick. Gently push the meat up the bone toward the joint to expose the drumstick bone and, with a heavy knife, cut away half of the drumstick bone. Then pull the meat back down again. If you're using chicken quarters with wings, remove all bones except the wing bones.

Season the chicken pieces on all sides with salt and arrange them, skin side up, in a single layer in the bottom of an ovenproof dish. (If they won't fit comfortably in one dish, use two smaller ones.)

Slice the tomatoes and lemons into thin rounds (reserving a few lemon slices for garnish) and arrange over the chicken pieces, alternating and overlapping the slices. (There should be about 2 slices of tomato and 2 of lemon for each piece of chicken.) Drizzle about 3 tablespoons of the oil over the chicken and set aside.

Preheat the oven to 425 degrees F.

Scrape the carrots. Wash the leeks thoroughly, trimming off the root and green part. Peel the onion. Slice all three of these into thin rounds.

Trim the celery. Remove the core and seeds from the pepper. Cut both into thick 1½-by-¼-inch julienne.

Place the coriander seed and peppercorns in a square of clean cheesecloth and tie securely with a string.

Place ¼ cup of the remaining oil in a medium saucepan. Add the carrots, leek, onion, celery, and red pepper and sauté, stirring, over medium heat until the vegetables are tender but still slightly crunchy. (Be careful not to let vegetables brown.) Add the wine, bouquet garni, bouillon cubes, garlic, coriander/pepper sachet, and ½ cup water. Cover the saucepan and simmer over low heat for 20 minutes.

Place the chicken in the oven to bake for 20 minutes.

When the vegetables have simmered 20 minutes, remove the bouquet garni and the coriander/pepper sachet, squeezing the sachet against the side of the saucepan to extract all the liquid. Stir the remaining 5 tablespoons oil into the vegetables.

Remove the chicken from the oven and reduce the oven temperature to 350 degrees F.

Skim off all the fat that has collected on the surface of the chicken. Then pour in the vegetables and their cooking liquid, distributing them evenly over the chicken. Return chicken to the oven for 20 minutes.

Remove from the oven, cover with aluminum foil and let rest for at least 1 hour before serving.

❧

**At serving time, remove the aluminum foil and garnish the chicken with sprigs of fresh parsley, chervil, tarragon, and the reserved lemon slices.

❧

Note: Organic lemons are best for cooking since they have not been treated. But if they are not available, buy ordinary lemons and wash them in warm water to remove the oil.

This dish is to be served at room temperature. It can, of course, be prepared several hours in advance, but it's best not to refrigerate it.

For me, this dish is best with thick slices of buttered country-style bread to dip in the juices of the chicken.

L'Anchoïade de Salade de Legumes

RAW VEGETABLES WITH PROVENÇAL
ANCHOVY DRESSING

Time required: *15 minutes*
advance preparation
Difficulty: *Very easy*
Cost: *Moderate*

I included this recipe in my previous book, but how can one put together a Provençal menu without including *anchoïade*? I assure you that this will be the only recipe I repeat (in this book).

A basic *anchoïade* is served with thick grilled slices of farmhouse bread or a baguette, and a salad—for example, some *mesclun* with black olives, slices of tomato, hard-cooked eggs. A full-scale *anchoïade*, on the other hand, is a meal in itself.

With the slices of bread, you serve a whole basket of raw vegetables: tomatoes, mushrooms, celery, radishes, carrots, fennel, cucumbers, red, yellow, and green peppers, lettuce hearts, the little violet artichokes known as *poivrades*, the small green onions known in the Midi as *cebettes*, fresh broad beans, cauliflower, lemon slices, hard-cooked eggs, black olives from Nice. Or, you can just as well cube or slice all these vegetables and arrange them, by color, on a large platter to make a marvelous tableau.

Ingredients

2   cans (2 ounces each) flat anchovy fillets, drained (see Note)
2   cups virgin olive oil
3   cloves garlic
1   teaspoon wild thyme flowers, or 3 teaspoons fresh thyme, or 1 teaspoon dried thyme
1½ tablespoons chopped fresh basil leaves
1½ tablespoons Dijon mustard

3   tablespoons wine vinegar
½   teaspoon freshly ground pepper
An assortment of fresh vegetables such as: green, red, and yellow peppers; cucumbers; fennel; carrots; cauliflower; baby artichokes; radishes; celery; mushrooms; and cherry tomatoes, each cut into strips or bite-size pieces

Utensils

Food processor, blender, or food mill with fine disc
Small skillet
Large bowl

Whisk
Wooden spoon
Rubber spatula
Measuring cups and spoons

Preparation

**This recipe can be made in advance using a food processor, blender, or food mill.

overleaf: *The* anchoïade *is a sauce, but it's also all the vegetables of Provence.*

USING A FOOD PROCESSOR
OR BLENDER

Combine the anchovies, olive oil, garlic, thyme, basil, mustard, vinegar, and pepper and process until reduced to a purée.

Scrape into one or two attractive small bowls or crocks that can be taken to the table for guests to dip into with the fresh raw vegetables.

USING A FOOD MILL

In a small skillet, combine the anchovies with 3 tablespoons of the olive oil and barely warm over *very* low heat, stirring with a wooden spoon just until the anchovies dissolve slightly.

Scrape the anchovies and the oil into a food mill placed over a large bowl. Add the garlic, thyme, and basil and turn through the mill, rinsing with some of the remaining oil as you turn.

Scrape off any of the mixture that clings to the bottom of the food mill and add to the bowl. Add the mustard, vinegar, pepper, and any remaining oil to the bowl, beating with a whisk until the oil is incorporated and the mixture is thoroughly blended.

Serve in the bowl in which you prepared the *anchoïade*, along with a small or large (depending on the appetite of your guests) assortment of crudités.

Note: Anchovies from Provence are less salty than many other varieties, so if you're using anything but the Provençal type, soak them in a little milk for 1 hour, then drain and pat dry with paper towels before using.

The *anchoïade* keeps well in a tightly sealed jar in the refrigerator. You can double the proportions indicated here and save half of it for another meal or for seasoning salads.

Le Biscuit au Chocolat Fourré de Marmelade d'Oranges Amères

CHOCOLATE SPONGE CAKE FILLED WITH
ORANGE MARMALADE

Time required: *1¼ hours*
advance preparation
Difficulty: *Easy*
Cost: *Moderate*

Ingredients

5	ounces semisweet chocolate
⅔	cup unsalted butter
⅓	cup flour
¾	cup granulated sugar
4	eggs, separated and at room temperature

4	tablespoons Grand Marnier or other orange-flavored liqueur
⅓	cup orange marmalade
3	tablespoons unsweetened cocoa powder
3	tablespoons powdered sugar

Utensils

8-inch round cake pan
Double boiler or makeshift bain-marie (composed of a metal or Pyrex mixing bowl set over a saucepan half-full of boiling water)
2 mixing bowls
Whisk
Wire rack
Rubber spatula
Large sharp knife

Sugar sifter or very fine sieve
8-inch round of sturdy cardboard
Heavy-duty waxed paper or parchment
Aluminum foil
Scissors
Measuring cups and spoons
1 yard decorative 1-inch satin ribbon

Preparation

***With scissors, cut 12 even strips of waxed paper or parchment paper, each ¼ inch wide by 8 inches long. Set aside until decorating the cake.

Preheat the oven to 300 degrees F.

Butter and lightly flour an 8-inch cake pan.

Place the chocolate and butter in the top of a double boiler over boiling water. (If you don't have a double boiler, half fill a saucepan with boiling water and place a mixing bowl containing the chocolate and butter over it.) Let the chocolate and butter melt, whisking frequently.

Meanwhile, in another mixing bowl combine the flour, granulated sugar, and egg yolks. Pour the melted chocolate and butter into this mixture and blend thoroughly.

In another bowl, beat the egg whites until stiff. Using a wooden spoon, gently fold the egg whites into the chocolate mixture, being very careful not to deflate them.

Pour the batter into the prepared cake pan. Place in the preheated oven and bake for about 50 minutes. (The cake will still be moist in the middle.) After the cake has baked for 15 or 20 minutes, place a sheet of aluminum foil, shiny side up, over the top of the cake to prevent the cake from drying out while cooking.

Remove the cake from the oven and let cool briefly. Turn onto a wire rack and let cool completely, about 2 hours.

When the cake is ready to be filled and decorated, use a large sharp knife to carefully slice crosswise through the center into two equal thin layers.

Sprinkle the cut side of each half with 2 tablespoons of the Grand Marnier. Spread half of the marmalade over each layer.

Stack the two layers again, cut sides facing, and place the cake on an 8-inch round of sturdy cardboard (so that it can be moved easily onto a clean serving platter once it has been decorated).

Using a sugar sifter or fine sieve, sprinkle the top of the cake with the cocoa.

Evenly arrange the reserved cut paper strips over the top of the cake, spaced about ¼ inch apart. Use the sugar sifter to sprinkle the powdered sugar evenly over the cake. Carefully remove the waxed paper strips; the cake will be decorated with white and brown zebra stripes.

Wrap a ribbon around the circumference of the cake and tie in a bow. Slide onto a clean serving platter.

Menu for 6 People

Un Dimanche à la Campagne

A Sunday in the Country

Difficulty:
Moderately difficult
Cost: *Moderate*

When I was a child on vacation, at a family farm in Allier where I was born, Sunday and holiday dinners were served in a great shadowy room that functioned as kitchen, bakery, dining room, living room, and even, in winter, as bedroom, since it was the largest and best-heated room on the farm.

At that time, red and white wine were stored in small, five-liter barrels. In summer, these would be lowered into the well the night before to chill the wine. Although restricted to water because of my age, I remember very well the agreeable "glug glug" as the wine was poured from the barrels. For that matter, I had only to look at the happy faces around the table to feel a pang of envy and vow to imitate them

La Terrine de Lotte en Gelée et sa Sauce d'Herbes Fines
Monkfish Terrine en Gelée with Fresh Herb Sauce

L'Entrecôte de Charolais à la Fondue d'Anchois et aux Herbes
Shell Steaks with Anchovies and Herbs

Les Beignets d'Aubergines Croustillants
Crisp Eggplant Beignets

La Tarte Fine aux Reinettes à la Compote d'Abricots
Delicate Apple Tarts with Apricot Compote

later on. And believe me, I fulfilled that vow!

Doing the Marketing

Order the monkfish in advance. *Lotte* is called monkfish in the U.S. for a very good reason—it actually looks as

if it has a monk's hood over its head. That is why this particular fish is generally served without the head.

What to Drink

For an apéritif, serve a dry white wine (St. Véran, Sancerre, or Sauvignon Blanc) with some dried sausage or cured ham. Or, make a cocktail by combining a bottle of white wine with 2 peaches quartered (with the pits), several fresh strawberries or raspberries, and 2 tablespoons sugar and letting the mixture marinate in the

refrigerator for several hours. Serve very, very cold.

For the wines, choose a fruity white wine such as a Chablis or a white Hermitage to serve with the monkfish terrine. With the entrecôte, serve a good

At my friend César's (indoors this time).

Bordeaux, such as a Margaux, or choose a Châteauneuf-du-Pape.

Table Linens and Decoration

A country house is often furnished and decorated in an eclectic fashion, so don't hesitate to mix styles and genres. Choose a tablecloth and napkins of white cotton, or of a check pattern. Decorate the table with wildflowers, blades of wheat, foliage—or don't decorate it at all.

Use stoneware pitchers and wicker utensils. You might place an enormous cauliflower stuck with candles in the center of the table.

Write the menus with a felt-tip pen on large leaves of maple, fig, or plane tree.

Tableware

Choose a lovely, rustic faïence:
- 6 plates for the monkfish terrine
- 6 dinner plates for the steaks
- 6 large plates for the apple tarts
- 1 sauce boat for the herb sauce
- 1 sauce boat for the apricot compote
- 1 platter and a linen napkin for the eggplant fritters

Silverware

- 6 fish knives and 6 fish forks
- 6 steak knives and 6 dinner forks for the steaks
- 6 dessert forks and 6 dessert spoons for the tart
- 2 sauce spoons
- 3 serving spoons and 3 serving forks
- 1 tart server

Glassware

18 rustic glasses for water, white wine, and red wine

Getting Organized

In this menu, several dishes can be prepared the day before or on the morning of the dinner—the monkfish terrine (which is best if prepared 24 hours ahead), its sauce, the puff pastry, almond cream, and apricot compote for the dessert.

These tasks are marked in each recipe with the symbol ✱✱✱. The symbol ✱✱ indicates those tasks that need to be done just before serving.

Put the white wine in the refrigerator to chill several hours in advance.

About an hour before the meal, warm 6 plates on the back of the stove or over a saucepan of hot water.

Peel and slice the eggplants and prepare the beignet batter. Core and slice the apples and assemble the tarts.

Thirty minutes before serving dinner, preheat the oven to 400 degrees F.

Begin frying the eggplant.

Fifteen minutes later, start cooking the steaks. Unmold and slice the monkfish terrine. Remove the apricot compote from the refrigerator.

Serve the monkfish terrine.

Place the steaks and beignets in the oven to keep warm while preparing the anchovy sauce.

Just before serving the steaks and beignets, place the tart in the hot oven to bake for 20 to 25 minutes.

A wine cocktail and a few slices of sausage to whet the appetite.

La Terrine de Lotte en Gelée et sa Sauce d'Herbes Fines

MONKFISH TERRINE IN GELEE WITH FRESH
HERB SAUCE

Time required: *1 hour*
preparation
(12 hours in advance)
10 minutes just before serving
Difficulty: *Moderate*
Cost: *Moderate*

Ingredients

TERRINE

1	can (10½ ounces) consommé with gelatin
1	sprig fresh tarragon, or 1 teaspoon dried tarragon
1¼	pounds monkfish fillets
	Salt
	Freshly ground pepper
½	pound ripe tomatoes (about 4 medium)
3	tablespoons finely chopped fresh tarragon
3	tablespoons finely chopped fresh mint
3	tablespoons finely chopped fresh parsley
3	tablespoons finely chopped fresh chervil

SAUCE

⅔	pound ripe tomatoes (about 5 medium)
2	tablespoons finely chopped fresh parsley
2	tablespoons finely chopped fresh mint
2	tablespoons finely chopped fresh tarragon
1	teaspoon Pernod or other anise-flavored liqueur
	Juice of 1 lemon
½	cup virgin olive oil
	Salt
	Freshly ground pepper

Utensils

	Couscousière with cover, or a roasting pan and a wire rack
	Medium saucepan
2	medium mixing bowls
1	6-inch-long rectangular terrine or pâté mold
	Roasting pan large enough to hold the terrine
	Long, thin knife or electric knife
	Chef's knife
	Paring knife
	Cutting board
	Aluminum foil
	Waxed paper

Preparation

❊❊❊This recipe should be made at least 12 hours before serving.

Place the consommé in a small saucepan with the sprig of tarragon and warm gently over low heat. Remove from the heat, cover, and set aside.

Cut the monkfish fillets into ½-inch-thick scallops. Then cut each scallop lengthwise into ½-inch-wide strips. Season with salt and pepper.

To steam the fish, fill a couscousière with water, place the fish strips in the top of the couscousière, and cover. If you don't have a couscousière, fill a roasting pan with water. Place the fish strips on a wire rack in the roasting pan (above the water level) and cover with aluminum foil. Place the couscousière or pan over high heat and steam over boiling water for 2 to 3 minutes. Remove the fish from the steam and let cool; it should be sufficiently cooked.

Plunge the tomatoes into a medium saucepan filled with boiling water for several seconds. Rinse under cold water and peel. Cut the tomatoes in half and squeeze out the seeds and juice. Chop coarsely and place in a medium mixing bowl. Add the tarragon, mint, parsley, and chervil and blend well.

Preheat the oven to 400 degrees F.

Spread a layer of the tomato/herb

mixture over the bottom of a buttered, 6-inch-long rectangular terrine or pâté mold. Top with a layer of the fish strips, placed in the terrine lengthwise, side by side. Spread another layer of the tomato/herb mixture over the top, followed by another layer of the fish. Continue layering in this manner until all of the ingredients have been used. Pour a layer of the cooled consommé over the top.

Place the terrine in a large baking pan filled with warm water to reach about halfway up the sides of the terrine. Cover the terrine loosely with waxed paper and bake for 20 minutes.

Remove the terrine from the oven and let cool. Chill until just before serving.

To make the sauce, plunge the tomatoes into a saucepan of boiling water for several seconds. Rinse under cold water and peel. Cut in half and squeeze out the seeds and juice. Cut into large dice and place in a mixing bowl. Add the parsley, mint, tarragon, Pernod, lemon juice, and oil, and season with salt and pepper.

**Fifteen minutes before serving, place 6 plates in the refrigerator to chill.

Just before serving, dip the bottom of the terrine in warm water and invert it onto a cutting board to unmold. Using a long, sharp knife or, better still, an electric knife, cut the terrine into 12 slices.

Spoon a little of the sauce onto each of the chilled plates, reserving some of

the sauce for the sauce boat.

Place 2 slices of the terrine on each plate and serve. Pass the remaining sauce separately.

For an added touch, accompany this terrine with a small fancy salad of green beans, small new carrots, tiny artichoke hearts, and fancy peas or seeded and thinly sliced cucumbers.

L'Entrecôte de Charolais à la Fondue d'Anchois et aux Herbes

SHELL STEAKS WITH ANCHOVIES AND HERBS

Time required: *20 minutes*
just before serving
Difficulty: *Easy*
Cost: *Expensive*

Ingredients

18 anchovy fillets (about two 2-ounce cans), drained
¼ cup milk
3 shell steaks (about 1 pound each), trimmed
Salt
Freshly ground pepper
8 tablespoons unsalted butter
Juice of 1 lemon
½ teaspoon thyme flowers, fresh thyme, or ¼ teaspoon dried thyme
½ teaspoon finely chopped fresh savory, or ¼ teaspoon dried savory
1½ tablespoons chopped fresh parsley
1 teaspoon very finely chopped garlic
½ teaspoon Worcestershire sauce

Utensils

2 large skillets
Large plate
Small plate
Cutting board
Chef's knife
Bowl
Aluminum foil

Preparation

***Place the anchovy fillets in a small bowl with the milk and let soak for 20 or 30 minutes. Drain and pat dry with paper towels.

**Fifteen or 20 minutes before serving, season the steaks on both sides with salt and pepper.

Melt 2 tablespoons of the butter in each of 2 skillets over medium heat. When the butter begins to turn brown, add the steaks and cook for 2 to 3 minutes on each side for rare, or more to suit your taste and the thickness of the meat.

Remove the steaks from the skillets and place them on a small inverted saucer set on a larger plate. This arrangement allows the steaks to sit above, not in, their juices. Cover the steaks with aluminum foil to keep them warm.

Drain off the butter from one of the skillets, but do not clean it. Add the anchovies and let them dissolve over medium heat. Add the remaining 4 tablespoons butter, the lemon juice, thyme flowers, savory, parsley, garlic, and Worcestershire sauce. Season generously with pepper.

Pour the juice that has accumulated on the plate under the steaks into the skillet with the sauce and warm the sauce through. Cut each steak in half and divide among 6 warmed plates. Spoon some of the sauce over each and serve.

Les Beignets d'Aubergines Croustillants

CRISP EGGPLANT BEIGNETS

Time required: *10 minutes*
advance preparation
15 minutes just before serving
Difficulty: *Easy*
Cost: *Inexpensive*

This recipe for beignet batter is wonderfully simple, light, and crisp—in short, it is marvelous! Often, before dinner, I cut a large onion into very thin slices, dip them into this batter, and deep-fry. Occasionally, when just the family is dining, we make an entire meal out of these crisp fritters and tender, young vegetables with herbs fresh from the garden.

Ingredients

½ cup flour
1 cup very cold beer

2 firm medium eggplants
1 quart peanut oil, for frying

Utensils

Large saucepan
Deep-frying or candy
thermometer
Mixing bowl
Whisk
Wire rack

Chef's knife
Paring knife
Fork
Paper towel
Slotted spoon or skimmer

Preparation

***Thirty minutes before dinner, place the flour and beer in a mixing bowl and blend with a whisk. The batter should be the consistency of a thick crêpe batter. Chill.

Peel the eggplants and cut into ¼-inch-thick rounds.

**Fifteen minutes before serving, heat the peanut oil in a large saucepan to 350 degrees F, verifying the temperature with a thermometer.

When the oil is hot, drop the eggplant rounds, one at a time, into the chilled batter and then into the hot oil. Do not put too many rounds into the oil at once or they will stick together.

Turn the beignets in the oil so that they brown lightly and evenly on all sides for 3 or 4 minutes. Remove from the oil with a slotted spoon or skimmer and drain on a wire rack covered with

Peel and core the apples and cut them into thin, uniform slices. Arrange the slices in a circular pattern on top of each pastry round.

Melt the remaining 4½ tablespoons butter and brush it over the apples. Sprinkle the remaining ¼ cup of sugar over the top of the tarts.

Place in the hot oven and bake for 20 to 25 minutes.

Serve hot, and pass the chilled apricot compote separately in a sauce boat. If you wish, serve a bowl of chilled whipped cream with the tarts as well. paper towels. Keep the beignets warm, but do not salt them until just before serving; the salt will soften their crispness.

Serve in a clean white linen napkin folded over a large plate.

La Tarte Fine aux Reinettes à la Compote d'Abricots

DELICATE APPLE TARTS WITH APRICOT
COMPOTE

Time Required: *2½ hours*
advance preparation
Difficulty: *Difficult*
Cost: *Moderate*

Ingredients

PUFF PASTRY
3   cups flour
1⅓ cups unsalted butter

1   tablespoon salt
⅔   cup cold water

APRICOT COMPOTE
Using fresh fruit:
2¼   pounds very ripe apricots
1   cup superfine sugar

½   cup water
Using canned fruit in syrup:
2   cans (17 ounces each) halved apricots in syrup

ALMOND CREAM AND APPLE TOPPING
8½   tablespoons unsalted butter
½   cup sugar
½   cup almond powder (see Appendix)

2   eggs
2   pounds Granny Smith or other firm, crisp apples
     Whipped cream (optional)

Utensils

2   large mixing bowls
     Large saucepan
     Rolling pin
     Food processor or food mill

with fine disc
Wooden spoon
Whisk
Paring knife

Chef's knife
6-inch round plate or bowl
2 or 3 baking sheets

Pastry brush
Measuring cups and spoons
Waxed paper

Preparation

✳✳✳The puff pastry and the apricot compote can be prepared a day in advance. Start with the puff pastry, so that you can turn it every half hour while preparing the apricot compote and the monkfish terrine, which should also be made in advance.

PUFF PASTRY

The quantities given here are for twice the amount of puff pastry required to make these tarts. However, it's difficult to make a small quantity of puff pastry, and the leftover dough can be kept in the freezer for 2 to 3 weeks and used for another recipe.

Begin by combining the flour, ½ cup of the butter, the salt, and the water in a large mixing bowl or the container of a food processor; blend well. This is known as the *détrempe*. Form the dough into a ball, cut a cross in the top to allow the dough to breathe, wrap in a damp cloth, and chill for 30 minutes.

Flatten the remaining butter between two sheets of waxed paper with a rolling pin, and return the tablet of butter to the refrigerator.

When the dough and butter have chilled for 30 minutes (they must be exactly the same temperature and consistency), place the dough on a lightly floured work surface and roll out to a large square, ½ inch thick. Place the butter in the center of the dough. Fold the four corners of the dough over the butter and roll out into a rectangle about ¼ inch thick. Be careful not to apply too much pressure while rolling out the dough or the butter will break through the dough.

Fold the rectangle into thirds, as you would a letter. Pinch the edges together, and roll out again into a rectangle. Fold into thirds again; fold in half. You have just finished 2 turns of the dough. To remember this, lightly press 2 fingerprints into the top of the dough, wrap the dough in a damp cloth, and chill for 30 minutes.

After half an hour, remove the dough from the refrigerator and give it 2 more turns, rolling it into a rectangle, folding in thirds, then in half, and repeating the process.

Make 4 fingerprints on the dough, wrap in a damp cloth, and chill for another 30 minutes. Then give the dough 2 last turns and chill until ready to use.

APRICOT COMPOTE

Wash the apricots and place them whole, with their pits, in a saucepan with the sugar and the water. Bring to a boil and simmer over medium-high heat for 10 minutes. Let cool slightly. Remove the pits and process the apricots with their cooking liquid in a food processor or pass through a food mill.

If using canned apricots, drain the fruit and combine all of the fruit with half of the syrup in a food processor or food mill. Process to a purée.

The resulting compote should be the consistency of thin jam. If it's too thick, add more syrup or liquid. If you wish, add a little apricot brandy or kirsch to this canned or fresh fruit compote.

ALMOND CREAM AND APPLE TOPPING
Place 4 tablespoons of the butter in a large mixing bowl and let soften slightly. Beat with a whisk until light and creamy. Add ¼ cup of the sugar, beating constantly until well blended. Beat in the almond powder. Add the eggs, one at a time, and beat until thoroughly incorporated. Chill.

**About an hour before serving, divide the pastry in half, reserving one half for another use. Roll out the pastry ⅛ to 1/16 inch thick. Using around 6-inch plate or bowl, cut out 6 rounds of dough. Place them on 2 or 3 baking sheets and refrigerate for 10 minutes.

Preheat the oven to 400 degrees F.
Remove the pastry from the refrigerator and, dividing evenly, spread the almond cream over the top of each round of dough, distributing it evenly and smoothing it out with the back of a spoon.

Peel and core the apples and cut them into thin, uniform slices. Arrange the slices in a circular pattern on top of each pastry round.

Melt the remaining 4½ tablespoons butter and brush it over the apples. Sprinkle the remaining ¼ cup of sugar over the top of the tarts.

Place in the hot oven and bake for 20 to 25 minutes.

Serve hot, and pass the chilled apricot compote separately in a sauce boat. If you wish, serve a bowl of chilled whipped cream with the tarts as well.

A savory variation of this recipe could be

ALMOND CREAM AND APPLE TOPPING
Place 4 tablespoons of the butter in a large mixing bowl and let soften slightly. Beat with a whisk until light and creamy. Add ¼ cup of the sugar, beat-

ing constantly until well blended. Beat in the almond powder. Add the eggs, one at a time, and beat until thoroughly incorporated. Chill.

**About an hour before serving, divide the pastry in half, reserving one half for another use. Roll out the pastry ⅛ to 1/16 inch thick. Using a round 6-inch plate or bowl, cut out 6 rounds of dough. Place them on 2 or 3 baking sheets and refrigerate for 10 minutes.

Preheat the oven to 400 degrees F.
Remove the pastry from the refrigerator and, dividing evenly, spread the almond cream over the top of each round of dough, distributing it evenly and smoothing it out with the back of a spoon.

A savory variation of this recipe could be prepared with pears instead of apples.

Menu for 6 People

Par une Belle Soirée d'Automne

On a Lovely Autumn Evening

Difficulty:
Moderately difficult
Cost: *Expensive*

I must confess it: I am no Fernand Point. Neither is Michel Guérard. On the other hand, Paul Bocuse, Pierre and Jean Troisgros, Alain Chapel, Louis Outhier, and a few others can boast of having studied with this indisputable master of our art. And they don't hesitate to let you know it, either!

One day they were going on about it in front of Michel Guérard and myself, who were feeling somewhat irritated at being unable to participate in the conversation. Michel said to me, "Here's what we'll do: create an Association of Chefs *Not* from the School of Point."

We laughed, but were not totally consoled. In truth, perhaps even more than his cuisine—which established him as the outstanding restaurateur of this century—it was the man's personality that so profoundly impressed all these great chefs: his character, his good humor, his generosity, his sub-

La Truite Farcie Mado Point
Stuffed Trout Mado Point

Le Filet de Boeuf en Chevreuil, Sauce Poivrade
Chateaubriand with Peppery Game Sauce

La Mousseline d'Epinards aux Poires
Spinach and Pear Purée

La Tarte aux Pommes Caramélisées
Caramelized Apple Tart

tlety. As Paul Bocuse described him, "Fernand Point was a nobleman who knew how to receive his equals—and his only equals were kings."

But Fernand Point left us more than a marvelous memory. His wife Mado Point has continued his work, and this menu is inspired by her example of nobility and courage.

Doing the Marketing

Everything can be purchased the day before, particularly the trout, which should be killed and cleaned a day in

advance to keep it from curling up during cooking.

What to Drink

For an apéritif, serve a sweet port or sherry, or, as Fernand Point would have liked, a very good Champagne, which he would have chilled in a large marble mortar that held 4 or 5 bottles

and plenty of ice.

For the wines, choose a white Côtes-

Mado Point, widow of the famous Fernand Point from Vienne, still runs their restaurant, Le Pyramide.

du-Rhône, such as a Condrieux whose aroma of violets marries very well with the flavor of port in the fish.

Table Linens and Decoration

Choose autumn colors—a beige or ecru tablecloth decorated with red, orange, and yellow leaves. Place some small flat candles in a glass with a bit of water and arrange some autumn leaves around the glass.

Tableware

Choose a faïence decorated with autumn leaves or hunting scenes:

6   plates for the trout
6   dinner plates for the chateaubriand

6   dessert plates for the tart
1   large platter for the chateaubriand
1   vegetable dish for the spinach
1   flat platter for the tart

Silverware

6   fish knives and 6 fish forks for the trout
6   dinner knives and 6 dinner forks for the chateaubriand

6   dessert spoons
2   serving spoons and 2 serving forks
1   pie server

Glassware

18   goblets for water, white wine, and red wine

Getting Organized

Many things in this menu can be prepared in advance. They are indicated in each recipe with the symbol ***. The symbol ** indicates those tasks that must be done just before serving.

The day before, place the beef in the marinade. Prepare the dough for the apple tart, wrap in a damp cloth, and place in the refrigerator to chill. The vegetables for the trout can also be prepared and kept in the refrigerator.

Put the white wines and Champagne in the refrigerator to chill several hours before serving.

Two hours before serving, drain the chateaubriand and place the marinade in the pan to reduce. Bone the trout and stuff them. Cook the spinach.

One hour before serving, warm 12 serving plates, 1 sauce boat, 1 platter, and 1 vegetable dish. Prepare the ap-

With the chateaubriand, serve a full-bodied red wine, such as a Pommard or a Côte-Rôtie.

Write the menu on some parchment with leaves glued to it, or else roll up the parchment and tie it with a ribbon into which you insert a branch of foliage.

ples and the caramel for the tart and cover them with the dough.

Preheat the oven to 500 degrees F. Twenty minutes later, put the meat in the oven to cook for 20 to 25 minutes.

After cooking, do not turn off the oven.

Remove the chateaubriand from the pan and keep warm. Deglaze the pan with the reduced marinade. Finish preparing the sauce and keep warm in a bain-marie. Prepare the spinach.

Ten minutes before sitting down to eat, put the trout in the oven. Prepare the sauce just before serving the trout. Reduce the oven temperature to 400 degrees and put the tart in the oven to bake.

After serving the trout, unmold the tart. Finish the spinach purée and serve with the chateaubriand.

La Truite Farcie Mado Point

STUFFED TROUT MADO POINT

Time required: *1¼ hours*
advance preparation
Difficulty: *Moderate*
Cost: *Moderate*

Ingredients

2	medium leeks
2	celery ribs
2	medium carrots
12	tablespoons unsalted butter
½	cup plus 3 tablespoons port
1	cup crème fraîche (see Appendix), or heavy cream
	Salt

	Freshly ground pepper
2	egg yolks, at room temperature
6	small whole fresh trout (about ½ pound each)
2	shallots, finely chopped
¾	cup dry white wine
1	tablespoon chopped fresh parsley

Utensils

Cutting board
Medium saucepan with cover
Chef's knife
Filleting knife
Kitchen shears

Wooden spoon
Large spatula
Whisk
Rimmed baking sheet

Preparation

***Several hours in advance or, if you wish, the day before, you can julienne the vegetables.

Trim and thoroughly wash the leeks, discarding the greens. Trim the celery and scrape the carrots. Using a very sharp knife, cut the vegetables into short julienne, about the size of the tines of a fork.

Melt 5 tablespoons butter in a medium saucepan. Add the vegetables, cover, and sauté over low heat for about 5 minutes, stirring from time to time to prevent sticking.

Remove the cover and add 3 tablespoons of the port, 3 tablespoons of the cream, and salt and pepper. Simmer, uncovered, for 8 minutes longer.

Remove from the heat and whisk in the egg yolks. Let cool to room temperature and refrigerate.

One or two hours before dinner, prepare the trout for cooking: With the aid of a sharp knife, separate the bones from the flesh on each side of the fish, then carefully separate the spine and remove it. Snip the spine away from the two ends with kitchen shears and discard it.

If all this seems too confusing and complicated, smile nicely at your fishmonger and ask him to bone the trout for you in this manner. You will be left with 6 boneless trout in the form of pouches.

**Thirty minutes before serving, preheat the oven to 475 degrees F. Season the trout with salt and pepper and place 1 tablespoon of the vegetables in the cavity of each. Butter a rimmed baking sheet and sprinkle with the chopped shallots. Place the trout on the baking sheet and pour the white wine and the remaining ½ cup port over the fish. Bake in the hot oven for 8 to 10 minutes.

Just before serving, remove the trout from the oven and use a large spatula to transfer them from the baking sheet to 6 warm plates. If you like, peel off the skin of each trout, but be very careful not to break them when turning.

Pour the cooking liquid into a medium saucepan and simmer over medium-high heat until reduced by half. Add the remaining ¾ cup plus 1 tablespoon cream, bring to a boil, and boil for several seconds. Whisk in the remaining 7 tablespoons butter. Add the parsley and adjust the seasonings. Pour generous amounts of the sauce over each trout and serve.

Le Filet de Boeuf en Chevreuil, Sauce Poivrade

CHATEAUBRIAND WITH PEPPERY GAME
SAUCE

Time required: *24 hours marinating*
25 minutes cooking just before serving
Difficulty: *Moderate*
Cost: *Expensive*

One can easily like the sauces that accompany game without liking game. That's the case with me. This sauce can very easily accompany any cut of venison, as well as a nice leg of lamb or a fillet of beef.

Ingredients

1   large onion

4   cloves garlic

2 carrots
1 celery rib
3 tablespoons olive oil
½ cup wine vinegar
1 bottle robust red wine, such as a Côte-Rôtie
2 tablespoons cracked black peppercorns
8 whole juniper berries
1 bouquet garni composed of 2 bay leaves, 1 sprig thyme, and the stems of 1 bunch parsley,

all tied together with string
1 chateaubriand (about 2½ pounds)
2 chicken bouillon cubes
1½ teaspoons tomato paste
Salt
Freshly ground pepper
9 tablespoons unsalted butter
1 tablespoon cornstarch
½ cup cold water or wine
1½ teaspoons currant jelly

Utensils

Paring knife
Cutting board
Large skillet with cover
Roasting pan
Large mixing bowl
Large saucepan
Fine sieve

Wire rack
Large plate
Small plate
Aluminum foil
Plastic wrap
Wooden spoon
Whisk

Preparation

***The meat should marinate for 24 hours, so you'll need to prepare the marinade the day before.

To do so, peel the onion and garlic. Scrape the carrots and trim the celery. Finely chop all of the vegetables.

Heat the olive oil in a large, deep skillet. Add the vegetables and cook over medium heat until the vegetables soften and begin to brown lightly. Add the vinegar and boil for 5 minutes. Add the wine, peppercorns, juniper berries, and the bouquet garni. Reduce the heat to low, cover, and simmer gently for 20 minutes.

Pour the marinade into a large mixing bowl and let cool.

Add the chateaubriand to the mixing bowl; it should be completely covered with the marinade. Cover with plastic wrap and set aside in a cool place (but not in the refrigerator) for 24 hours.

About 2 hours before dinner, remove the meat from the marinade and place on a rack over a large saucepan to drain. When the meat is well drained, set aside on a plate. Pour the marinade into the saucepan, add the bouillon cubes and tomato paste, and simmer over medium heat until reduced to 1 cup. Remove from the heat and set aside.

It's best to cook the meat a little in advance so that it will have time to rest before being carved. This way, the blood will have time to collect in the meat, giving flavor and preventing the juices from running out and being lost when cut. This advice is applicable to any red meat that needs to be sliced.

**About 1 hour before serving dinner, preheat the oven to 475 degrees F. Thoroughly dry the drained chateaubriand and season it on all sides with salt and pepper.

Place 2 tablespoons of the butter in a roasting pan and place in the oven to melt. Place the roast in the hot butter to sear it, turning to coat all sides. Bake for 20 to 25 minutes, depending on the size of the roast.

When the meat is cooked, remove the roasting pan from the oven. Place the chateaubriand on a small plate inverted on a large plate, to prevent the meat from bathing in its juices. Cover with aluminum foil and place the plate over a small saucepan filled with hot, but not boiling, water to keep the meat warm while you prepare the sauce.

Pour off any excess fat from the roasting pan. Pour the reduced marinade into the roasting pan and use a wooden spoon to scrape up the browned bits that cling to the bottom of the pan. Strain the sauce through a fine sieve back into the saucepan and place over low heat.

Mix the cornstarch with the water or wine and add it, a small amount at a time, to the simmering sauce until thickened to the desired consistency. The sauce should be light, but slightly thick. Be careful not to add too much of the cornstarch mixture or the sauce will thicken too much.

Remove the saucepan from the heat and season the sauce with salt, if necessary. Cut the remaining 7 tablespoons butter into small pieces and gradually whisk them into the sauce along with the currant jelly. If not serving immediately, keep the sauce warm in a bain-marie until serving time.

Just before serving, slice the roast and arrange the slices on a warmed (but not hot) serving platter. Season with freshly ground pepper and serve. Pass the sauce separately in a sauce boat.

La Mousseline d'Epinards aux Poires

SPINACH AND PEAR PUREE

Time required: *15 to 20 minutes*
advance preparation
10 minutes cooking just before serving
Difficulty: *Easy*
Cost: *Inexpensive*

Ingredients

2½ pounds fresh spinach, or 3 packages (10 ounces each) frozen spinach
2 tablespoons coarse salt
½ pound whole Bartlett pears in syrup, or 1 can (7 ounces) pear halves in syrup
7 tablespoons unsalted butter
Pinch of freshly grated nutmeg

Utensils

Large saucepan
Food processor or food mill with fine disc
Large skillet
Wooden spoon

Colander

Beef replaces game, but is served with a peppery game sauce.

Preparation

***If you're using fresh spinach, remove the stems and wash the spinach leaves in several changes of cold water; drain.

In a large saucepan, bring 3 quarts of water and the coarse salt to a boil. Add the spinach and let the water return to a boil. Immediately turn the spinach into a colander and drain. Fill the saucepan with cold water and plunge the spinach into it to refresh the leaves; drain again. Squeeze handfuls of the spinach between the palms of your hands to extract all the excess water and form the spinach into compact balls. All this can be done several hours ahead and the spinach refrigerated like this until you prepare the purée.

If you're using frozen spinach, simply thaw it before preparing the purée.

Drain the pears and, if they are whole, remove the stems and cores.

**Shortly before serving, place the spinach and pears in a food processor or a food mill and reduce to a fine purée. Melt the butter in a large skillet. When the foam subsides and the butter is a light, nut brown color, add the spinach and pear purée. Season with salt and a pinch of freshly grated nutmeg and stir with a wooden spoon until heated through.

Serve in a warmed vegetable dish.

Certain foods don't like extreme cold. Keep your cheese in a cool larder or pantry instead of the refrigerator.

Note: Although the spinach can be cleaned and blanched in advance, the purée should not be sautéed too far in advance or the spinach will lose its nice dark green color.

La Tarte aux Pommes Caramélisées

CARAMELIZED APPLE TART

Time required: *1 hour*
advance preparation
15 minutes just before serving
Difficulty: *Moderately easy*
Cost: *Inexpensive*

This recipe is inspired by the famous tart Tatin, the immortal masterpiece of the Tatin sisters of La Motte-Beuvron. It's said that they invented that recipe when an ordinary apple tart had fallen and broken and they had to disguise the catastrophe. Their customers were delighted with the result.

Alas for the Tatin sisters! What crimes have been committed in their name, with all those spongy, floury, or sugary things misnamed Tatin. Copying is a difficult art, because it requires simplicity and modesty—two extremely rare qualities!

Ingredients

1⅔	cups all-purpose flour
14	tablespoons unsalted butter
	Salt
1	cup water
1	cup plus 2 tablespoons sugar

½	cup crème fraîche (see Appendix), or heavy cream
2	pounds Golden Delicious apples
1	tablespoon semolina flour

Utensils

8- or 9-inch springform pan or other round baking pan, at least 2 inches deep
2 medium saucepans
Small saucepan
Food processor or electric mixer (optional)

Baking sheet
Large mixing bowl
Rolling pin
Paring knife
Whisk
Wooden spoon

Preparation

***The dough for this tart can be prepared the day before or on the morning of the dinner.

Place the flour in a food processor or mixing bowl.

In a small saucepan, combine 7 ta-blespoons of the butter, a pinch of salt, and ½ cup of the water; bring to a boil. Immediately pour the boiling liquid into the flour and process until the dough is well blended and forms a ball. Wrap in a damp cloth and chill.

The caramel and apples can also be prepared several hours before baking the tart.

In a medium saucepan, combine 1 cup of the sugar with ½ cup of the water and cook over high heat until the sugar turns to a rich brown caramel. Just as it reaches this point, add the crème fraîche, whisking vigorously. Remove from the heat, still whisking, and gradually add the remaining 7 tablespoons butter, cut into small pieces.

Pour the warm caramel immediately into the springform pan; let cool.

Preheat the oven to 550 degrees F or to your oven's highest setting.

Peel and core the apples; cut them into quarters. Place on a rimmed baking sheet and sprinkle with the remaining 2 tablespoons sugar. Place in the hot oven for 10 minutes. Remove from the oven and let cool.

Arrange the apples on top of the caramel. Chill.

Roll the dough out ⅛ inch thick and prick in several places with a fork. Drape the dough over the top of the springform pan and trim evenly around the edge.

Shortly before sitting down to eat, preheat the oven to 400 degrees F. Fifteen minutes later, place the tart in the oven and bake for 20 to 25 minutes, until the dough is cooked.

Remove from the oven and place the pan over high heat for a few seconds to unmold the caramel. Invert a serving plate on top of the pan, hold your breath, and invert the pan and plate together. Carefully remove the pan. Keep warm until serving time.

Be careful not to burn yourself when turning the tart out onto a serving platter.

Menu for 6 People

Un Repas de Chasse

A Hunt Dinner

Difficulty: *Moderate*
Cost: *Expensive*

There are dinners that call for porcelain, crystal, sterling silver, and lace tablecloths—and then there are others, no less delicious, that need no elaborate trimmings: some oilcloth, a bare wooden table, and the shade of a tree.

I remember safari nights in Africa, when our dinner consisted of a guinea fowl roasted plain over the embers of the campfire. I pulled off the firm golden meat in strips. I licked my fingers, both literally and metaphorically. Then I wiped off my hands on boots scratched bare by thousands of thorns and completed my ablutions on pants bleached by the sun.

The pleasure of such a moment—and the pleasure was intense—came from satisfying hunger, of course, but also and perhaps above all from the sensuous enjoyment of eating with my hands and using my shirt or my pants as a napkin; to abandon for a moment so-called civilized habits in order to rediscover tastes, smells, sensations, and make contact with the truly natural.

La Quiche Crémeuse aux Morilles
Creamy Wild Mushroom Quiche

Le Suprême de Poule Faisane au Poivre et aux Fruits
Breast of Pheasant with Cracked Pepper and Fruit

Les Petits Grillons de Chavignol aux Brins de Sarriette
Goat Cheese Toasts

Le Soufflé Léger aux Reinettes
Light Apple Soufflés

Doing the Marketing

To be sure of obtaining them for the dinner, order the pheasants, the fresh morels, the dried Martin pears, and the crottins de Chavignol in advance.

What to Drink

For an apéritif, serve a Vermouth-Cassis, made by adding 1 tablespoon of cassis to a glass of dry vermouth, or simply serve the white wine that you will drink with the first course. For the wines, choose a white Hermitage or a Pouilly-Fumé for the quiche and a Burgundy (Pommard or Chambol) for the pheasants and cheese.

Table Linens and Decoration

Choose a thick, gray-brown tablecloth. You can decorate the table with

A hunt party can be an occasion to entertain in high style.

pheasant feathers, autumn leaves, and chestnuts with their burrs.

Write the menu on gray-brown pa-per. Roll up the paper and insert it in the cartridge from a rifle shell—empty, of course.

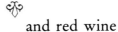

Tableware

For this meal, a faïence decorated with hunting scenes or fall motifs is a must:

- 1 large round platter for the quiche
- 6 plates for the quiche
- 6 plates for the pheasant
- 6 small plates for the goat cheese toasts
- 6 small plates for the soufflés
- 6 individual soufflé molds

Silverware

- 6 forks and 6 knives for the quiche
- 6 forks, 6 knives, and 6 sauce spoons or dessert spoons for the pheasant
- 6 dessert forks and 6 dessert knives for the goat cheese toasts
- 6 dessert spoons for the soufflés
- 1 pie server and 1 large knife for the quiche
- 1 serving spoon and 1 serving fork

Glassware

- 18 goblets for water, white wine, and red wine

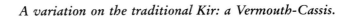

A variation on the traditional Kir: a Vermouth-Cassis.

Getting Organized

Many things in this menu can be prepared in advance. They are indicated in each recipe with the symbol ❊❊❊. The symbol ❊❊ indicates those tasks that must be done just before serving.

Prepare the dough for the quiche the day before.

Several hours in advance, put the white wine in the lower part of the refrigerator to chill, begin the preparation of the pheasants, and prepare the apples for the soufflés.

Fifty minutes before the meal, preheat the oven to 400 degrees F. Warm 12 large plates on the back of the stove or over a saucepan filled with hot water. Prepare the filling for the quiche.

Thirty minutes before serving, bake the quiche. Meanwhile, finish preparing the pheasants and keep them warm while you begin the preparation of the grilled goat cheese toasts.

When the quiche is ready, serve it, leaving the oven on.

After serving the quiche, place the pheasants in the hot oven to warm for 2 minutes. Arrange them on warmed plates and serve.

Return to the kitchen, set the oven on broil, and finish preparing the grilled goat cheese toasts.

Just before serving them, set the oven temperature to 400 degrees F, finish preparing the soufflés, and place in the oven to bake.

Serve the goat cheese toasts, but don't forget to return to the kitchen in time to reduce the oven temperature to 300 degrees to finish cooking the soufflés.

Return to the table to finish eating the goat cheese toasts. Serve the soufflés 10 minutes later.

La Quiche Crémeuse aux Morilles

CREAMY WILD MUSHROOM QUICHE

Time required: *15 minutes*
preparation
(6 hours in advance)
25 minutes advance preparation and cooking
30 minutes cooking just before serving
Difficulty: *Easy*
Cost: *Moderately expensive*

Ingredients

DOUGH
½ cup unsalted butter
2½ cups flour

1 whole egg
1½ teaspoons salt
5 tablespoons cold water

FILLING
14 ounces fresh morel mushrooms, or 3 ounces dried morels

2 tablespoons unsalted butter
2 tablespoons chopped shallots
1½ cups crème fraîche (see Appendix), or heavy cream

Salt

Freshly ground pepper

2 whole eggs

2 egg yolks

Freshly grated nutmeg

2 tablespoons chopped chives

Utensils

Electric mixer or food processor (optional)

Mixing bowl

Rolling pin

Medium skillet

Paring knife

9- or 10-inch round tart pan

Baking sheet

Whisk

Dishcloth

Aluminum foil

Aluminum pie weights or dried beans

Preparation

***The dough for this recipe must be made at least 6 hours before rolling it out and baking. Prepare the day before, if you wish.

Cut the ½ cup butter into small pieces.

If using an electric mixer or food processor, combine the butter, flour, egg, salt, and water until a ball forms, adding more water if the dough seems too dry.

If you're making the dough by hand, pour the flour onto a clean work surface. Make a well in the center and add the butter, egg, salt, and water. Incorporate the flour into the wet ingredients little by little with a fork. In either case, don't overwork the dough.

Wrap the dough in a damp cloth and chill for at least 6 hours. (These quantities make more dough than is needed for this recipe, but it is difficult to make a smaller quantity. You may even want to prepare a larger quantity than this and keep it for use in other recipes. The dough is suitable for fruit tarts, for encasing pâtés, or for any kind of savory tartlets topped, for example, with poached eggs and spinach or asparagus tips, ham mousse, smoked salmon, etc. The dough keeps well, wrapped in plastic wrap for a week in the refrigerator or for much longer in the freezer.)

When the dough has chilled for 6 hours, roll it out ¹⁄₁₆ to ⅛ inch thick. Drape the pastry over a 9½-inch round tart pan, pressing it gently into the bottom and sides of the pan and being careful not to tear it. Roll the rolling pin quickly and firmly over the rim of the tart pan to cleanly trim off the excess dough. Pinch the edges between your thumb and index finger to raise it slightly. Place the pie shell in the freezer for at least 1 hour to stabilize the dough and prevent it from shrinking during baking.

Preheat the oven to 425 degrees F.

Cut a sheet of aluminum foil into a round to just fit the bottom of the tart pan. Spread pie weights or dried beans over the bottom of the tart to prevent the dough from puffing up. Place in the hot oven and bake for 15 minutes.

Remove the tart shell from the oven and remove the pie weights or beans and foil. Set the pastry shell aside. (This pre-cooking is not absolutely necessary, but it will prevent the sides of the tart from collapsing and will prevent the bottom from becoming soggy.)

If using dried morels, place in a bowl

In this quiche, ordinary cultivated mushrooms can be substituted for morels.

with 2 cups warm water and let soak for 1 hour.

**Fifty minutes before serving, preheat the oven to 400 degrees F.

Drain the morels and squeeze gently to extract any excess water.

If using fresh morels, do not wash them (they'll become soggy). Simply wipe off the dirt and cut off the base end of each.

Melt the butter in a medium skillet. Add the shallots and sauté over high heat until lightly browned. Add the morels and sauté, stirring, until any liquid the morels give off evaporates completely. (This will take longer if you're using fresh morels.) Stir in ½ cup crème fraîche, season with salt and pepper, and simmer for 4 to 5 minutes.

Remove from the heat and set aside.

In a large mixing bowl, combine the whole eggs and egg yolks and whisk for 2 minutes. Add the remaining 1 cup crème fraîche, a pinch of nutmeg, and the chives. Season with salt and pepper and blend well.

Thirty minutes before serving, pour the morels and their sauce into the bottom of the tart shell. Pour the egg mixture into the tart. Place in the hot oven and bake for 30 minutes, until the quiche is cooked and lightly browned on top. To test for doneness, insert the tip of a knife into the center of the quiche. If it comes out clean, the quiche is cooked.

Place on a round serving platter and serve.

Le Suprême de Poule Faisane au Poivre et aux Fruits

BREAST OF PHEASANT WITH CRACKED
PEPPER AND FRUIT

Time required: *50 minutes
advance preparation
1 hour advance cooking
35 minutes just before serving*
Difficulty: *Moderately difficult*
Cost: *Expensive*

Ingredients

6	pitted prunes
2	tablespoons golden raisins
4	shallots
3	tablespoons whole black peppercorns
3	pheasants (about 1½ pounds each), plucked and cleaned, or 3 guinea hens, of the same weight

⅔	cup peanut oil
1	strip orange zest, ½ inch wide by 2 inches long
1	bouquet garni composed of 1 sprig thyme, the stems of a bunch of parsley, 1 bay leaf, and 1 small celery rib, all tied together with string
1	tablespoon flour

2 bottles strong red wine, such as
Côtes-du-Rhône
Salt
6 small dried Martin pears, or 3

ripe, but not soft, fresh Bartlett
pears
7 tablespoons unsalted butter
¼ cup plus 1 tablespoon Cognac

Utensils

Large saucepan
2 medium saucepans
Large skillet
Fine sieve
Boning knife
Paring knife

Wooden spoon
Slotted spoon
Cutting board
Small bowl
Plate
Cheesecloth

Preparation

***Much of the preparation of this dish can be done several hours in advance.

Begin by placing the prunes and raisins in a small bowl and covering them with warm water. Set aside to soak. Peel and thinly slice the shallots. Tie the peppercorns in a square of cheese-

cloth and crush them with a mallet or the bottom of a saucepan. Set aside.

To prepare the pheasants for cooking, cut off the feet and discard them. Remove the legs and thighs. Remove the wings. With a small boning knife, lift off the fillets from the breasts. Remove the skin from the fillets and

The fruits accentuate the aroma of the pepper while softening its pungency.

wings. Chop or break up the carcasses into large pieces.

Heat the peanut oil in a large saucepan until hot. Add the carcasses and legs and cook, stirring with a wooden spoon, for about 15 minutes, until the bones turn golden brown. Add the shallots, orange zest, and bouquet garni. Sprinkle all with the flour and stir. Add 1½ bottles (4½ cups) of the wine. Season generously with salt, bring to a boil, and simmer for 5 minutes.

If the bones are not completely covered with liquid, add water to cover. Reduce the heat to medium and simmer gently, uncovered, for about 30 minutes. Be careful: the simmering should be very gentle; the liquid should not reduce too much.

Meanwhile, if using dried pears, peel them, keeping them whole with their stems. Arrange the pears in a medium saucepan and add the remaining ½ bottle (1½ cups) wine. Place over medium heat and simmer, adding a little water if necessary to cover the pears entirely, for about 30 minutes.

Drain the prunes and raisins. Set the raisins aside. When the pears have sim-

⁕⁕Thirty-five minutes before serving, season the fillets and wings with salt on all sides. Spread the cracked pepper on a large plate and roll the fillets and wings in it to coat well.

Melt 2 tablespoons of the butter in a large skillet. When the butter turns nut brown, add the pheasant fillets and sauté for 3 to 4 minutes over medium heat. Turn and sauté for about 2 minutes on the other side.

Remove the pheasant fillets from the skillet and keep warm while finishing the sauce.

mered for 30 minutes, add the prunes and simmer for 10 minutes. Remove the saucepan from the heat and set aside, allowing the fruit to steep in the liquid.

If using fresh pears, peel them, cut in half, and remove the cores. Arrange, cut sides down, in a saucepan and add the prunes and the remaining wine, adding a little water if necessary to cover the fruit. Simmer over medium heat for 10 minutes only.

When the pheasant bones and legs have simmered for 30 minutes, strain the sauce through a fine sieve into a medium saucepan. Place over medium-high heat and reduce until only ⅔ cup of sauce remains. Remove the oily film that forms on the surface of the sauce and set the sauce aside.

Discard the carcasses. Place the legs in a small bowl, cover with a little of the sauce, and set aside for another meal. (They need only be reheated and served with buttered noodles.)

At this point you should have the sauce, the prunes and pears in their cooking liquid, the drained raisins, the cracked peppercorns, and the pheasant breast fillets and wings.

Add the raisins to the skillet and stir to coat in the butter. Add the Cognac and ignite. When the flames subside add the reduced sauce and boil briefly.

Cut the remaining 5 tablespoons butter into small pieces and stir them into the sauce with a wooden spoon until the butter is completely incorporated. Adjust the seasoning if necessary, remove from the heat, and keep warm. Drain the prunes and pears.

To serve, divide the breast fillets among 6 warmed serving plates and garnish with the drained fruit. Spoon the sauce over all. If necessary, place the plates in a hot oven for 2 minutes to warm before serving.

Les Petits Grillons de Chavignol Aux Brins de Sarriette

GOAT CHEESE TOASTS

Time required: *15 minutes*
Difficulty: *Very easy*
Cost: *Moderate*

Ingredients

18	slices baguette (each cut ¼ inch thick)
6	tablespoons virgin olive oil
6	small crottins de Chavignol, 4 rigottes sèches, or 1 log Montrachet goat cheese
2	sprigs fresh savory
	Freshly ground black pepper
	Several leaves radicchio or other peppery lettuce leaves

Utensils

Large baking sheet
Cutting board

Small knife

Preparation

***Assemble these in advance; they'll only need a final toasting just before serving.

Arrange the baguette slices on a baking sheet (or 2 if necessary). Drizzle about 4 tablespoons of the olive oil over all of the slices of bread. Place under the broiler and toast on one side.

Cut the goat cheese into ¼-inch slices and place a slice on each bread slice. Sprinkle each with a pinch of savory and freshly ground pepper.

** Ten or 15 minutes before serving, preheat the broiler.

Drizzle the remaining olive oil over the cheese, place under the broiler, and cook until the cheese is lightly browned.

Place 1 or 2 lettuce leaves on each of 6 serving plates. Arrange 3 toasts on each plate and serve immediately.

Le Soufflé Léger aux Reinettes

LIGHT APPLE SOUFFLES

Time required: *20 minutes*
advance preparation
30 minutes preparation and
cooking just before serving
Difficulty: *Moderately difficult*
Cost: *Inexpensive*

Ingredients

4 firm tart apples, such as Granny Smiths
1 tablespoon water
½ cup plus 2 tablespoons superfine sugar

4 tablespoons unsalted butter
12 eggs, at room temperature
¼ cup plus 2 tablespoons Calvados or other apple brandy

Utensils

Medium saucepan with cover
Medium skillet
6 individual soufflé molds
Baking sheet
2 mixing bowls

Whisk
Rubber spatula
Paring knife
Cutting board
Wooden spoon

Preparation

***The apples and soufflé molds can be prepared several hours in advance.

Peel and core the apples. Cut 2 apples into quarters and place in a medium saucepan with the water and 2 tablespoons of the sugar. Cover and cook until the apples begin to break down, stirring with a wooden spoon to produce a compote-like mixture. Remove from the heat and set aside to cool.

Cut the remaining 2 apples into ¼-inch cubes.

Melt 2 tablespoons of the butter in a medium skillet. When the butter starts to foam, add the diced apples and sauté over high heat for 3 to 4 minutes. Set aside to cool.

Soften the remaining 2 tablespoons butter and use it to coat the inside of the soufflé molds. Pour ¼ cup sugar into the first mold and rotate to distribute the sugar over all of the inside surfaces of the mold. Shake out the excess sugar into the second mold, and continue in this manner until all the molds are dusted with sugar. Place the soufflé molds on a baking sheet, making sure they are well spaced and not touching each other, and chill.

**Twenty-five minutes before serving dessert, preheat the oven to 400 degrees F.

Separate the egg whites from the yolks, being careful to leave no trace of the yolk in the whites, and place in 2 separate mixing bowls. (The eggs should not be cold or the whites won't

The Calvados in this apple soufflé recipe can be replaced by a pinch of cinnamon.

beat well.)

Add the remaining ¼ cup sugar to the yolks and whisk for about 5 minutes, until light and fluffy. Whisk in the apple compote and Calvados, blending well. Gently fold in the diced apples.

Beat the egg whites, at first slowly, then rapidly, until stiff.

Fold one-third of the egg whites into the apple mixture with a rubber spatula. Gently fold in the remaining egg whites, being careful not to deflate the whites.

Divide the mixture among the 6 prepared soufflé molds, letting it spill over the rims slightly. Run your thumb around the rim of each mold to clean it.

Place the soufflés in the preheated oven. Bake for 3 to 4 minutes; reduce the oven to 300 degrees F. Continue to bake for 17 minutes longer, and, by all means, do not open the oven!

Remove the soufflés from the oven and place one on each of 6 dessert plates lined with paper doilies or folded linen napkins. Serve immediately.

Menu for 6 people

Les Parfums Gaillards

Robust Flavors

Difficulty: *Easy*
Cost: *Moderately expensive*

Yes, there are meals that are eaten at the edge of the lips and the edge of the fork, with the little finger in the air, the spine erect, and with a somewhat dazed air. But that's not for me. When it comes to eating, only comfort and satisfaction count. How can you appreciate a fine meal without being natural and at ease?

So be a gourmand without restriction—in other words, simply be yourself, and be simple.

Doing the Marketing

Choose a beautiful, well-marbled piece of tenderloin that has been aged for about 15 days.

What to Drink

For an apéritif, serve a Cardinal, which is a kir made with red wine flavored with 1½ teaspoons of cassis. If you wish, place a few black peppercorns in the wine to macerate in advance and chill. Strain before pouring into individual glasses and adding the cassis.

For a meal with such robust flavors, you'll need a good, robust red wine, such as a Cahors or a Côte-Rôties.

Table Linens and Decoration

If you have a nice country-style table, lay out the tableware directly on it. If not, choose a thick tablecloth and large napkins of unbleached linen. Keep the table simple, with good thick candles and a large wicker bread basket. You can decorate the table with wildflowers, but don't expect to benefit much from the aroma.

As for the menu, simply read it out loud.

Tableware

Use rustic white stoneware dishes, or a faïence:

6   soup plates for the soup

Le Tourin d'Ail Doux
Sweet Garlic Soup

La Piecè de Faux-Filet au Poivre Noir à la Façon d'Eddie
Roast Tenderloin of Beef in Black Pepper, Eddie's Style

La Salade de Cocos Frais à la Menthe
White Bean and Fresh Mint Salad

Les Croutes de Roquefort
Roquefort Toasts

Les Pêches ou Poires au Vin de Poivre et de Laurier
Peaches or Pears Poached in Wine Scented with Pepper and Bay Leaf

A menu in which robust aromas replace the delicate bouquet of flowers.

6	dinner plates for the tenderloin		1	soup tureen
6	salad plates for the white bean salad		1	large platter for the meat
			1	sauce boat
6	salad plates for the Roquefort toasts		2	shallow bowls for the bean salad and the peaches
6	bowls for the peaches			

Silverware

6	soup spoons		1	large ladle to serve the soup
6	dinner knives and forks Use your hands for the Roquefort toasts		1	serving fork and 1 serving spoon
			2	spoons, 1 for the sauce boat and 1 for the beans
6	dessert knives and forks for the peaches		1	small ladle for the peaches

Glassware

6   goblets for the red wine

Getting Organized

Many things in this menu can be prepared well in advance. They are indicated in each recipe with the symbol ***. The symbol ** indicates those tasks that must be done just before serving.

If you're using dried beans for the salad, plan to soak them in water for at least 24 hours before beginning the preparation.

Several hours before the meal, prepare the bean salad, the peaches or pears in wine, and most of the Roquefort toast recipe.

About 1½ hours before sitting down to eat, preheat the oven to its highest setting. Warm 6 soup plates, 6 dinner plates, 1 platter, and 1 sauce boat on the back of the stove or over a large saucepan filled with hot water.

Prepare the meat for cooking and put in the hot oven.

Thirty-five minutes before the meal, while the meat is still cooking, start preparing the garlic soup.

Remove the meat from the oven and let it rest in a warm place while you serve the soup.

Assemble the Roquefort toasts and finish making the sauce for the meat by adding the Cognac to the roasting pan and stirring over very low heat. Finish the sauce. Slice the meat and serve, along with the bean salad and the Roquefort toasts.

Le Tourin d'Ail Doux

SWEET GARLIC SOUP

Time required: *35 minutes*
just before serving
Difficulty: *Easy*
Cost: *Inexpensive*

Don't worry about the odors of this *tourin* bothering your guests, because the two preliminary cookings will have largely dissipated the heavy aroma of the garlic.

And in any case, don't forget that garlic is a remedy for many ills. When I was a child, I knew an old couple in the neighborhood who amazed the whole village with their vitality and good humor. Each year they harvested 800 garlic plants in their little garden solely for their personal use: enough for one big head of garlic each, every day of the year.

I won't say that they smelled like Chanel No. 5, but I can tell you that they lived to the age of 90 without problems, and that they died, as the saying goes, in perfect health.

Ingredients		
6	slices white bread	2 tablespoons unsalted butter
3	or 4 whole heads of garlic	Salt
4	chicken bouillion cubes	Freshly ground pepper
1¼	cups crème fraîche (see Appendix), or heavy cream	6 egg yolks (optional)

Utensils

Large saucepan   Colander
Food processor or blender   Paring knife

Preparation

✽✽ This soup should be prepared just before serving. Start making it about 35 minutes before sitting down to eat.

Trim off the crusts from the bread slices.

Separate and peel the garlic cloves. Half-fill a large saucepan with water, add the garlic, and bring to a boil. Pour off the water. Refill the saucepan with water, and bring to a boil again. Drain

and reserve the garlic.

Return the garlic to the saucepan, along with 3½ cups water and the bouillon cubes. Place over low heat and simmer until the garlic begins to soften, 7 to 8 minutes. Add the bread and bring to a boil. Stir in the crème fraîche, and let the soup return to a boil.

Pour the soup into a food processor

Don't be stingy with the pepper.

or blender, add the butter, season with salt and pepper, and process or blend until smooth.

Pour into individual soup bowls and add a fresh egg yolk to each just before serving.

La Pièce de Faux-Filet au Poivre Noir à la Façon d'Eddie

ROAST TENDERLOIN OF BEEF IN BLACK
PEPPER, EDDIE'S STYLE

Time required: *10 minutes
advance preparation
30 minutes cooking*
Difficulty: *Moderate*
Cost: *Expensive*

Aside from his well-known abilities as a musician, Eddie Barclay cultivates several other passions. Cooking is one of them, and he gives it the same warmth of feeling he brings to everything he does.

I remember a time when a group of us stayed with friends, and Eddie literally took over the kitchen in order to prepare some of his specialities for us. The cook herself had fled, chased away not by Eddie but, more probably, by the odor of pepper.

Actually, I must warn you that you should ventilate your kitchen when you make this recipe. As it heats, the pepper makes the atmosphere red hot. Don't be surprised if your eyes sting, your throat gets sore, and you start sneezing. But do as my friend Eddie does: forget all these minor inconveniences with a glass of good Bordeaux.

❧

Ingredients

1	cup black peppercorns
4½	pounds beef tenderloin, trimmed

	Salt
8	tablespoons unsalted butter
½	cup Cognac

❧

Utensils

Roasting pan
Cutting board
Wooden mallet
Wooden spoon

Sharp carving knife
Large plate
Small plate
Aluminum foil

❧

Preparation

***It's important to start cooking the meat at least 1 hour before serving so that it will have time to rest, allowing the juices to coagulate in the meat before cutting it. Otherwise, the juices and all their flavor are lost when the meat is cut.

About 1¼ hours in advance, preheat the oven on its highest setting.

Meanwhile, wrap the peppercorns in a dishcloth and crush them with a wooden mallet or the bottom of a heavy skillet. Place the crushed peppercorns on a large plate. Season the meat with salt on all sides. Then roll it in the crushed pepper, coating all of the surfaces of the meat completely.

Melt 2 tablespoons butter over high heat in a roasting pan just large enough to hold the meat. When the butter begins to sizzle, add the beef and sear quickly on all sides. Place in the oven

to roast for about 30 minutes, turning once during that time. The cooking time will vary depending on the thickness of the meat. Consult your butcher about cooking time, if you like. After 30 minutes, the meat should be rare.

When the meat has reached the desired degree of doneness, place on a small plate inverted onto a large plate. This arrangement allows the meat to rest without sitting in its juices. Cover the meat with aluminum foil and place in the oven with the heat off and the door slightly ajar, to keep warm.

Pour off the fat that has collected on the surface of the juices in the roasting pan. Add the Cognac and place over very low heat, being careful not to ignite the Cognac. Stir with a wooden spoon to dislodge the bits of meat and pepper that stick to the bottom of the pan.

❧

**Just before serving, pour the juices from the meat that have accumulated on the plate into the roasting pan and stir over low heat until warmed

through. Cut the remaining 6 tablespoons butter into small pieces.

Remove the roasting pan from the heat and add the butter, a little at a time, whisking between each addition until the butter is completely incorporated in the sauce. Pour into a sauce boat.

Quickly cut the meat into ½-inch-thick slices, arrange on a platter, and serve. Pass the sauce separately.

La Salade de Cocos Frais à la Menthe

WHITE BEAN AND FRESH MINT SALAD

Time required: *45 minutes
advance preparation
2 to 3 hours cooking and resting*
Difficulty: *Easy*
Cost: *Inexpensive*

This recipe—so simple, yet redolent of aromas filled with sunshine—I owe to my friend César, the great sculptor.

Ingredients

2½	pounds fresh white beans in their shells, or 1 pound dried white beans, such as Great Northern
1	large leek
1	carrot
1	onion
1	clove
1	tablespoon salt

DRESSING
1	small celery heart
30	fresh mint leaves
1	small bunch parsley
1	small clove garlic
1½	tablespoons Dijon mustard
3	tablespoons wine vinegar
	Salt
7	tablespoons virgin olive oil
	Freshly ground pepper

Utensils

Large saucepan with cover
Mixing bowl
Colander

Whisk
Chef's knife
Paring knife

Preparation

***This salad can be prepared several hours in advance. But if you're using dried beans, don't forget to put them in water to soak for 24 hours before beginning to make the dish.

If using fresh beans, you'll need only to shell them before cooking.

Trim and thoroughly wash the leek. Scrape the carrot. Peel the onion and stick the clove in it.

Place the vegetables and beans in a large saucepan and fill with enough water to cover the vegetables by about 1 inch. Bring to a boil over high heat. Skim off the residue that floats to the surface. Add the salt. Reduce the heat to low, cover, and simmer until the beans are tender, 30 to 40 minutes for fresh beans or 1½ to 2 hours for dried.

Trim and wash the celery heart. Chop coarsely. (Save the leaves to make your own celery salt. To do so, lay the celery leaves out to dry thoroughly in a dry, shady spot. Place them in a jar and fill the jar with sea salt. Seal tightly.)

Coarsely chop the mint leaves and parsley and set aside.

Peel the garlic. Scrape the garlic into a mixing bowl, using the tines of a fork, or crush through a garlic press.

When the beans are tender, drain in a colander. Remove and discard vegetables.

Place a tablespoon of the beans in the mixing bowl with the garlic, and mash to a fine purée with a fork. Add the mustard and vinegar and season with salt. Whisk to blend.

Gradually pour the olive oil into the mixing bowl in a thin, steady stream, whisking constantly, until the dressing attains the consistency of mayonnaise.

Add the beans, celery, mint, and parsley, and season generously with pepper. Toss to mix well. Turn into a salad bowl and serve with the roast.

Les Croutes de Roquefort

ROQUEFORT TOASTS

Time required: *10 to 20 minutes*
Difficulty: *Easy*
Cost: *Moderate*

Ingredients

3½	tablespoons fromage blanc, whipped cream cheese, or yogurt (see Note)
1½	tablespoons unsalted butter
2½	ounces Roquefort cheese
	Pinch of celery
	Freshly ground pepper

½	bunch fresh chives, chopped
18	slices baguette (cut ½ inch thick)
1	clove garlic
	Virgin olive oil
6	leaves Romaine lettuce
18	celery leaves

Utensils

Large mixing bowl, electric mixer or food processor

Baking sheet
Whisk

The celery leaf adds a slightly sweet note.

Plate	Sieve
Fork	2 dessert spoons

Preparation

***Prepare the cheese and toast several hours in advance.

Place the fromage blanc or yogurt in a sieve to drain. (If using whipped cream cheese, this isn't necessary.)

Remove the butter from the refrigerator and let it soften.

Preheat the oven to broil.

If you're using a food processor, blender, or electric mixer, crumble the Roquefort into the bowl. Add the softened butter, celery salt, and a few grinds of fresh pepper and blend until creamy. Add the drained fromage blanc and chives; blend until creamy.

If mixing the cheese by hand, mash the Roquefort on a plate with a fork until creamy. Place in a mixing bowl with the softened butter, celery salt, and pepper and beat until creamy. Stir in the fromage blanc and chopped chives.

Arrange the baguette slices on a baking sheet. Place under the hot broiler and toast lightly on both sides. Rub each slice with the cut side of a garlic clove. Drizzle a thin stream of olive oil over the toasts.

Rinse and dry the lettuce leaves.

**Just before serving, use 2 dessert spoons to form the cheese mixture into quenelles, or firm ovals. To do so, scoop out a spoonful of the mixture with one spoon, place the second spoon on top of the cheese, and turn the spoons over and over, pressing gently to form a neat, compact quenelle.

Place one cheese quenelle on each baguette slice. Arrange the lettuce leaves on 6 serving plates and place 3 toasts on each plate. Tuck a celery leaf into each quenelle and serve.

Note: Fromage blanc is a fresh white cheese similar to cottage cheese but without curds. In recipes such as this one that call for a small quantity, you can substitute whipped cream cheese or yogurt. Or whisk several tablespoons of buttermilk into a package of farmer's cheese until it has the creamy consistency and slight tartness of fromage blanc.

Les Pêches ou Poires au Vin de Poivre et de Laurier

PEACHES OR PEARS POACHED IN WINE
SCENTED WITH PEPPER AND BAY LEAF

Time required: *30 minutes*
advance preparation
Difficulty: *Easy*
Cost: *Inexpensive*

When I was a child, my Aunt Celestine made a dessert like this, to which she added, just before serving it, a generous glass of crème de cassis. Astonishingly enough, I wasn't permitted to eat the fruit, but on the other hand I *was* allowed a bit too much of the syrup, into which I dipped ladyfingers by the spoonful. . . .

With such an upbringing, how could I not have become a gourmand?

Ingredients		
2	tablespoons black peppercorns	
2	cups Port	
	Zest of 1 lemon	
1	vanilla bean (if using peaches)	
6	bay leaves, fresh if possible	

1 bottle strong red wine, such as Côtes-du-Rhône or Pinot Noir
¼ cup plus 1 tablespoon honey
12 ripe peaches or Bartlett pears

Utensils

2 large saucepans with covers
Paring knife
Cheesecloth

Wooden spoon
Large bowl

Preparation

***Prepare this recipe at least 2 hours in advance, or longer if possible, to

give the fruit time to cool and steep.

Place the peppercorns in a square of cheesecloth and tie securely with string.

In a large saucepan, combine the Port, lemon zest, vanilla bean, bay leaves, wine, and pepper sachet, and bring to a boil. Stir in the honey and remove the saucepan from the heat. Cover the saucepan and set aside.

If you're using peaches, half-fill a large saucepan with water and bring to a boil. Plunge the peaches into the boiling water for 1 to 2 minutes, rinse them under cold water, and peel. If using pears, peel them, leaving the stems attached.

Place the peaches or pears in the warm wine, place over medium-high heat, and bring to a boil. Reduce the heat and let simmer for 10 minutes. Remove from the heat, cover, and let cool.

Remove the fruit from the sauce and arrange in a large shallow bowl. Pick out the bay leaves and stick them in the fruit at the stem, where the leaves would be. If using peaches, cut the vanilla bean into 12 small segments and place one in each peach to make a stem.

Set aside in a cool place, ouside the refrigerator, until serving time.

Peaches or pears work equally well in this recipe, but a strong red wine is essential.

Au Bistrot

At the Bistro

Menu for 6 people

Difficulty: *Moderate*
Cost: *Moderate*

This is a very rustic menu, for sure, but a delicious one nonetheless. It is inspired by the old Halles district of Paris. There one mingled with the strong market porters, concessionaires, butchers, vegetable growers, fish mongers, buyers, and the inevitable early morning visitors who came to finish off the evening after closing the fashionable nightclubs.

Everybody, it seemed, would end up in the bistros. The menu was always the same: onion soup, pigs' feet, snails, tripe, pot-au-feu, kidneys, undercut of sirloin. Bottles of wine freshly tapped from large barrels and huge baskets of bread were on every table.

At this time of the morning, and presented with such a copious meal, nobody ate lightly. Bread was abundant, both on tables and plates. And the dishes were as succulent as they were traditional. Personally, I admit

La Soupe à l'Oignon
Les Halles Onion Soup

L'Omelette aux Crottins de Chavignol
Chavignol Goat Cheese Omelet

Les Pieds de Cochon avec les Pommes de Terre Rôties
Braised Pigs' Feet with Roasted New Potatoes

La Salade aux Lardons
Chicory and Bacon Salad

Les Tartelettes aux Pommes et aux Noix
Individual Apple and Walnut Tarts

liking them more than many that are more exotic and complicated.

So, invite to your "bistro" some good friends who, like you, love simple and natural things.

Doing the Marketing

This menu can be quickly pulled together, except perhaps for the pigs' feet, which may have to be ordered in advance from your butcher. If you can't find them cooked, prepare them the day before, if possible. The other ingredients can be picked up the day before or the morning of the dinner.

What to

For an apéritif "au bistrot," the Kir is a must. But you can vary the pleasure and create new versions of the traditional Kir. The original Kir formula of 3½ ounces of white wine (Sancerre, Mâcon, or even Champagne) and 1 teaspoon of crème de cassis, can be varied by substituting Campari, crème de fraises (strawberry liqueur), framboises (raspberry brandy), etc. for the crème de cassis. The same flavorings can be added to a light, chilled red wine to make a pleasant apéritif called a Cardinal.

For the wines, if you wish to serve only one, choose a white wine that can also be used in the preparation of the Pigs' Feet. I suggest a Sancerre or a Mâcon, two years old or more. Serve it very cold, 42 to 45 degrees F.

If you prefer a red wine to pour into the last drops of the onion soup with a turn of the pepper mill, as the connoisseurs used to do at Les Halles, choose a Beaujolais Villages or a Beaujolais Nouveau and serve it at 50 to 54 degrees F. A young Côtes-du-Rhône, Morgon, or Brouilly at room temperature (55 to 60 degrees F) would also complement this menu.

Be careful about Beaujolais Nouveau—it is served from mid-November on, but loses its bouquet by springtime.

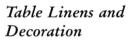

Table Linens and Decoration

For a bistro dinner, a marble-top table would be perfect. Otherwise, use a red and white checked tablecloth, a simple white cloth, or even one of oilcloth. Choose napkins of assorted colors and roll them in napkin rings made of colorful cardboard.

The menu can be written in chalk on a blackboard or on old-style bistro menus, and you can decorate the table with all the traditional bistro accessories such as water carafes, metal bread baskets, thick glass salt and pepper shakers, and promotional ashtrays.

Tableware

Choose thick, white, rustic china:
- 6 deep ovenproof soup crocks or bowls
- 6 dessert plates for under the soup bowls
- 12 large plates for the omelette and the pigs' feet
- 6 finger bowls
- 6 salad plates

- 6 dessert plates
- 1 large oval serving platter for the omelette
- 1 large salad bowl
- 1 large plate for under the salad bowl
- 1 bread basket with a crisp folded napkin for the potatoes

Silverware

- 6 soup spoons
- 12 dinner forks
- 6 knives

overleaf: *The dining room of Café de la Poste in Biot.*

IMAGES DU TRAVAIL EN FRANCE
DANS LES COLLECTIONS FRANÇAISES
PEINTURES ET DESSINS

DU 6 JUILLET AU 7 OCTOBRE 1985
MUSÉE NATIONAL FERNAND LÉGER BIOT 06

| 6 | dessert forks and knives | | forks |
| 3 | serving spoons and 3 serving | 1 | set wooden salad servers |

Glassware 12 goblets for water and wine

Getting Organized

Many things in this menu can be prepared in advance. They are indicated in each recipe with the symbol ✻✻✻. The symbol ✻✻ indicates those tasks that must be done just before serving.

Put the wine in the refrigerator to chill several hours in advance.

Forty-five minutes before sitting down to eat, preheat the oven to 400 degrees F. Warm 12 plates over a large pan of hot water or in a warm place on the back of the stove.

Join your guests for 15 minutes, then return to the kitchen to put the potatoes into the oven. Start reheating the onion soup over *very* low heat (it should not reduce) and return to your guests to finish the apéritif.

Five minutes before serving time, remove the potatoes from the oven and cover with aluminum foil. Turn on the broiler, fill the soup bowls, and garnish with the toast and cheese.

Seat your guests at the table and serve the onion soup when it's nicely browned. At the same time, reduce the oven temperature to 400 degrees F, remove the aluminum foil from the potatoes, and return them to the oven to continue cooking.

After serving the soup, slip away to prepare the omelette. But before serving it, put the pigs' feet in the oven with the potatoes. (Remove the potatoes when they've cooked for 35 to 45 minutes; test with a knife to make sure they are thoroughly cooked.)

Preparation of the salad takes a little more time away from the table (10 to 15 minutes). Just before serving the salad, place the tarts in a warm but *un-lighted* oven. (The oven will still be warm from cooking the pigs' feet and potatoes.) Or reheat for 3 minutes in a very low oven just before serving. They should be served slightly warm.

La Soupe à l'Oignon

LES HALLES ONION SOUP

Time required: *40 minutes
advance preparation
15 minutes preparation and
cooking just before serving*
Difficulty: *Moderately easy*
Cost: *Inexpensive*

The most famous of all onion soups is unquestionably that of Les Halles in Paris. In the old days, high-living night people and early-rising simple folk used to eat onion soup elbow to elbow on the zinc of the bistros and brasseries of the "*Ventre de Paris*" (literally, belly of Paris, the nickname for Les Halles). When they got to the bottom of the bowl, the connoisseurs used to give a good grind to the pepper mill and throw in a glassful of red wine—this was known as the "*chabrot*" style. And believe me, if you do that at four or five in the morning—at Les Halles or anywhere else—you'll have nothing

to fear for the rest of the day.

Today the Halles area is no longer what it was, but the onion soup remains the same, that is to say delicious, honest, and simple. Simple—well, perhaps not altogether. It requires patience and attention, if you don't want it to look like dishwater with some old crusts swimming around in it.

Ingredients

2	or 3 large onions (about 1⅓ pounds total weight)
3	tablespoons unsalted butter
6	cloves garlic
1	tablespoon flour
2½	quarts beef or chicken stock, or 12 bouillon cubes dissolved

	in 2½ quarts hot water
1	sprig fresh thyme, or ½ teaspoon dried thyme
	Salt
½	of a 30-inch baguette
	Freshly ground pepper
¾	pound Gruyère or Swiss cheese

Utensils

Large saucepan or soup pot
Rimmed baking sheet
Cutting board
Paring knife

Wooden spoon
Measuring cups and spoons
6 deep ovenproof soup crocks or bowls

Preparation

***Peel the onions and cut into very thin slices.

In a large saucepan or soup pot, melt the butter, add the onions, cover and cook briefly over low heat. Remove the cover and continue cooking until onions are softened and just golden.

Meanwhile, peel and crush the garlic.

Sprinkle the flour over the onions

and stir with a wooden spoon. Add the garlic, stock, and thyme. Season with salt and let simmer over medium heat for 30 minutes.

While it simmers, cut the baguette into thin slices. Toast lightly on both sides.

Shred the cheese.

Stop at this point if preparing the soup in advance.

**Fifteen minutes before serving time, preheat the broiler and place the soup over low heat to simmer, covered, for 5 minutes.

Place the soup crocks on a rimmed baking sheet and fill each crock to the rim with soup. Float toasted baguette slices on top of each crock, covering the soup entirely. Grind fresh pepper

over the top and generously sprinkle each with shredded cheese, making sure that the cheese covers the bread and soup completely and spills over the rim slightly.

Place the soup under the hot broiler and broil for 2 to 3 minutes, until the cheese melts, runs over the edge, and forms a beautiful golden crust.

Note: Many ingredients can be added to this soup. For example, a quart of white wine or a cup of semi-dry sherry can be substituted for an equivalent amount of the stock. Or, a raw egg yolk can be slipped under the golden crust as the soup comes out of the broiler. Just lift up the edge of the cheese crust, slide the egg yolk under, and replace the crust. Even a jigger of port or kirsch can be drizzled over the top of the golden crusts.

These are all very good additions. But personally, I prefer it in its simplest form, straight from the hot oven.

L'Omelette aux Crottins de Chavignol

CHAVIGNOL GOAT CHEESE OMELETTE

Time required: *10 minutes*
advance preparation
10 minutes preparation and
cooking just before serving
Difficulty: *Moderately difficult*
Cost: *Moderate*

Ingredients

4	very dry crottins de Chavignol (see Note)
20	¼-inch-thick slices baguette
¾	cup virgin olive oil
3	teaspoons fresh wild thyme

flowers or fresh thyme, or 1 teaspoon dried thyme

12	eggs
	Salt
	Freshly ground pepper

Utensils

12-inch omelette pan or nonstick skillet
Paring knife
Medium knife
Large mixing bowl

Baking sheet
Brush
Aluminum foil
Measuring cups and spoons
Fork

Preparation

***The cheese and bread slices can be prepared in advance if you wish.

Carefully scrape off any mold from the outside of the cheese. Slice each crottin thinly, put slices back together, wrap tightly in aluminum foil, and set aside.

**Ten minutes before serving time, preheat the broiler.

Break the eggs into a large bowl, season lightly with salt and pepper, and

Place the baguette slices on a baking sheet and brush generously with ½ cup plus 2 tablespoons of the olive oil. Sprinkle with 2½ teaspoons of the fresh thyme flowers (or ¾ teaspoon of the dried thyme).

beat with a fork. Add the cheese and remaining ½ teaspoon thyme flowers (or ¼ teaspoon dried thyme) and blend well.

In a 12-inch omelette pan or skillet, heat the remaining 2 tablespoons oil. Add the eggs and stir briefly with a fork. Cook over medium heat until the eggs are just set. Don't overcook.

(If you prefer, divide the eggs in half and make 2 smaller omelettes in an 8-inch omelette pan or skillet. It will be easier to handle if you're not accustomed to making omelettes.)

Meanwhile, place the bread slices under the hot broiler to brown lightly on both sides.

Carefully roll the omelette in thirds and slide it onto a large platter. Surround with the toasted bread and serve.

Note: Crottins de Chavignol, small firm discs of a dry, flavorful goat cheese, are found in better cheese shops in the United States. If unavailable, however, substitute about 9 ounces of the driest goat cheese available. Even the softer, moister Montrachet, for example, could be substituted.

Individual crottins de Chavignol and the finished omelette.

Les Pieds de Cochon

BRAISED PIGS' FEET

Time required: *30 minutes*
advance preparation
10 minutes reheating just before serving
Difficulty: *Moderately easy*
Cost: *Moderate*

Pigs' feet from Les Halles! This is another of those nighttime dishes that you can eat with your fingers and without ceremony. (All the same, don't forget the fingerbowls!)

Ingredients

3	tablespoons unsalted butter
5	tablespoons minced shallots
6	pre-cooked pigs' feet, split in half lengthwise (see Note)
1	cup dry white wine
¼	cup Meaux-style mustard or mild Dijon mustard

Utensils

Ovenproof baking dish large enough to hold 6 pigs' feet, halved

Chef's knife
Spoon
Measuring cups and spoons

Preparation

***Preheat the oven to 400 degrees F.

Melt the butter in a large ovenproof baking dish. Sprinkle the shallots evenly over the bottom of the dish and arrange the pigs' feet on top, skin side up. Pour ¾ cup of the wine over the pigs' feet and bake in the preheated oven for 20 minutes. Check the pigs' feet from time to time during the cooking to make sure that the wine doesn't cook away too fast. If it does, add the remaining ¼ cup wine.

Remove the baking dish from the oven and spread each halved pigs' foot with 1 teaspoon of the mustard. Baste each with a little of the cooking liquid (or with the remaining ¼ cup wine if you did not use it during the cooking.)

If preparing in advance, stop at this point and put the pigs' feet aside in a cool place.

**Twenty-five minutes before serving, preheat the oven to 400 degrees F.

Ten minutes before serving, place the pigs' feet in the preheated oven and reheat for 10 minutes. (There should be no need to season the pigs' feet, as they are salted during the pre-cooking.)

This dish can be brought to the table as it is, unadorned. Serve with the same white wine the pigs' feet cooked in. And enjoy!

Note: Cooked pigs' feet *en gelée* are readily available in French charcuteries. This recipe calls for the un-breaded variety, with a little of the

Pigs' feet in the style of Les Halles.

cooking gelée still on them.

If you cannot find them pre-cooked, order fresh pigs' feet from your butch-er and prepare them the day before or several hours ahead, in the following manner:

Rinse the pigs' feet, then soak in cold water for 3 hours. Drain and place in a large stockpot with 1 cup dry white wine, 1 peeled onion stuck with 2 cloves, 1 rib celery, 2 carrots, and a bouquet garni composed of parsley stems, 2 bay leaves, and 2 sprigs fresh thyme, tied together with string. Fill the pot with enough water to cover the pigs' feet and bring to a boil. Skim off the residue that rises to the surface. Re-duce the heat to medium and simmer gently until tender, about 1½ hours. Remove pigs' feet from the broth and let cool. Split each in half lengthwise and proceed as indicated in the recipe.

Les Pommes de Terre Rôties

ROASTED NEW POTATOES

Time required: *10 minutes*
advance preparation
30 to 45 minutes
cooking just before serving
Difficulty: *Very easy*
Cost: *Inexpensive*

Ingredients

30 small new potatoes (each about the size of an egg)

⅔ cup milk

Salt

3 tablespoons unsalted butter, melted (optional)

Utensils

Shallow baking dish large enough to hold 30 small new potatoes

Shallow bowl
Vegetable peeler
Measuring cups and spoons

Preparation

*** Wash the potatoes *before* peeling them so that their white flesh doesn't get dusty from the skins. Peel, trimming as you go to make all about the same size.

Place peeled, trimmed potatoes in a large shallow bowl, pour in the milk, and roll and soak potatoes in the milk until well coated. Drain potatoes and arrange in one layer on the bottom of a shallow baking dish.

If preparing in advance, stop at this point and set potatoes aside in a cool place.

** About 1 hour before serving, preheat the oven to 400 degrees F.

Put the potatoes in the oven and bake for 30 to 45 minutes, turning from time to time during the cooking so that they brown lightly and evenly on all sides. Pierce potatoes with the tip of a knife to test for doneness. If not tender, continue to bake for a few

Serve hot potatoes instead of bread with the pigs' feet.

more minutes.

When the potatoes are tender, remove from the oven and sprinkle with salt. To give the potatoes a glossy sheen, roll in the melted butter just before serving, if desired.

Arrange them in a bread basket lined with a crisp folded napkin.

Note: These potatoes can be served instead of bread and are delicious when mashed under the fork on the plate to absorb the juices from the pigs' feet.

La Salade aux Lardons

CHICORY AND BACON SALAD

Time required: *15 minutes*
advance preparation
10 minutes just before serving
Difficulty: *Very easy*
Cost: *Inexpensive*

Ingredients

½   pound slab bacon
6   eggs (optional)
1½   teaspoons Dijon mustard
2   tablespoons wine vinegar
    Salt
⅓   cup virgin olive oil or
    walnut oil
1½   pounds chicory or other crisp
    greens (see Note)
1   clove garlic
    Freshly ground pepper

Utensils

Large salad bowl
Small saucepan
Medium saucepan
Small skillet
Chef's knife
Fork
Measuring cups and spoons
Wooden salad servers
6 salad plates

Preparation

✳✳✳ Cut the bacon into short, thick julienne, 1¼-by-¼-by-¼-inch.

Place in a small saucepan of boiling water and blanch for 30 seconds. Drain and set aside.

If you choose to include the eggs,

soft boil them as follows: To prevent eggs from cracking during the cooking, be sure there are no hairline cracks and add about 2 tablespoons of salt per quart of boiling water. Plunge the eggs into a saucepan of the salted boiling water for only 7 minutes. Another method to prevent cracking (question it if you like, but I've tried it and it works!) is to burn several wooden matches halfway down, then toss them into the boiling water.

To remove shells without damaging the eggs, peel under a stream of cold running water.

In a large salad bowl, combine the mustard, vinegar, and a pinch of salt and mix well. Add the oil and blend thoroughly.

Wash and dry the salad greens.

Stop here if preparing in advance.

❧

** Just before serving, place the bacon in a small, dry skillet (no butter or oil needed) and sauté over medium heat to render the fat. Drain bacon on paper towel.

Add the salad greens to the bowl with the dressing. Add the bacon. Cut the soft-boiled eggs into large pieces and add to the salad. Scrape the garlic over the salad with the tines of a fork or crush the garlic through a press. Season with a grind or two of pepper.

Toss (or *"fatiguez"* as they say in Provence) the salad, turning it carefully with wooden (never metal) salad servers. Don't worry if the soft egg yolks run; it's inevitable and they give a creamy smoothness to the dressing.

Serve at once on salad plates.

❧

Note: The greens for this salad should be very crunchy, with the texture of frisée, chicory, or dandelion greens. Mix in radicchio and endive if you wish, but for the best harmony of textures, the greens should all have a similar crispness.

Since there is an omelette in this menu, the soft-boiled eggs in this salad can be omitted if you wish. Normally this salad is served with croutons rubbed with crushed garlic. But as toasted baguettes are served with the soup and the omelette here, bread is not necessary with the salad.

Les Tartelettes aux Pommes et aux Noix

INDIVIDUAL APPLE AND WALNUT TARTS

Time required: *50 minutes*
advance preparation
3 to 5 minutes warming
just before serving
Difficulty: *Moderately easy*
Cost: *Moderate*

Ingredients

⅔ cup unsalted butter, softened
⅔ cup granulated sugar
3 eggs
1¼ cups flour

⅔ cup coarsely chopped walnuts
3 tart apples, such as Granny Smiths
⅓ cup powdered sugar

Utensils

Medium mixing bowl
6 individual tart molds, 3½ to 4 inches in diameter
Vegetable peeler

Medium knife
Wooden spoon
Cutting board
Measuring cups and spoons

Preparation

*** Preheat the oven to 350 degrees F.

In a mixing bowl, combine the butter and granulated sugar and blend thoroughly. Add the eggs one at a time, blending well after each. Stir in the flour and walnuts and blend well.

Divide the batter among 6 buttered tart molds, patting it evenly over the bottom of each.

Peel and core the apples; thinly slice.

Divide the apple slices among the 6 tarts, arranging them attractively on top of the batter.

Place in the preheated oven and bake for 15 to 20 minutes, until the batter puffs slightly and the edges are golden. Sprinkle the tarts with the powdered sugar and return them to the oven to brown slightly, about 5 minutes.

** These tarts need be reheated in a very low oven for only about 3 minutes before serving. They are best served warm, not hot.

Note: Prunes cooked in wine can be substituted for the apples. To prepare, place about 20 prunes in a medium saucepan and cover with 1 cup water and 1 cup red wine. Stir in 2 tablespoons sugar and a piece of lemon peel. Let simmer over low heat for 10 minutes. Let cool.

Drain the prunes and remove the pits. Arrange 3 to 4 prunes, depending on their size, on each tart and bake as indicated above.

These tarts are best served slightly warm.

Aux Chandelles

By Candlelight

Difficulty: *Difficult*
Cost: *Expensive*

I cannot think of a candlelight meal without remembering a certain Christmas dinner, a very memorable Christmas dinner. . . . It took place near the awe-inspiring Zambesi Falls in a country then called Northern Rhodesia and since re-baptized Zimbabwe.

I had been invited, along with a dozen friends, to celebrate Christmas with some English farmers. In that part of the world, the Christmas season is as hot as the Fourth of July. However, in order to re-create a Christmas atmosphere, a large, festive table had been set; it was covered with a fine lace tablecloth, beautiful plates rimmed with gold, and the sparkling silverware the English are so well known for. The Christmas tree looked more like a mimosa than a pine tree, but its decorations made it a very presentable specimen. Nevertheless, what really created a festive atmosphere were six large, silver candelabra with ivory-colored candlesticks. These gentle and warm sources of light constituted the only light in the vast room, and they

Les Escalopes de Saumon Crû avec la Crème aux Graines de Moutarde et le Bouquet de Champignons
Fresh Raw Salmon Slices with Whole-Grain Mustard Sauce and Mushrooms

Les Huîtres Chaudes en Crème Safranée
Warm Oysters in Saffron Cream Sauce

Les Filets d'Agneau en Croûte en Duxelle de Cèpes
Fillet of Lamb in Puff Pastry with Duxelle of Wild Mushrooms

Le Gâteau Nélusko
Chocolate Nélusko Cake

transported us away from the tropical night with its croaking frogs and noisy insects.

At the stroke of midnight, the sound of "Oh, Holy Night" came from a record player and was taken up by a chorus of guests and domestics of the farm. This was perhaps my most memorable Christmas evening and my most beautiful candlelight dinner.

Doing the Marketing

Order the saddle of lamb in advance and ask the butcher to trim it.

Also order the salmon and oysters.

If you don't already own them, buy 2 cutting boards, each about 9 by 4½

inches, to serve and cut the fillets on.

For a warm atmosphere nothing equals the soft glow of candles.

What to Drink

For an apéritif, serve Champagne or Champagne cocktails.

For the wines, I suggest that you drink a dry white wine with the salmon and the oysters—a Blanc de Palette, for example, a Graves, or a brut Champagne. With the lamb fillets, choose a good Bordeaux such as a Margaux.

Table Linens and Decoration

Make this dinner into a gentle feast of warm lights and the mingled scents of candle wax and flowers and your delightful meal. Get out the candelabra and candle holders. Forget about electricity tonight.

Choose your candles carefully. Buy good ones that will last until the end of the evening. Avoid placing them near drafts or they will burn down too quickly.

If you have no glass or metal drip-catchers for the candles, cut out colored cardboard circles that match the color of the candles. You can also use small crowns of dried or artificial flowers that serve the same function. After taking these precautions, you can bring out your best lace or damask tablecloth and all the silver.

Write the menu with a black felt-tip pen on gold doilies placed on pleated napkins. You also could print the names of your guests on small, heart-shaped lace doilies.

Tableware

The dishes should be elegant and subtle. Choose flowered porcelain plates or a service of white plates rimmed in gold:

6 large plates for the salmon
6 large plates for the oysters (or oyster plates)
6 large plates for the lamb
6 dessert plates for the cake
1 large serving platter for the lamb
1 large round plate for the cake
1 sauce boat

Silverware

6 fish knives and fish forks for the salmon
6 oyster forks
6 teaspoons or saucespoons for the oyster sauce
6 dinner forks and dinner knives for the lamb
6 dessert forks for the cake
2 pie servers for the lamb and the cake
1 serving spoon
1 large knife

Glassware

18 Bordeaux glasses for water, white wine, and red wine

Getting Organized

Many things in this menu can be prepared in advance. They are indicated in each recipe by the symbol ✳✳✳. The symbol ✳✳ indicates those tasks that must be done just before serving.

Put the white wine in the refrigerator to chill several hours in advance.

Thirty minutes before sitting down to eat, warm 6 plates over a pan of hot water or on the back of the stove.

Finish the lamb stock and keep it warm in a bain-marie and give the pastry over the lamb fillets a second brushing with the egg wash.

Preheat the broiler.

In a bain-marie, warm the sauce for the oysters and the julienne of vegetables separately. In a small bowl, whip the crème and the egg yolks. Place a bed of seaweed on each of 6 plates.

Just before sitting down to eat, remove the Nélusko cake from the refrigerator. Place the oyster shells on a bed of coarse salt on a rimmed baking sheet. Finish preparing the salmon and serve.

After the salmon, blend the crème and egg mixture into the sauce for the oysters. Place the oysters in their shells, cover each with some of the vegetable julienne, coat with sauce, and place under the broiler. When they are browned, reduce the oven to 460 degrees F. Give the puff pastry a last coat of egg wash and place the filets en croûte in the oven for 20 minutes. Serve the oysters.

Before serving the lamb, you'll only have to incorporate the remaining butter into the warmed fond d'agneau, put it in a sauce boat, and serve with the fillets.

Les Escalopes de Saumon Crû avec la Crème aux Graines de Moutarde et le Bouquet de Champignons

FRESH RAW SALMON SLICES WITH WHOLE-GRAIN MUSTARD SAUCE AND MUSHROOMS

Time required: *20 minutes
advance preparation
10 minutes just before serving*
Difficulty: *Very easy*
Cost: *Expensive*

Ingredients

1⅓ pounds very fresh salmon, preferably cut from the tail (see Note)

¼ cup plus 2 tablespoons crème fraîche (see Appendix), or heavy cream

2 egg yolks, at room temperature

1 teaspoon Dijon mustard
Juice of 2 lemons

Salt
Freshly ground pepper

½ cup virgin olive oil

2 teaspoons Meaux-style grainy mustard

6 large, fresh white mushroom caps
Fresh parsley leaves
Fresh chervil leaves

Utensils

3 mixing bowls
Whisk
Paring knife

Filleting knife
Measuring cups and spoons

Preparation

***Ask your fishmonger to scale and fillet the salmon and to slice it diag- onally into very thin slices. (If you have a good knife with a long slim

The salmon must be served very cold.

blade, you can slice the salmon yourself. Hold the knife on a slight angle and cut into thin diagonal slices. The salmon should be sliced in the same way that properly cut smoked salmon is sliced.)

In a small mixing bowl, beat the crème fraîche with a whisk until thick but not fully whipped. Chill. Place 6 plates in the refrigerator to chill.

In another bowl, combine the egg yolks, Dijon mustard, and the juice of 1 lemon. Season with salt and pepper

and blend well. Add the oil in a very thin, steady stream, whisking constantly, until the sauce thickens (in the same way you would make a mayonnaise). Stir in the Meaux-style mustard and the whipped crème fraîche. Adjust the seasonings if necessary.

Arrange the salmon on 6 well-chilled serving plates, spreading the slices out flat. Season with salt and pepper and spoon the sauce over the salmon. Chill until serving time.

**Just before serving, rinse the mushroom caps briefly and cut them into large julienne strips. Place them in a small bowl, season with salt and pepper, and toss with the juice of the remaining 1 lemon to prevent the

mushrooms from discoloring.

Arrange a fan-shaped bouquet of julienned mushrooms on each plate of salmon. Garnish with the parsley and chervil leaves and serve.

Note: If salmon is not available, you can substitute any number of other fresh white-fleshed salt-water fish, such as sea bass or sea trout.

Les Huîtres Chaudes en Crème Safranée

WARM OYSTERS IN SAFFRON CREAM SAUCE

Time required: *30 minutes advance preparation 25 minutes just before serving*
Difficulty: *Moderately easy*
Cost: *Expensive*

Ingredients

2	medium carrots
1	leek (white part only)
1	or 2 celery ribs, preferably from the heart
1½	teaspoons unsalted butter
	Salt
⅔	cup crème fraîche (see Appendix), or heavy cream
1	clove garlic
1	large shallot

36	fresh raw oysters, preferably Belon or Marennes or other small, plump oysters
1	pound coarse salt
⅔	cup dry white wine
2	egg yolks
½	teaspoon saffron threads
	Freshly ground pepper
2	to 3 handfuls seaweed
1	bunch fresh parsley

Utensils

2	medium saucepans
	Rimmed baking sheet
2	mixing bowls
	Paring knife
	Oyster knife
	Chef's knife

Fine sieve
Colander
Slotted spoon
Measuring cups and spoons
Plate
Cheesecloth

Preparation

***Scrape the carrots. Trim and thoroughly wash the leek and celery. Cut all of the vegetables into fine julienne. Place the julienne in a saucepan with the butter and enough water to cover. Season with salt. Bring to a boil and let simmer, uncovered, until all of the water evaporates, about 20 minutes. Remove from the heat and set aside.

Place the crème fraîche in a mixing bowl and refrigerate until both bowl and crème are thoroughly chilled.

Peel and crush the garlic. Peel and chop the shallot.

Open the oysters over a large bowl, being careful to catch the oyster liquor and not to damage the shells. Rinse the rounder half of each shell under cold water and reserve; discard the other half.

Pour a thick layer of coarse salt over a rimmed baking sheet. Set the shells on the salt and place in a very low oven (less than 200 degrees F) to dry. (When heated like this, the oyster shells give off the warm aroma of seaweed that will later permeate the oysters and their sauce. But beware, high heat will crack the shells.) Meanwhile, strain the oyster liquor through a fine sieve lined with cheesecloth to remove any pieces of shell and dirt. Place the oysters and their liquor in a medium saucepan. Add the white wine, garlic, and shallot. Set aside in a cool place. Remove the oyster shells from the oven and set aside.

**Just before serving, place the saucepan with the oysters and their cooking liquid over high heat and bring quickly to a boil. Immediately remove the oysters from their cooking liquid with a slotted spoon and set aside on a plate. Let the cooking liquid continue to simmer until reduced to 3 or 4 tablespoons. Stir in 3 or 4 tablespoons of the crème fraîche and remove from the heat.

Preheat the broiler.

Remove the remaining crème fraîche and chilled bowl from the refrigerator and beat with a whisk until whipped. Stir in the egg yolks and saffron and blend well. Fold this mixture into the reduced oyster cooking liquid and season with salt and pepper.

Arrange a bed of the julienned carrots, leek, and celery on each oyster shell and place an oyster on each. Divide the sauce equally among the oysters. Place under the broiler and heat until the sauce turns golden, about 30 seconds.

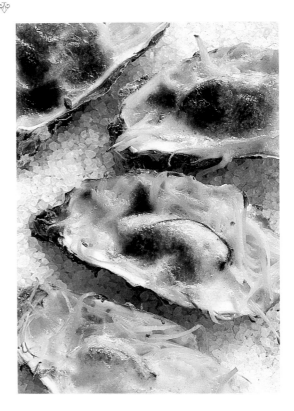

Divide the seaweed among 6 warmed serving plates. Place 6 oysters on each plate, garnish each oyster with a parsley sprig, and serve immediately.

Les Filets d'Agneau en Croûte en Duxelle de Cèpes

FILLET OF LAMB IN PUFF PASTRY WITH
DUXELLE OF WILD MUSHROOMS

Time required: *4 hours*
advance preparation
30 minutes cooking before serving
Difficulty: *Very difficult*
Cost: *Expensive*

Ingredients

PUFF PASTRY
1⅔ cups unsalted butter
3 cups flour

1 tablespoon salt
⅔ cup cold water

LAMB STOCK
1 pound lamb bones
4 shallots
1 small head garlic
1 medium carrot
3 tablespoons olive oil
1 sprig fresh thyme, or ½ tea-

spoon dried thyme
1 bay leaf
1½ teaspoons tomato paste
1⅓ cups red wine, preferably the same that will be served with the lamb
Freshly ground pepper

LAMB AND DUXELLE
1 saddle of lamb (about 3 pounds)
Salt
Freshly ground pepper
2 tablespoons virgin olive oil
6 tablespoons unsalted butter
¾ pound fresh cèpes, or 1 ounce dried cèpes *and* ¾ pound fresh white mushrooms

1 shallot
2 slices white bread
½ cup milk
5 ounces skinless, boneless chicken breast
¾ cup crème fraîche (see Appendix), or heavy cream
2 egg yolks
1 teaspoon sugar
2 tablespoons water

Utensils

2 small roasting pans
Food processor
Medium skillet
Small saucepan
Roasting pan to serve as bain-marie
2 small cutting boards
2 small bowls

Rolling pin
Mixing bowl
Paring knife
Chef's knife
Large, fine sieve
Brush
Fork
Dishcloth

Waxed paper
Plate

Wooden spoon
Measuring cups and spoons

***The majority of the preparation and assembling of this dish can be done several hours in advance.

PUFF PASTRY

Begin by tackling the puff pastry, which will need "turning" every 30 minutes during the preparation of the lamb and its garniture.

Remove the cold butter from the refrigerator and flatten it between two sheets of waxed paper with a rolling pin to soften and make it more malleable. Wrap half of the butter in waxed paper and return it to the refrigerator.

Place the remaining butter in a large mixing bowl, add the flour, salt, and ⅔ cup cold water and blend together well. Form the dough, called the *détrempe*, into a ball, cut a cross in the top of it to allow it to breathe, and wrap it in a damp cloth. Refrigerate for about 30 minutes.

On a lightly floured work surface, roll out the chilled dough into a large square, about ½ inch thick. Shape the remaining butter into a smaller square, and place it in the center of the dough. The butter should be the same consistency and temperature as the dough. Fold in the four corners of the dough square over the butter, covering it completely, and roll out quickly into a rectangle about ¼ inch thick. Be careful not to use too much pressure when rolling the dough or the butter will break through.

Fold the rectangle into thirds as you would a letter; then fold in half. Pinch the ends together, and roll out again into a rectangle. Fold into thirds and then in half, as before. You have given the dough 2 "turns"; to remind yourself, make 2 light marks with your fingers in the top of the dough, wrap it in a damp cloth, and refrigerate for 30 minutes.

Proceed with the preparation of the stock and the duxelle, remembering to give the dough another two turns (i.e., roll into a rectangle, fold in thirds, then in half and repeat) after 30 minutes. Make 4 marks on top of the dough this time and return it to the refrigerator for another 30 minutes.

Finally, give the dough its last two turns, for a total of 6 turns.

LAMB STOCK

Ask your butcher to saw the lamb bones into pieces.

Peel and chop the shallots and garlic cloves. Scrape the carrot and chop.

Heat the oil in a roasting pan, add the bones, and brown them over medium heat for about 15 minutes. Pour off the excess oil and grease and return the pan to the heat. Add the shallots, garlic, carrot, thyme, bay leaf, and tomato paste, and sauté over medium heat.

Add the wine and a grind of fresh pepper and let reduce by three-quarters.

Pour in enough water to cover the bones (about 2 cups) and simmer for 40 to 50 minutes, until the liquid is reduced by half.

Meanwhile, there are other tasks to be done. Don't forget about the puff pastry dough, waiting for its 2 turns. Then proceed with the preparation of the lamb and the duxelle, but don't forget about the stock simmering quietly on the stove. When the 40 to 50 minutes have elapsed, strain the stock through a large, fine sieve into a small saucepan, and set aside in a cool place until needed.

LAMB AND DUXELLE

If you have an obliging butcher, he will have boned the saddle of lamb and trimmed it neatly of all fat and skin to make 2 fillets. Season the fillets with salt and pepper.

Heat the oil and 1 tablespoon of the butter in a roasting pan. Place the fillets in the hot oil and brown evenly on all sides. This should be done very rapidly over high heat, for only 1 or 2 minutes, so that the meat is simply seared. Remove the meat from the pan and set aside while preparing the duxelle. (And don't forget about the pastry and the stock.)

If you're using fresh cèpes, coarsely chop them. (To reconstitute dried cèpes, soak in 2 cups of warm water for about 15 minutes. Then drain thoroughly and squeeze to extract all of the excess water. Coarsely chop the cèpes and the white mushrooms and mix the two together.) Peel and chop the shallot.

Melt 1 tablespoon butter in a medium skillet, add the shallot and cèpes, season with salt and pepper, and sauté over very high heat, stirring with a wooden spoon until all the water from

A golden crust, with its little "chimney," encloses the lamb fillet.

the mushrooms has evaporated. Adjust the seasoning if necessary. Turn the mixture onto a plate and refrigerate.

Cut the crusts from the bread and soak the slices in a small bowl with the milk.

Place the chicken in a food processor and pulse until finely chopped. Gently squeeze out the bread and add to the processor. Season well with salt and

pepper and process briefly. Add half the crème fraîche and process. Add the remaining crème and process briefly. Place half of this mixture in a mixing bowl and combine thoroughly with the sautéed cèpes; chill.

Refrigerate the leftover chicken mixture and save for another use (see Note).

ASSEMBLING

Prepare an egg wash by combining the egg yolks, sugar, and 2 tablespoons of water in a small bowl and beating with a fork.

Divide the puff pastry into 4 equal parts and roll out each part on a lightly floured surface until about ⅛ inch thick and slightly larger than a lamb fillet (see Note).

Spread a layer of the duxelle mixture over 2 of the pastry rectangles and place one of the fillets on top of each. Spread half of the remaining duxelle over the top of each fillet. Position the

remaining pastry rectangles on top of the fillets.

Brush the egg wash along the edges of each piece of pastry and crimp the top and bottom pastry, pressing the edges together firmly.

Make a ½-inch "chimney" on top of the pastry on each fillet and insert a piece of waxed paper rolled into a 2-by-½-inch tube into each hole. This will allow the steam to escape and will prevent the pastry from bursting. Brush a generous layer of the egg wash over the top of each fillet.

**Thirty minutes before sitting down to eat, preheat the oven to 425 degrees F. Brush a second layer of egg wash over the pastry.

Place the saucepan containing the stock in a bain-marie (or in a large baking dish filled with 1 to 2 inches of water and placed over medium heat to warm).

Place the fillets in the preheated oven

and cook for 15 to 20 minutes, until the pastry is golden.

Just before serving, whisk the remaining 4 tablespoons butter into the stock and pour into a sauce boat.

Place the fillets on two small cutting boards placed on a large platter and take triumphantly to the table. Cut into slices at the table.

Note: It is difficult to make the poultry stuffing in less than the quantities indicated. But whatever you do, don't throw away the surplus. You can make

little poultry pies to serve as appetizers or to garnish another dish. Or you can cook mousses in small molds in a bain-marie and refrigerate for several days.

Le Gâteau Nelusko au Chocolat

CHOCOLATE NELUSKO CAKE

Time required: *45 minutes
advance preparation*
Difficulty: *Moderately easy*
Cost: *Moderate*

Ingredients

CAKE
5 eggs, separated and at room temperature

½ cup superfine sugar
1 cup flour
½ cup unsweetened cocoa powder

FILLING AND FROSTING
5 ounces bittersweet or semi-sweet chocolate
6 tablespoons unsalted butter

2 eggs, separated and at room temperature
½ cup superfine sugar

"PUNCHAGE"
½ cup superfine sugar
¾ cup light or dark rum, depend-

ing on your taste
1 ounce bittersweet or semisweet chocolate

Utensils

8-inch round cake pan
2 large mixing bowls
Small mixing bowl
Double boiler or medium saucepan
Long, serrated knife
Sifter
Whisk

Wire rack
Brush
Waxed paper
Rubber spatula
Aluminum foil
Vegetable peeler
Measuring cups and spoons
8-inch round of cardboard

Preparation

***This cake can be prepared very successfully a day in advance or several hours ahead and stored in the refrigerator. It should be removed from the refrigerator when you sit down to eat so that it will not be too cold when served.

To make the cake, preheat the oven to 450 degrees F.

In a large mixing bowl, combine the egg yolks and sugar and beat with a whisk until the mixture thickens and becomes pale yellow.

Sift the flour and cocoa powder onto a sheet of waxed paper. Add the dry ingredients to the egg yolk mixture and blend well.

In a large, very clean bowl (not plastic or aluminum), beat the egg whites until stiff.

Fold one-third of the egg whites into the batter with a rubber spatula. Gently fold the remaining egg whites into the batter, being careful not to deflate

them.

Line the bottom of a generously buttered cake pan with an 8-inch round of buttered aluminum foil. Pour the batter evenly into the pan and bake for 20 minutes, or until a thin crust forms on top of the cake. Remove from the oven and let cool for 30 minutes before turning onto a wire rack to cool for another hour before assembling.

To make the filling, melt the chocolate and butter in the top of a double boiler or in a mixing bowl held over a saucepan of simmering water. Remove from the heat and whisk the egg yolks into the warm chocolate. Add the sugar gradually, whisking constantly.

In a small mixing bowl, beat the remaining 2 egg whites until very stiff. Fold one-third of the egg whites into the melted chocolate until well incorporated. Gently fold in the remaining egg whites. Let cool.

When the cake has cooled completely, place it on an 8-inch round of cardboard so that it can be easily transferred to a serving plate when it has been decorated.

Cut the cake in half horizontally with a long, serrated knife and "punch" it! Be careful: when it comes to baked goods, "to punch" does not mean to hit or beat them; it simply means to infuse with what we call a *punchage*, in this case a mixture of rum and sugar. To prepare this *punchage*, combine the sugar and ⅓ cup water in a small saucepan and bring to a boil. Remove from the heat, let cool, and stir in the rum. Brush the mixture generously over the cut side of each cake layer. Spread the bottom layer of the cake with the filling. Replace the top half of the cake and frost it with the remaining filling.

Draw a vegetable peeler over the top of the chocolate to make chocolate shavings. Scatter them over the top of the cake. (Or you can sprinkle the cake with store-bought chocolate bits, but this is cheating!)

The irresistible finale: Chocolate Nelusko Cake.

Menu for 6 People

Au Coin du Feu

By the Fireside

Difficulty:
Moderately difficult
Cost: *Expensive*

Throughout most of history, fire has been at the center of the home for all civilizations, and its importance is stressed in the word *foyer*, which in French means both "a place where one builds a fire" and "home." Since my father was a blacksmith, I was literally raised by the fireside, and for me life without a fireplace is unthinkable.

What could be more pleasant and beautiful than these flames that are reflected on friends' faces, that create dancing shadows on the walls, that forge a mysterious link among people, that invite one to dream? You'll probably tell me that television also is reflected on people's faces and makes shadows dance upon walls. But I challenge you to serve this dinner "by the television."

Moreover, do you have any idea of how good a soup can be when cooked in the fireplace? The smoke gives the pot a lovely patina and imparts a delicately smoky flavor to the stock. After

Les Huitres aux Agrumes
Oysters with Citrus Fruits

La Poule Faisane Rôtie à la Liqueur des Pères Chartreux
Roast Pheasant with Chartreuse

La Fondue de Chicons à la Bière
Belgian Endives Braised in Beer

Les Meringues Glacées à l'Infusion de Grains de Café avec la Sauce Chocolat à la Cannelle
Coffee Ice Cream and Meringues with Cinnamon-Chocolate Sauce

the soup is finished, there will always be enough embers to grill the meat. If there is plenty of soup, you may want to forget about the grilled meat. All you need to do to complete the meal is to spear a thick slice of peasant bread with your fork and toast it over the fire. Then rub the slice lightly with a clove of garlic and pour plenty of olive oil on it.

If you haven't made your own meringues before, consider buying them.

Doing the Marketing

Order the oysters and pheasants in advance.

What to Drink

For an apéritif, serve Champagne or a cocktail made by mixing one bottle of Champagne with ½ cup fresh orange juice and a jigger of apricot brandy, all

well chilled.

For the wines, you can continue with Champagne cocktails with the oysters or serve a still white wine from the Champagne region. With the pheasant, choose a red wine such as a Volnay, a Mercurey, or a Saint-Emilion.

Table Linens and Decoration

Pick a white damask tablecloth and matching napkins; use large candle holders. If you want to play the autumn décor to the hilt, use dark-colored candles (green or brown) and decorate the table with branches, leaves, and flowers.

Write the menu with brown ink, on parchment paper decorated with small pheasant feathers. And, if you have a fireplace, build a roaring fire.

Tableware

A Champagne cocktail.

6	plates for the oysters
6	dinner plates for the pheasant
6	salad plates for the endives
6	ice cream dishes, 6 doilies, and 6 dessert plates for the meringues glacées
1	large platter for the pheasant
1	sauce boat for the sauce for the pheasant

| 1 | sauce boat for the chocolate sauce |

Silverware

| 6 | oyster or dessert forks and 6 sauce spoons |
| 6 | forks and 6 knives for the pheasant |

| 6 | dessert spoons for the meringues |
| 2 | serving spoons and 2 serving forks |

Glassware

| 6 | Champagne glasses |
| 12 | stemmed glasses for water and |

| | red wine |

Getting Organized

Many things in this menu can be prepared well in advance. They are indicated in each recipe by the symbol ✳✳✳. The symbol ✳✳ indicates those tasks that must be done just before serving.

Prepare the dessert the day before.

Put the white wine in the refrigerator to chill several hours in advance. You can start preparing the pheasants and the fruit for the oysters in advance, too.

An hour before serving dinner, preheat the oven to 500 degrees F. Warm 12 plates, 1 large platter, and a sauce boat on the back of the stove or over a saucepan of hot water.

Finish preparing the pheasants and start the Belgian endive.

overleaf: *Fireside at the home of Denis Mornet, who has sampled many recipes in this book.*

When the oven is hot, put the pheasants in to cook and begin braising the endives.

Thirty minutes before sitting down to eat, remove the pheasants from the oven and keep warm. Prepare the sauce for the pheasant and keep warm in a bain-marie.

Finish preparing the oysters and warm them in the oven just before serving.

Reduce the oven temperature to 400 degrees F and place the endives in the oven to finish cooking while you serve the oysters.

After serving the oysters, cut the pheasant, finish the sauce, and remove the endives from the oven.

To serve the dessert, you'll need only a few minutes for assembly.

Les Huitres aux Agrumes

OYSTERS WITH CITRUS FRUITS

Time required: *10 minutes*
advance preparation
30 minutes preparation
just before serving
Difficulty: *Easy*
Cost: *Moderately expensive*

Ingredients		
3	oranges	
3	lemons	
1	teaspoon coriander seeds	
30	Belon or other small fresh oysters in their shells	
2	handfuls seaweed or 2 bunches parsley	
	Few drops of olive oil	
	Freshly ground pepper	

Utensils

Large bowl
Fine sieve
Paring knife

Oyster knife
Cheesecloth
Rolling pin

Preparation

***Several hours before serving, peel the oranges and lemons, removing the skin and all the white membrane underneath.

Separate the fruit into segments, re-moving the membrane and seeds from each segment.

Tie the coriander seeds in a square of cheesecloth and crush them to a powder under a rolling pin.

**No more than 30 minutes before serving, open the oysters over a large bowl, catching the liquor and discarding the shallower half of each shell.

Arrange the seaweed or parsley on 6 serving plates and place 5 oysters in their shells on each plate.

Twenty minutes before serving, preheat the oven to 500 degrees F.

Place 1 orange and 1 lemon segment on top of each oyster. Strain the oyster liquor through a fine sieve and divide it among the 30 oysters. Top each with a drop of olive oil and a pinch of the crushed coriander seed. Season with a grind of fresh pepper.

Just before serving, place the oysters in the preheated oven to warm for about 2 minutes. Serve immediately.

La Poule Faisane Rôtie à la Liqueur des Pères Chartreux

ROAST PHEASANT WITH CHARTREUSE

Time required: *1½ hours
advance preparation
45 minutes cooking time*
Difficulty: *Moderately difficult*
Cost: *Expensive*

Ingredients

3	young pheasants (about 1½ pounds each)
6	petits suisses, or 2¼ cups plain yogurt, drained (see Note)
¼	cup green Chartreuse liqueur

1½	teaspoons salt
	Freshly ground pepper
4½	tablespoons unsalted butter
¼	cup plus 1 tablespoon port
2	chicken bouillon cubes

Utensils

Large roasting pan
Small saucepan
Fine sieve
Cutting board
Medium knife

Trussing string
Plate
Whisk
Measuring cups and spoons

Preparation

***The pheasants can be prepared for cooking several hours in advance. If using wild pheasants, you'll have to remove the feathers and singe the birds. Thoroughly clean them, removing the feet, necks, and wing ends. Coarsely chop the necks and wing ends and reserve. If you're using a farm-raised pheasant, ask your butcher to prepare it, reserving the neck and wing ends.

In a small bowl, combine the petits suisses, Chartreuse, salt, and a few grinds of pepper, and blend together well. Using a spoon, daub the mixture generously inside the cavity of each pheasant. Truss the birds.

**One hour before serving, preheat the oven to 500 degrees F. Place the necks and wing ends in a large roasting pan. Season the outside of the pheasants with salt and rub each with 1½ teaspoons butter. Place the pheasants in the roasting pan.

After 15 minutes, place the birds in the oven and bake for 35 minutes, turning 2 or 3 times during the cooking and basting with their juices.

Remove the pheasants from the oven, baste generously with the port, and return to the oven for 7 minutes longer.

Remove the roasting pan from the oven and transfer the pheasants to a platter. Place the roasting pan over high heat and add the bouillon cubes and ½ cup water. Bring to a boil and cook over high heat for 5 minutes.

Meanwhile, carve the pheasants, removing the legs and breasts, and arranging them on a platter. Place in the warm unlighted oven to keep warm while finishing the sauce.

Strain the liquid from the roasting pan through a fine sieve into a small saucepan. Scoop out the cheese-Chartreuse mixture remaining in the cavities of the pheasant carcasses and add to the juices in the saucepan. Bring the sauce to a boil.

Cut the remaining 3 tablespoons butter into small pieces and add to the sauce little by little, whisking constantly, until the butter is thoroughly incorporated. Adjust the seasonings, if necessary. Strain the sauce through a sieve into a sauce boat.

Grind a little fresh pepper over the pheasant pieces and serve. Pass the sauce in the sauce boat. Serve the braised endive at the same time on separate salad plates.

Note: Petit suisse is a fresh unsalted cheese, packaged in small cylinders. Yogurt can be substituted, but must be drained first. To do so, line a fine sieve with cheesecloth, add the yogurt, and let drain over a bowl for 2 hours.

La Fondue de Chicons à la Bière

BELGIAN ENDIVE BRAISED IN BEER

Time required: *45 minutes*
preparation and cooking
just before serving
Difficulty: *Easy*
Cost: *Moderate*

Ingredients

12	medium Belgian endives
½	cup plus 1 tablespoon unsalted butter
1	cup beer
1	tablespoon sugar

2	chicken bouillon cubes
	Salt
	Freshly ground pepper
¼	cup fine dry bread crumbs
¼	cup shredded Gruyère cheese

Utensils Large, heavy skillet with cover Large gratin dish

Preparation **Begin preparing this dish about 45 minutes before serving. Remove any bruised outer leaves from the endives, leaving the heads intact. Trim the bases and tips and wipe with a damp cloth.

Melt 7 tablespoons of the butter in a large, heavy skillet. Arrange the endives in the skillet in a single layer, cover, and simmer over medium heat until the butter begins to sizzle and the endives start to brown. Turn the endives to brown on all sides.

Add the beer, sugar, and bouillon cubes and season with salt. Cover and simmer for 20 minutes over medium-low heat.

Preheat the oven to 400 degrees F.

When the endives have simmered for 20 minutes, remove the cover and reduce the liquid over medium heat until only 1 or 2 tablespoons of syrupy liquid remain in the bottom of the skillet.

Arrange the endives in a single layer in a large gratin dish. Sprinkle with the bread crumbs and the shredded cheese. Pour any liquid remaining in the skillet over the endives. Cut the remaining 2 tablespoons butter into small pieces and sprinkle over the top of the endives. Ten minutes before serving, place the endives in the preheated oven to bake until a light golden crust forms. Serve immediately, in the gratin dish.

The Belgian endives are braised in beer rather than in wine.

Les Meringues Glacées à l'Infusion de Grains de Café avec la Sauce Chocolat à la Cannelle

COFFEE ICE CREAM AND MERINGUES WITH
CINNAMON-CHOCOLATE SAUCE

Time required: *Meringues—15 minutes*
advance preparation
2½ hours baking
Crème Glacée—1 hour
advance preparation
Difficulty: *Moderately difficult*
Cost: *Moderate*

Ingredients

MERINGUES
4 egg whites, at room
temperature
Pinch of salt

½ cup plus 2 tablespoons granulated sugar
¾ cup powdered sugar
All-purpose flour

CREME GLACEE
3 cups milk
1 cup coarsely ground coffee
beans

6 egg yolks, at room temperature
1 cup superfine sugar
2 cups crème fraîche (see Appendix), or heavy cream

CHOCOLATE SAUCE
4½ ounces semisweet chocolate
½ cup milk

½ cup crème fraîche, or heavy
cream
Pinch of ground cinnamon

WHIPPED CREAM
1 cup crème fraîche, or heavy

cream
⅓ cup superfine sugar

Utensils

Ice cream or sorbet machine
3 large mixing bowls
Medium mixing bowl
2 baking sheets
Large saucepan with cover
Medium saucepan
Fine sieve

Electric mixer
Pastry bag
Spatula
Whisk
Wooden spoon
Ice cream scoop

Preparation

***This dessert can be prepared well in advance. Make the meringues several days in advance and the crème glacée and chocolate sauce a day ahead or the morning of serving.

MERINGUES

Begin with the meringues. There are two alternatives here. The easiest approach is to buy six meringues at your local pastry shop.

Or, take things in hand and make your own. The preparation of meringues, in fact, is extremely simple. Baking them, on the other hand, is tricky. If the oven is too hot, the meringues will brown and a sticky mass will form in the center. If the oven isn't hot enough, they will take on the marvelous texture of chewing gum, a delicacy that requires chewing and rechewing to appreciate its flavor fully. But enough of apprehension. Let's roll up our sleeves and attack these meringues. If you spoil them, the pastry shop isn't far away.

First, some general advice about beating egg whites to their maximum volume. To begin with, the egg whites should not be cold. Next, there should be no traces of yolk in the whites. Finally, all the utensils used must be completely clean, without any traces of grease. To make sure there is no residual grease, rub the utensils with half a lemon or with vinegar, rinse in water, and dry with a clean towel. You can also add a pinch of salt to the egg whites before beating to aid the stiffening. If the whites become grainy, discard them and begin again.

Now, you're ready to begin.

Preheat the oven to the lowest setting (around 150 degrees F).

Place the egg whites in a large mixing bowl with a pinch of salt and 1 tablespoon granulated sugar. If you're using an electric mixer, start at medium speed and beat for 3 minutes, then increase the speed to high and add 1 tablespoon more sugar. If beating the eggs by hand, whip with a vertical circular motion.

When the egg whites are very stiff, add the remaining ½ cup granulated sugar and beat for 30 seconds longer.

Gently fold the powdered sugar into the egg whites, using a spatula and stirring in a slow, regular movement to avoid deflating the egg whites.

Sprinkle 2 generously buttered baking sheets with flour until they are completely white. Invert each sheet over the sink, and tap firmly to remove excess flour.

Using a pastry bag fitted with a plain tip, pipe the meringue onto the baking sheets in balls about the size of large walnuts. If you like, outline the size in the flour on the baking sheets with the rim of a liqueur glass.

Place the meringues in the preheated oven and bake for 2 to 2½ hours, being careful not to let them brown.

Remove the meringues from the oven and let cool. Place in a clean, airtight tin with a tight-fitting lid. They will keep well like this for several weeks.

While you're at it, you may want to make a larger quantity of meringues. It's always good to have them on hand.

CREME GLACEE (ICE CREAM) AND CHOCOLATE SAUCE

***To make the crème glacée, place the milk in a large saucepan and bring to a boil. Stir in the coffee and let the milk return to a boil. Remove from the heat, cover, and let stand for 45 minutes.

Meanwhile, prepare the chocolate sauce. Break or chop the chocolate into small pieces. In a medium saucepan, combine the milk, crème fraîche, and cinnamon and bring to a boil. Remove from the heat and add the chocolate, whisking until completely melted.

Pour the mixture into a large mixing bowl and chill for at least 2 hours. When well chilled, whisk for 2 to 3 minutes to achieve a light, creamy texture.

To finish the crème glacée, combine the egg yolks and superfine sugar in a large mixing bowl and blend well. Strain the milk and coffee mixture through a sieve into the mixing bowl and stir in the 2 cups crème fraîche. Pour the mixture into an ice cream machine and freeze according to the manufacturer's directions. The ice cream will keep in the freezer for several hours. But keep in mind that the longer it is frozen, the heavier it will become.

Finally, make the whipped cream. Place the crème fraîche in a medium mixing bowl and beat with a whisk, slowly incorporating the superfine sugar, until thick; do not overwhip. Chill until serving time.

❧

**Just before serving, arrange 2 scoops of ice cream between 2 small meringues on each dessert plate. Decorate each serving with a wreath of whipped cream piped through a pastry bag.

Serve at once and pass the chocolate sauce on the side.

There are many ways to present this dessert; the sauces can be varied any way you like.

Menu for 6 People

Les Petits Plats dans les Grands

A Grand Occasion

Difficulty: *Difficult*
Cost: *Expensive*

Certain menus, this one in particular, will appear too copious to some people. But I believe that the best parties need a degree of abundance and opulence.

Let's take one of my Aunt Celestine's ordinary Sunday meals as an example.

It was the time just before World War II. My aunt and uncle used to get up around 5 in the morning to begin preparing for friends who would arrive that morning. They would have a snack around 7 o'clock: a small, grain-fed chicken for each of them, some cheese, and plenty of white wine.

Around 9 o'clock our friends would arrive, famished by a long walk. We would immediately be seated at a well-appointed table for a welcome snack of sausages and ham, accompanied by a crock of pickled onions and gherkins. Then came shell steaks or huge slabs of rump steak (weighing nearly a pound each), followed by a little cheese. All of this was generously washed down with white and red wines straight from the casks.

Around 10:30 we rose from the table. The men would walk to the village café where they met their friends every Sunday. There they would remake the world around a few glasses of Picon, Suze, or Gudron—their apéritifs being

Les Petites Pommes au Caviar Pressé
New Potatoes with Caviar

Le Gratin d'Homard aux Macaroni, Selon Mon Ami Jacques
Jacques' Lobster and Macaroni Gratin

Le Sirop de Tomate aux Citrons Verts
Tomato and Lime Soup

Le Pâté Chaud de Cailles aux Truffes, Sauce Foie Gras
Heart-Shaped Hot Quail Pies with Truffles and Foie Gras Sauce

Le Soufflé Vanillé en Confiture de Fruits Frais à l'Armagnac
Individual Vanilla Soufflés with Fresh Fruit and Armagnac Sauce

the only bitter part of their lives.

Twelve-thirty was the time for the real meal. We started with an enormous platter of cold cuts. There were at least ten or twelve varieties of pâtés, sausages, and sundry meats. After that came a cold salmon with mayonnaise; then chicken vol-au-vents; then young guinea fowl, pigeons, partridges, or other fowl with gravy. Then we had a roast with a variety of vegetables and salads, followed by different cheeses; and dessert, including the traditional floating island, chocolate mousse, fruit tarts (at least three or four varieties), fruit in syrup, brioche mousseline, and crisp noisette biscuits. All of this was washed down with simple wines, ending with a splash of the local brandy in our coffee cups.

Well, after that, everyone was ready for a long siesta. One knew how to live a long and happy life in those days. My uncle lived heartily and well until his eighty-seventh year.

Doing the Marketing

Order the quail and lobsters in advance, but be sure that the lobsters are alive and kicking just before they are cooked.

The remaining ingredients can be purchased the day before or the same day. Choose unbruised, uniformly round little new potatoes about the size of small eggs.

What to Drink

For an apéritif, Champagne is a must.

For the wines, Champagne is most fitting with the new potatoes and caviar. For the lobsters, choose a great white Burgundy such as a Corton-Charlemagne or a Chassagne-Montra-

above: *Great wines like these should be treated with respect and moved with care.*

overleaf: *An occasion to bring out the family heirlooms.*

chet. With the quails, serve a Margaux or a Châteauneuf-du-Pape from a good year. And, if it's a special party, put a Sauternes in to chill for dessert.

❧

Table Linens and Decoration

Choose a tablecloth and napkins of cotton net or organdy, decorated with flower motifs. Use silver candlesticks, and at the base of the candles you can tie little velvet ribbons of the same color as the patterning of the plates.

❧

Tableware

Choose fine porcelain plates with gold rims or discreet designs:

- 6 dessert plates for the potatoes and caviar
- 6 finger bowls
- 6 individual gratin dishes for the lobster
- 6 large plates for under the lobster gratins

- 6 coffee cups for the tomato soup
- 6 saucers for under the cups
- 6 large plates for the quail
- 6 small plates for the soufflés
- 1 silver platter with a linen napkin for the potatoes and caviar
- 1 large silver platter for the quail

❧

Silverware

The fingers of your guests for the new potatoes and caviar

- 6 fish forks and 6 dessert spoons for the lobster
- 6 soup spoons for the tomato

soup
- 6 knives and 6 forks for the quail
- 6 dessert spoons for the soufflés
- 1 pie server for the quail
- 1 sauce boat for the quail sauce

❧

Glassware

- 30 goblets (tulip-shaped for the Champagne, balloons for the white Burgundy, tulips or bal- loons for the Margaux, and chilled tulips for the Sauternes)

❧

Getting Organized

Many things in this menu can be prepared well in advance. They are indicated in each recipe by the symbol ✳✳✳. The symbol ✳✳ indicates those tasks that must be done just before serving.

The tomato soup, the fruit sauce for the soufflés, and most of the quail dish can be made the day before, or several hours in advance. (Remember to marinate the chicken and bacon for at least 10 hours before assembling the quail dish.)

Put the Champagne and white wines in the refrigerator to chill several hours in advance.

Start preparing the lobster about 1½ hours before serving. About an hour before sitting down to eat, warm 12 large plates on the back of the stove or over a large saucepan of hot water.

Preheat the oven to 500 degrees F.

Place the potatoes in the oven to bake for 20 to 30 minutes.

Just before serving the potatoes, turn on the broiler.

Five minutes before serving the lobster, place it under the hot broiler.

After removing the lobster from the broiler, reduce the oven temperature to 425 degrees and place the quail in the oven.

Just before serving the quail, reduce the oven temperature to 300 degrees.

Beat the egg whites for the soufflé, fold into the yolk mixture, and pour into the soufflé molds. Place in the oven 20 minutes before serving.

Les Petites Pommes au Caviar Pressé

NEW POTATOES WITH CAVIAR

Time required: *1 hour and*
10 minutes just before serving
Difficulty: *Easy*
Cost: *Expensive*

Ingredients

40 small new potatoes, about the size of small eggs (see Note)
1½ cups coarse salt

5 ounces fresh Sevruga caviar, or pressed caviar
1 small bunch fresh chives

Utensils

Large rimmed baking sheet
Small saucepan
Small serrated knife
2 demitasse spoons

Plate
40 small pleated paper liners for petits fours

Preparation

** This recipe should not be prepared in advance. Start making it about 1½ hours before serving.

Preheat the oven to 475 degrees F and place a plate in the refrigerator to chill.

Wash and scrub the potatoes; drain thoroughly.

Spread the salt over a large rimmed baking sheet and place the potatoes on top. Place in the hot oven and bake for 20 to 30 minutes, until the potatoes are tender.

Meanwhile, half-fill a small saucepan with water and bring to a boil. Dip one of the demitasse spoons into the boiling water, and use the hot spoon to scoop out a spoonful of caviar. Dip the second spoon into the boiling water and place on top of the caviar, using the two spoons to turn the caviar over and over to form a neat, small oval "egg" of caviar. Place the caviar on a chilled plate. Continue to scoop out the caviar with the hot spoons until

The humble potato is ennobled in this preparation.

you have formed 40 "eggs." Be sure that the water continues to boil while you work so that the heat evaporates excess moisture instantly when the spoons are removed from the water. If the spoons are wet when they touch the caviar, the caviar will turn white. Place the caviar eggs on the chilled plate, cover with plastic wrap, and chill.

Remove the potatoes from the oven and reduce the oven temperature to 200 degrees F.

Wipe off any salt that clings to the potatoes. Using a serrated knife, slice off the top quarter of each potato and reserve. Scoop out a cavity large enough to hold a caviar egg in the top of each potato with a demitasse spoon. Place the potatoes in the small pleated paper liners.

Return the potatoes to the oven to warm for 10 minutes more.

Meanwhile, cut the chives into 2-inch lengths.

At serving time, remove the potatoes from the oven, place a chilled caviar egg in the cavity of each, and stick 2 or 3 chive blades in each. Replace the tops of the potatoes and arrange on a serving platter with a small bouquet of flowers in the center.

It is essential that these potatoes be served hot, particularly if you're using pressed rather than fresh Sevruga caviar. And though I know iced vodka is the traditional beverage with caviar, I personally prefer a good brut Champagne.

Note: Choose potatoes that are as small and uniformly round as possible, without bruises or spots.

Le Gratin d'Homard aux Macaroni, Selon Mon Ami Jacques

JACQUES' LOBSTER AND MACARONI GRATIN

Time required: *50 minutes
advance preparation
10 minutes just before serving*
Difficulty: *Moderately easy*
Cost: *Expensive*

One knows a cook by his sauces.

In this recipe my friend Jacques combined subtle flavors the way a painter combines colors on his palette. Good cooking is as noble an art as painting or music. Why should one think that the tongue is less worthy than the eye or the ear? The fine nuances of a sauce can be as marvelous as a symphony or a painting.

As a token of my friendship with Jacques Maximin, chef at Chantecler in Nice, I have included his recipe for Lobster and Macaroni Gratin.

Ingredients

1	medium carrot
1	celery rib
4½	pounds live lobster (preferably three 1¼- to 1½-pound lobsters)
2	tablespoons unsalted butter
¼	cup plus 1 tablespoon Cognac
3	tablespoons chopped shallots
½	cup port wine
1	bouquet garni composed of several sprigs parsley, several sprigs thyme, and a bay leaf,

all tied together with string
3 cups plus 2 tablespoons crème fraîche (see Appendix), or heavy cream
Salt
7 ounces elbow macaroni or small shell pasta
Freshly ground pepper
1 egg yolk
3 tablespoons shredded Gruyère cheese

Utensils

Large skillet with cover
Large saucepan
2 small mixing bowls
Fine sieve
Chef's knife
Paring knife
Cutting board

Whisk
Slotted spoon
Wooden spoon
Colander
6 individual heatproof gratin dishes
Measuring cups and spoons

Preparation

✳✳✳Prepare this recipe about 1½ hours before serving dinner.

Scrape the carrot and trim the celery. Cut both into ¼-inch dice. (You should have about ¼ cup diced carrot and 2 tablespoons diced celery.)

You can deal with the lobsters in two ways: Either plunge the live lobsters into a large pot of boiling water and cook for 2 minutes, or cut them live, as we sadistic chefs do. If you do the latter, do not cut them until just before cooking and assembling the dish.

In either case, cut each lobster tail cleanly into 1½-inch sections. Remove the legs and claws. Cut the bodies in half lengthwise. Remove and discard the sand sacks in the heads. Remove the coral and tomalley and set aside in a small bowl.

Melt the butter in a large skillet over very high heat. When it starts to foam, add the piece of lobster tail, the bodies, legs, and claws, and sauté, stirring with a wooden spoon, until all sides of the lobster pieces have turned red. Add the Cognac and ignite, making sure that all of the lobster pieces are engulfed in the flames.

Stir in the carrot, celery, and shallots. Add the port, bouquet garni, and 2¾ cups of the crème fraîche. Cover the skillet, reduce the heat to very low, and simmer slowly for 15 minutes.

Place the remaining ¼ cup plus 2 tablespoons crème fraîche in a small mixing bowl and chill in the refrigerator.

Fill a large saucepan with 2 quarts of salted water and bring to a boil. Add the macaroni and boil until tender but still slightly resistant to the bite, or *al dente*. Turn the macaroni into a colander and drain.

Remove the skillet from the heat and remove the lobster with a slotted spoon. Set the bodies and legs aside for decorating the plates. Remove the meat from the claws and tail pieces and cut into ¼-inch-thick slices. Set aside.

Return the skillet to the heat and gently warm the cream and vegetables. Whisk in the reserved coral and tomalley. Add the lobster meat and macaroni. Bring to a boil and season with salt and pepper.

If not serving immediately, cover the skillet and place in a warm place on the stove.

**Ten minutes before serving, preheat the broiler. Divide the lobster, macaroni, and sauce among 6 individual gratin dishes.

Whisk the remaining chilled crème fraîche until thick. Fold in the egg yolk and Gruyère. Divide the mixture among the 6 portions. Place under the broiler and cook until lightly browned, 2 to 3 minutes.

Decorate each gratin dish with half a lobster body and several legs. Place each dish on a plate covered with a paper doily or a folded napkin and serve.

Le Sirop de Tomate au Citron Vert

TOMATO AND LIME SOUP

Time required: *20 minutes*
advance preparation
5 minutes just before serving
Difficulty: *Easy*
Cost: *Inexpensive*

This very simple dish serves as a palate freshener and an agreeable pause between two courses.

Ingredients

1⅓   pounds tomatoes
1½   teaspoons Worcestershire sauce
     Salt
 1   tablespoon virgin olive oil
     Juice of 2 limes
     Dash of Tabasco sauce
 1   tablespoon ketchup
 1   to 2 tablespoons vodka (optional)
     Fresh mint leaves or small fresh flowers

Utensils

     Food processor or food mill with fine disc
     Fine sieve

Preparation

Mixing bowl
6   coffee cups

6   saucers

***Prepare this recipe several hours in advance if you like.

Place 6 coffee cups in the freezer to chill.

Wash the tomatoes and remove the stems. Cut in half and squeeze out the juice and seeds; discard. Place the remainder in a food processor or food mill and process to a purée. Add the Worcestershire, season with salt, and

blend well. Add the oil, the juice of 1 lime, the Tabasco, ketchup, and vodka, if using, and blend well. Taste and adjust the seasonings, adding the juice of another lime if needed.

Strain the mixture through a fine sieve into a mixing bowl and chill until serving time. The dish should be served very cold.

**Just before serving, pour the mixture into the 6 chilled cups, place on

6 saucers, and decorate each saucer with mint leaves or a small flower.

Farm-bred quail are available year-round and can be served when wild ones cannot be obtained.

Le Pâté Chaud de Cailles aux Truffes, Sauce Foie Gras

HEART-SHAPED HOT QUAIL PIES WITH
TRUFFLES AND FOIE GRAS SAUCE

Time required: *10 minutes preparation*
(10 hours in advance)
2 hours advance preparation
30 minutes cooking just before serving
Difficulty: *Difficult*
Cost: *Expensive*

Ingredients

MARINADE

1	small boneless chicken breast (about 5 ounces)
¼	pound bacon
1½	teaspoons salt
⅓	cup Cognac
	Pinch of fresh thyme flowers

or fresh thyme
Pinch of sugar

1½	teaspoons chopped shallots
3½	ounces truffles (with juice, if canned)
	Freshly ground pepper

DOUGH

5	cups flour
10	tablespoons unsalted butter

1	tablespoon salt
⅔	cup water

STUFFING AND QUAIL

½	pound fresh mushrooms
4	tablespoons unsalted butter

3	large fresh quails
2	eggs

SAUCE

2	large shallots
½	cup red wine
⅓	cup port
1	sprig fresh thyme

1	bay leaf
2	juniper berries
1½	teaspoons cracked peppercorns
3	ounces foie gras, or 6 tablespoons unsalted butter

Utensils

2	medium skillets with covers
	Medium saucepan
3	large mixing bowls
	Food processor or meat grinder
2	large baking sheets
	Cutting board
	Paring knife
	Chef's knife

Fine sieve
Colander
Rolling pin
Wooden spoon
Fluted round pastry cutter, 2 inches in diameter (or a coffee cup)
Brush

Small bowl
Plate
Plastic wrap

2 tablespoons
Measuring cups and spoons

Preparation

✳✳✳Marinate the chicken for the filling at least 10 hours before assembling the dish. The pastry dough can also be made in advance, and the rest of the dish can be assembled several hours before cooking and serving.

Begin by placing the chicken and bacon in a mixing bowl along with the salt, Cognac, thyme flowers, sugar, shallots, and the juice from the truffles. (Reserve the truffles for later use.) Season with pepper. Cover and set aside in a cool place (but do not refrigerate) to marinate for 10 hours.

To prepare the pastry dough, place the flour in a large bowl or in the bowl of an electric mixer or food processor. In a small saucepan, combine the butter, salt, and water and bring to a boil. Pour the boiling mixture into the flour and mix or process until the dough is well blended and forms a ball. Wrap in a damp cloth and chill for at least 1 hour.

Meanwhile, prepare the stuffing. Rinse the mushrooms quickly in water, but do not let them soak. Drain and thinly slice. Thinly slice the truffles.

Melt 2 tablespoons butter in a medium skillet over high heat until it turns nut brown. Add the mushrooms, season with salt, and sauté until the mushroom liquid evaporates. Add the truffles and blend into the mushrooms. Place the mushroom mixture on a plate and let cool slightly. Cover and refrigerate until needed.

To prepare the quails for cooking, cut off and discard the feet. Cut off the wing ends and reserve them. Cut off the head and neck even with the body.

Remove the entrails, if this has not already been done. Using the tip of a small knife, remove the eyes and take off the lower beak, pulling close to the base, to remove the esophagus. Remove the skin from the neck and head. Cut the neck from the head. Cut the neck into 1-inch pieces.

Melt the remaining 2 tablespoons butter in a medium skillet over high heat. Add the 3 quails and their heads (reserving the other pieces for the sauce) and sauté quickly over high heat to sear the birds and heads on all sides. Reduce the heat to low, cover the skillet, and cook for 5 minutes.

Remove the skillet from the heat and let the quails cool slightly. Place the quails and heads on a plate and set aside in a cool place. Set the skillet and its cooking butter aside; you'll use it again to make the sauce.

After 10 hours of marinating, remove the chicken and bacon from the marinade and drain, reserving the marinade. Place the chicken and bacon in a meat grinder or a food processor and grind or process until fine. If using a grinder, pass the meat through it a second time.

Add the chopped meat to the mixing bowl with the marinade and blend together well. Chill.

Meanwhile, roll out the dough about ⅛ inch thick.

Using an inverted dessert plate or other 6-inch round as a guide, cut out six 6-inch rounds of dough. Place the rounds on 2 baking sheets.

Roll out the dough trimmings ⅟₁₆ inch thick and cut into six 2-inch rounds, using a fluted round pastry cutter or by cutting with the rim of an inverted coffee cup. Make a ¾-inch-round hole in the center of each small round, place them on the baking sheets, and chill.

While they chill, prepare the filling and the quails. With the aid of 2 table-spoons, form "quenelles," or small ovals about the size of eggs, with the chicken mixture. To do this, scoop a ball of the mixture out with one spoon. Place the other spoon on top and turn the mixture over and over between the spoons. Form 6 quenelles and set aside.

Remove the legs and thighs from the quails. Lift off the fillets, following the breastbone, and remove the skin. Reserve the carcasses for making the sauce.

Remove the dough rounds from the refrigerator. Spread ⅓ cup of the truffle/mushroom mixture over 3 of the large rounds, forming it into the shape of a heart and leaving a ¾-inch border of dough all around the edge.

Place 2 quenelles side by side on the mushroom beds. Place a quail breast half and a thigh on each quenelle.

Place the eggs in a small bowl with 1 tablespoon water and beat to make an egg wash. Brush the edges of each dough heart with the egg wash and cover with one of the remaining large rounds of dough. Gently press down the edges, flattening the dough out into the shape of a heart. Trim off any excess dough. Press down lightly on the top of each quail with the flat side of a knife and mark a separation between the two halves of the heart. With the tip of a knife, make a herringbone pattern on the hearts. Cut several small steam vents in the dough to prevent it from bursting during the baking.

Brush the small dough rounds with the egg wash and stack them together in pairs. Refrigerate the hearts and the small rounds until baking time.

To make the sauce, peel and chop the shallots and place them in the skillet in which the quails cooked. Break up the quail carcasses and add them to the skillet along with the wing ends, necks, and heads. Brown the bones and shallots over medium heat. Add the red wine, Port, thyme, bay leaf, juniper berries, pepper, and a pinch of salt. Simmer until the liquid is reduced to about ⅔ cup. Strain through a fine sieve, reserving the heads for decoration and discarding the remaining bones.

❧

**About 45 minutes before serving, preheat the oven to 425 degrees F.

Brush the remaining egg wash over the hearts and top each with one of the small pastry rounds. Place in the hot oven and bake for 30 minutes.

Five minutes before serving, place the sauce in a small saucepan and bring to a boil. Pour into a mixing bowl or the container of a food processor. Cut the foie gras or butter into small pieces, and add to the sauce. Mix or process until blended. Season with salt and pepper and pour into a warmed sauce boat.

Tuck a quail's head in the cutout circle of each pie and place the heart pies on a large platter decorated with leaves. To serve, cut each heart in half along the center line and serve half a heart to each guest. Pass the sauce separately.

You can accompany this dish with a simple salad of field or red leaf lettuce, drizzled with virgin olive oil and sprinkled with salt.

Le Soufflé Vanillé en Confiture de Fruits Frais à l'Armagnac

INDIVIDUAL VANILLA SOUFFLES WITH FRESH
FRUIT AND ARMAGNAC SAUCE

Time required: *40 minutes
advance preparation
35 minutes just before serving*
Difficulty: *Moderately difficult*
Cost: *Moderate*

When I was a child, I discovered that by sucking diligently on a stick of vanilla and then plunging it, wet with saliva, into some powdered sugar and leaving it to dry, I obtained an absolutely delicious candy. This is not, of course, something that should be told to children. But, just between ourselves, try my little recipe the next time you find yourself alone in your kitchen.

Ingredients

FRUIT SAUCE
¼ pound fresh strawberries (about 1 cup)
¼ pound fresh raspberries (about 1 cup)
3 fresh apricots

1 large fresh peach
½ cup superfine sugar
Juice of 1 lemon
3 tablespoons Armagnac or Cognac

SOUFFLES
6 tablespoons butter, softened
1 cup superfine sugar
10 egg yolks, at room temperature
2 tablespoons vanilla sugar (see

Appendix)
8 egg whites, at room temperature
¼ cup flour
¾ cup cold milk

Utensils

Large skillet
Small saucepan
2 large mixing bowls
Shallow baking dish large enough to hold 6 small ramekins
6 individual soufflé molds or ramekins, 2½ or 3 inches in

diameter
Colander
Paring knife
Wooden spoon
Whisk
Rubber spatula
Brush
Sugar sifter

Preparation

❊❊❊Prepare the fruit sauce several hours ahead.

Wash the strawberries and remove the stems. (Always wash strawberries before removing the stems so that sand does not wash into the cavities left by the stems. Never wash raspberries or wild strawberries; they will become soggy.) Sort through the raspberries. Wipe the apricots, remove the pits, and cut into 1-inch cubes. To peel the peach, plunge into boiling water for a few seconds, remove, and drain. The skin will peel off easily. Cut into 1-inch cubes.

In a large skillet, combine the strawberries and raspberries with the sugar and lemon juice and cook briefly over high heat. The berries will render

**Forty minutes before serving, preheat the oven to 300 degrees F.

In a non-aluminum saucepan, melt 4 tablespoons of the butter. Whisk in the flour and cook over low heat for about 1 minute. Remove from heat and add cold milk. Return to heat and bring to boil for 2 or 3 minutes, whisking constantly. Then turn into a large bowl and mix in the superfine and vanilla sugars.

In a separate bowl, whisk the egg yolks until well mixed. Add several tablespoons of the sweetened cream sauce to warm the yolks, then add yolks to the sauce, whisking well.

In a third bowl, beat the egg whites until stiff peaks form. Stir about one-third of the beaten whites into the yolk-cream mixture with a whisk.

Note: Replace or vary the fruits according to the season, but be sure to

enough juice to dilute the sugar to a thin syrup. Add the apricots and peaches and cook, stirring occasionally with a wooden spoon, for about 10 minutes. Remove from the heat and set aside. When cooled, stir in the Cognac.

Using 2 tablespoons of the softened butter, brush the inside of each soufflé mold. Pour ½ cup of the sugar into the first buttered mold, turning it to coat the bottom and sides entirely with sugar. Turn the excess sugar out into the next soufflé dish and turn to coat, continuing in this manner until all 6 molds are coated with sugar. Chill.

Then gently fold in the remaining whites, being careful not to deflate them.

Fill each of the chilled soufflé molds with the mixture and place them in a large baking dish filled with enough cold water to reach halfway up the sides of the molds. Place over medium-high heat until the water begins to boil. Then place in the hot oven and bake for 20 minutes.

About 5 minutes before serving, warm the fruit sauce over medium heat. Divide the sauce among 6 plates.

Remove the soufflés from the oven, unmold one onto each pool of the fruit sauce; or place on the plates in the soufflé molds, make an indentation in the top of each soufflé, and spoon the fruit sauce on top. Serve immediately.

maintain the ratio of about 14 ounces of fruit to ½ cup of sugar.

Menu for 6 People

Un Dîner en Famille

A Family Dinner

Difficulty:
Moderately difficult
Cost: *Expensive*

This menu originates largely in Lyons, since I owe the idea for the macaroni gratin to Lea (a famous Cordon-Bleu from Lyons), and the inspiration for the poultry recipe to Jean Vignard. This great chef from Lyons, whom few of us knew, understood how to elevate simplicity to the level of an art. And, in cooking, nothing is more difficult than to keep things simple. The whole secret of his sublime dishes rested on one unshakable principle: to cook well one needs to take one's time. For him, "real" cooking could only happen in earthenware pots seasoned with garlic, in which simmering could go on for hours.

But, who among us—with a few rare exceptions—could expect his customers to have enough patience to wait that long for their order? Happily, at home one is able to take the time to let a dish simmer as long as one desires.

Les Petits Flans d'Asperges, Sauce Crème aux Petits Pois
Asparagus Flans with Cream of Baby Pea Sauce

L'Escalope de Saumon en Brouillade de Ciboulette
Escalopes of Salmon with Scrambled Eggs and Chives

L'Étuvée de Volaille Mijotée à la Façon de Jean Vignard
Braised Chicken and Puréed Vegetables à la Jean Vignard

Le Gratin de Macaronis Compotés au Lait
Gratin of Creamy Macaroni

Le Soufflé Glacé aux Fraises
Frozen Individual Strawberry Soufflés

Doing the Marketing

Order the fresh salmon in advance. Ask for a piece cut from the tail: It will be easier to cut into very thin slices. (Avoid using frozen salmon; it's not as good and would be very difficult to cut into thin escalopes.) If necessary, order the chickens in advance to make sure that you will have the freshest birds of the best quality. I prefer the chickens of Allier near the Bresse region, which produces the most famous poultry in France. If these are not available, I suggest using free-range chickens.

This raw salmon is sliced as for smoked salmon.

What to Drink

For an apéritif, this family dinner calls for a fine sherry or a sweet apéritif wine such as Banyuls. Note that sherry is never served cold—nor is a Banyuls, for that matter.

For the wines, I would choose a white wine from the Loire or from the Côtes-du-Rhône. With the chicken serve a good Burgundy such as a Mercurey or, perhaps, a Volnay, lightly chilled (50 to 55 degrees F).

Table Linens and Decoration

If you're ever going to do it, this dinner is the occasion to get out grandmother's white lacework or embroidered tablecloths, the family silver, the silver candlesticks, and the ceramic or brass flowerpot holders for the bouquets of cyclamens.

For the menu, set a stylish tone with large, simple, white placecards on which you write (with elaborate penmanship) the name of the guest and a list of the courses and wines.

Tableware

To play on the family dinner theme, use white china plates with silver or gold rims:

- 12 dessert plates for the flan and the macaroni
- 12 dinner plates for the salmon and the chicken
- 6 dessert plates for the soufflés
- 1 deep serving platter for the chicken

Silverware

- 12 dessert spoons or sauce spoons for the flans and for tasting the sauce of the chicken
- 6 fish knives and forks
- 6 dinner knives and forks
- 6 dessert spoons for the soufflés
- 2 serving spoons
- 2 serving forks

Glassware

- 18 goblets for water, white wine, and red wine

Getting Organized

Many things in this menu can be prepared in advance. They are indicated in each recipe with the symbol ✽✽✽. The symbol ✽✽ indicates those tasks that must be done just before serving.

The strawberry soufflés can be made the day before your dinner, or as much as 2 or 3 days in advance, if you choose. Start preparing the other dishes several hours in advance. Put the white wine in the refrigerator to chill several hours in advance.

Thirty minutes before serving, preheat the oven to 450 degrees F. Place 12 large dinner plates and 12 medium plates on the back of the stove or over a large pan of hot water.

Twenty minutes before serving, remove the soufflés from the freezer and place in the refrigerator to soften slightly.

Reheat the asparagus flans in a bain-marie and prepare the sauce.

Before serving the flans, beat the

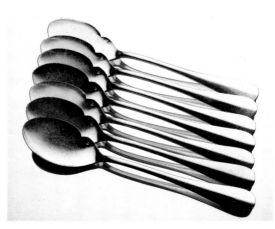

Sauce spoons.

eggs and chop the chives for the scrambled eggs. Place the macaroni in the preheated oven to cook.

After serving the flans, return to the kitchen for 15 minutes. Cover the macaroni with aluminum foil and reset the oven to "broil." Prepare the scrambled eggs and place the salmon under the broiler. Remove the salmon, reset the oven temperature to 450 degrees F and remove the aluminum foil from the macaroni.

Serve the salmon and scrambled eggs. Meanwhile, reheat the chicken over low heat. Remove the macaroni from the oven, finish the chicken, and serve.

To serve the dessert, just sprinkle the soufflés with cocoa powder and garnish with the whole berries.

Les Petits Flans d'Asperges, Sauce Crème aux Petits Pois

ASPARAGUS FLANS WITH CREAM OF BABY
PEA SAUCE

Time required: *1 hour
advance preparation
20 minutes just before serving*
Difficulty: *Moderately difficult*
Cost: *Moderate*

Ingredients		
18	fresh green asparagus spears, or 1 package (10 ounces) frozen asparagus spears, or 2 cans (10 ounces each) white or green asparagus Salt	
6	tablespoons unsalted butter	
3	eggs	

	Freshly ground pepper
2⅓	cups crème fraîche (see Note)
¾	cup fresh, shelled baby peas, or 1 package (10 ounces) frozen baby peas
2	tablespoons chopped onion
	Pinch of curry powder
3	large slices white bread

Utensils

Food processor, blender, or food mill
Large saucepan
Small saucepan
Bain-marie or shallow roasting pan
6 individual dariole molds, 2½ inches deep by 2½ inches in diameter
Colander

Mixing bowl
Sieve
Paring knife
Vegetable peeler
Brush
String

overleaf: *The simple elegance of a table set for a family gathering.*

A small asparagus flan, in cream sauce with peas.

Preparation

***Using a vegetable peeler, trim the fresh asparagus, removing any tough, woody ends, and cut all the spears to the same length. Tie in a bunch with string.

In a large saucepan, bring 2 quarts of salted water to a boil. Stand the asparagus bunch in the water, tapered ends up and extending just above the water line, and cook for about 20 minutes, depending on their size and texture. To avoid overcooking, test for doneness after 15 minutes: If the tines of a fork can be inserted easily into the stems, the asparagus is cooked. Rinse briefly under cold water to stop the cooking. (If using frozen asparagus, omit the above; simply thaw, drain thoroughly, and pat dry. It's essential that all excess water be removed.) Cut the tips from the asparagus and set them aside.

Preheat the oven to 225 degrees F.

Melt 2 tablespoons of the butter and brush evenly over the sides and bottoms of the dariole molds.

Place the well-drained asparagus stems in a food processor and add the eggs and 1 cup of the crème fraîche. Season with salt and pepper and process to a smooth, creamy consistency. Strain through a sieve.

Divide the asparagus among the buttered dariole molds, filling each with the mixture. Place the darioles in a roasting pan filled with enough water to come about halfway up the sides of the molds. Place in the oven and bake for 30 minutes.

Meanwhile, bring a small saucepan of salted water to a boil. Add the peas and boil for about 3 minutes. Turn into a colander, rinse with cold water, and drain. (If using frozen peas, just thaw and drain thoroughly.)

If you're preparing this dish in advance, remove the flans from the oven and let cool slightly, then refrigerate. Place the peas in the refrigerator.

**Twenty minutes before serving, place the asparagus flans in a bain-marie (or a shallow roasting pan filled with enough water to come halfway up the sides of the molds). Set over low heat and warm for about 15 minutes.

Melt 2 tablespoons of the butter in a skillet, add the onions, and sauté briefly. Sprinkle with a pinch of curry powder and add the remaining 1⅓ cups crème fraîche. Season with salt and pepper and simmer for 3 to 4 minutes.

Pour this crème mixture into a food processor and add the peas and the remaining 2 tablespoons butter. Process to a thoroughly homogeneous sauce. Adjust the seasoning if necessary.

Reheat the reserved asparagus tips in a saucepan with a little salted water. Drain well. Toast the bread slices, cut off the crusts, and cut each into 2 triangles.

Spoon some of the pea sauce onto each of 6 salad plates. Unmold the flans and place one in the center of each plate. Garnish each with 3 asparagus tips. Place a toast triangle on the edge of each plate and serve.

Note: Heavy cream does not substitute for crème fraîche in this recipe. However, if you cannot buy or make crème fraîche (see Appendix), substitute ¾ cup heavy cream mixed with 1 egg for the 1 cup crème fraîche used in the flans. The results will, however, be less desirable than when crème fraîche is used.

L'Escalope de Saumon en Brouillade de Ciboulette

ESCALOPES OF SALMON WITH SCRAMBLED
EGGS AND CHIVES

Time required: *10 minutes*
advance preparation
25 minutes preparation
and cooking just before serving
Difficulty: *Very easy*
Cost: *Expensive*

Ingredients

2 to 2¼ pounds very fresh salmon, preferably cut from the tail
Salt
Freshly ground pepper

1 bunch fresh chives
9 eggs
2 ounces fresh black truffles (optional)
5 tablespoons unsalted butter

Utensils

Medium skillet
Heavy baking sheet

Sharp filleting knife
Medium knife

Cutting board   Mixing bowl
Whisk   Measuring spoons
Large stainless steel spatula

Preparation

***Ask your fishmonger to scale and fillet the salmon and slice it diagonally into 6 thin slices, about 5 ounces each.

If your fishmonger isn't amiable, scale the salmon yourself and use a sharp knife to slit it open along the belly and back. Lift off the fillets and remove all the bones. With a very sharp filleting knife held slightly at an angle, cut each fillet diagonally into three very thin slices, without cutting through the skin. (The slices should be as thin and delicate as properly sliced smoked salmon.)

If you're preparing this in advance, separate the salmon slices with plastic wrap and refrigerate.

**About 20 minutes before serving, moisten a heavy baking sheet with several drops of water to prevent the salmon from sticking. Spread out the salmon slices on the baking sheet so that they do not overlap. Season lightly with salt and pepper.

Chop 1 tablespoon of the chives. Set the remaining chives aside for decorating the plates.

Break the eggs into a mixing bowl, season with salt and pepper, and beat with a whisk.

Preheat the broiler.

Slice the truffles thinly, if using.

Melt 2 tablespoons of the butter in a skillet. Add the eggs and cook over low heat, stirring, until the eggs are firm but still creamy. Remove from the heat. Cut the remaining 3 tablespoons butter into small pieces and stir into the eggs; stir in the chopped chives and truffles, if using.

Place the salmon under the broiler and cook just until opaque, about 2 minutes. (They should be just barely cooked.)

Meanwhile, divide the eggs among 6 warm plates.

When the salmon is ready, use a large spatula to carefully lift the salmon slices onto the eggs, and garnish each plate with a small bunch of chives.

L'Etuvée de Volaille Mijotée à la Façon de Jean Vignard

BRAISED CHICKEN AND PURÉED VEGETABLES
À LA JEAN VIGNARD

Time required: *1 hour and 25 minutes*
advance preparation
20 minutes reheating just
before serving
Difficulty: *Moderately easy*
Cost: *Inexpensive*

Ingredients

2	chickens (3 to 3½ pounds each)
2	or 3 large yellow onions (about 1⅓ pounds total weight)
6	tablespoons unsalted butter
3	tablespoons water
3	ripe tomatoes (about ⅔ pound total weight)
3	cloves garlic
1	bouquet garni composed of 1 celery rib, 1 sprig fresh thyme,

1 small bay leaf, and ½ bunch parsley all tied together with a string

Salt

Freshly ground pepper

1⅔ cup wine vinegar

1⅔ cup red wine, preferably the same that will be served with the chicken

Utensils

2 earthenware or cast-iron casseroles with covers (Jean Vignard would choose the earthenware)

Food processor or food mill with fine disc

Fine sieve

Wooden spoon
Medium knife
Cutting board
Large plate
Measuring cups and spoons

Preparation

***Cut the chickens in quarters. Peel the onions and slice thinly.

In a large earthenware or cast-iron casserole, melt 2 tablespoons of the butter with the water. Add the onions, cover, and cook over very low heat for 30 minutes, stirring occasionally to keep the onions from burning. If they begin to color, stir in another 2 tablespoons water and reduce the heat.

Meanwhile, remove the stems from the tomatoes, cut them in half, and squeeze gently to remove the seeds and juice. Cut into large dice. Peel and crush the garlic.

When the onions have cooked for 30 minutes, add the tomatoes to the casserole and cook for 5 minutes. Remove from the heat, add the bouquet garni and garlic, and set aside, uncovered.

Season the chicken pieces on all sides with salt and pepper. Melt 2 tablespoons of the butter in a second casserole. Add the chicken pieces and let them brown quickly on all sides over high heat. Transfer the browned chicken pieces to the first casserole and place on the bed of onions and tomatoes. Cook over low heat, making sure that the cooking liquid does not cover the chicken. The chicken should sit on top of the vegetables above the liquid so that it is cooked by the steam. Let simmer for 25 minutes. Then remove the chicken and set aside on a plate to cool.

Discard the butter from the casserole in which the chicken browned, but do not rinse. Add the vinegar to it and place over medium heat to simmer and reduce until only a glaze-like film remains. Add the red wine and reduce to ½ cup. Remove from the heat.

(At this point you should have a casserole of braised vegetables, a plate of browned and steamed chicken quarters, and a casserole of reduced wine and cooking liquids.)

Remove the bouquet garni from the vegetables and place them in the container of a food processor or in a food mill, and purée. Add the purée to the wine reduction and bring to a boil, stirring. Strain the mixture through a fine sieve and return it to the casserole. Add the chicken quarters and any juices that have accumulated on the plate.

If you're preparing this dish in advance, cover the casserole and refrigerate.

**Before serving, bring the casserole to room temperature and reheat, covered, over medium heat for 15 to 20 minutes. Remove from the heat and add the remaining 2 tablespoons butter, swirling the casserole in a circular motion to incorporate the butter.

This dish can be served from the casserole, presented on a large plate covered with a folded white napkin. Or if you wish, serve it on a large, deep platter.

Le Gratin de Macaronis Compotés au Lait

GRATIN OF CREAMY MACARONI

Time required: *20 minutes*
advance preparation
15 minutes cooking
just before serving
Difficulty: *Very easy*
Cost: *Inexpensive*

Ingredients

1⅓ cups elbow macaroni
     Salt
3   cups milk
6   tablespoons crème fraîche (see Appendix), or heavy cream
2   tablespoons unsalted butter

     Pinch of freshly grated nutmeg
     Freshly ground pepper
2   egg yolks
3   tablespoons shredded Gruyère cheese

Utensils

Medium saucepan
9-inch-long, oval gratin dish
Colander
Mixing bowl

Whisk
Wooden spoon
Measuring cups and spoons

Preparation

***In a medium saucepan, bring 1 quart of water to a boil. Add the macaroni and a pinch of salt and boil for 3 minutes. Turn the macaroni into a colander and drain.

Pour the milk into the saucepan and bring to a boil. Add the drained macaroni and simmer over very low heat for 12 minutes. While it's simmering, stir in 3 tablespoons of the crème fraîche and the butter. Season with a pinch of nutmeg, salt and pepper to taste.

Turn the macaroni into the gratin dish.

Place the remaining 3 tablespoons crème fraîche in a medium mixing bowl, season lightly with salt, and beat with a whisk until foamy. Add the egg yolks and cheese and blend gently. Pour this mixture over the macaroni.

If you're preparing this dish in advance, set macaroni aside in a cool place.

**About 30 minutes before serving, preheat the oven to 450 degrees F. After 15 minutes, place the macaroni in the hot oven and bake for 10 minutes.

Turn the oven to broil. Heat the macaroni under the broiler until the top is nicely browned, 3 to 5 minutes.

Le Soufflé Glacé aux Fraises

FROZEN INDIVIDUAL STRAWBERRY SOUFFLES

Time required: *1 hour*
advance preparation
5 to 6 hours freezing time
Difficulty: *Difficult*
Cost: *Moderate*

Ingredients

1	cup crème fraîche (see Note)
1	pint fresh strawberries or raspberries, or 1 package (10 ounces) quick-frozen whole strawberries or raspberries
4	egg whites, at room temperature

	Salt
1	lemon wedge
1	cup superfine sugar
⅔	cup water sugar
2	tablespoons unsweetened cocoa powder

Utensils

	Food processor, blender, or food mill

	Electric mixer
3	mixing bowls

Fine sieve
Small stainless-steel or
enameled saucepan
Candy thermometer (optional)
6 individual cold soufflé molds, 3
to 3½ inches in diameter and
1½ inches deep
Large sheet of heavy-duty

waxed paper or parchment
Scissors
6 rubber bands
Whisk
Wooden spoon
Sugar sifter
Measuring cups and spoons

Preparation

***These soufflés keep well and can be prepared a day in advance.

Place the crème fraîche in a mixing bowl and refrigerate until the crème and the bowl are thoroughly chilled, about 1 hour.

Rinse, drain, and hull the strawberries. Set 6 large, unblemished berries aside in the refrigerator for decorating the soufflés.

Place the remaining berries in a food processor, blender, or food mill and process to a purée. Strain the purée through a fine sieve over a small bowl. Refrigerate.

Place the egg whites in a mixing bowl and add a pinch of salt.

Rub the lemon wedge over the bottom and sides of a small stainless steel or enameled saucepan to make sure it is clean of any residual grease. Rinse and dry thoroughly. (It's essential that the pan be very clean and dry.) Add the sugar and water, stir together, and place over high heat.

Begin immediately to beat the egg whites with an electric mixer, slowly at first, then increasing the speed to fast.

Meanwhile, keep an eye on the sugar syrup. It should reach the desired temperature of 234 to 238 degrees F (soft ball stage) about the time the egg whites are very stiff. (The simplest way to tell when the syrup reaches 235 degrees is with a candy thermometer. But if you don't have one, use the following method: Fill a small bowl with ice

water. When the syrup begins to bubble, drop a bit of the syrup into the ice water. If you can gather it together into a soft ball, the syrup is ready.)

When the syrup reaches 235 degrees, remove it from the heat. Reduce the speed of the electric beater and pour a thin, steady stream of the syrup into the egg whites, continuing to beat at low speed and turning the bowl until the mixture has cooled. Refrigerate.

Remove the crème fraîche from the refrigerator and beat with a whisk or electric beater until whipped. Return it to the refrigerator.

Cut the parchment or waxed paper into 6 strips, each 2½ inches wide by about 12 inches long. Wrap a strip around the outside of each soufflé mold and secure with a rubber band to form a raised collar extending about an inch above the edge of the mold. Place the molds in the refrigerator.

When the egg white mixture is well chilled, remove from the refrigerator and fold in half the strawberry purée, blending well. Fold the remaining strawberry purée into the whipped crème fraîche with a wooden spoon. Then fold the two mixtures together. (The crème fraîche and the egg white mixture should be the same temperature, both very cold, when mixed together.)

Divide the soufflé mixture among the 6 chilled soufflé molds and freeze for 5 to 6 hours.

Cocoa-glazed strawberry soufflés.

**Twenty minutes before serving, remove the soufflés from the freezer and place in the refrigerator. Just before serving, remove the paper collars and sprinkle the cocoa powder through a sugar sifter or fine sieve over the top of each soufflé. Place 1 of the reserved berries on top of each soufflé and serve.

Note: Crème fraîche is very important to the success of this recipe. If heavy cream is substituted, the soufflés will not set. If you cannot buy or make crème fraîche (see Appendix), it is possible to use heavy cream and thicken the soufflés with gelatin. To do so, strain the strawberry purée into a small saucepan (see recipe), add 1 package of unflavored gelatin, and let soften for a minute or so. Place over very low heat and warm, stirring until the gelatin dissolves. Remove from the heat, let cool slightly, and refrigerate. The results, however, will be less delicious than when made with crème fraîche.

Menu for 2 People

Un Dîner d'Amoureux

A Dinner for Lovers

Difficulty:
Moderately easy
Cost: *Expensive*

When I first began courting my wife, I invited her for dinner one evening to a modest but good restaurant, so as not to overwhelm her and not to let myself be tempted by excessively appetizing dishes.

I stoically ordered asparagus vinaigrette and grilled sole, and Denise followed my lead. It's enough to say that I rose from the table with a happy heart but an unsatisfied stomach.

As much in love as I was, and anxious to see my lovely guest again as soon as possible, I knew I was incapable of living solely on love and asparagus vinaigrette. Thus Denise discovered very rapidly both my profession and my love of eating.

Several months later, moreover, she admitted that she had hesitated to accept a second invitation, discouraged by the frugal dinner after which she too had felt a serious desire to eat some more. But strong budding emotions

La Coquille de Brouillade d'Oeufs au Caviar
Scrambled Eggs in Their Shells with Caviar

La Fricassée d'Homard à la Crème d'Estragon
Fricassee of Lobster with Tarragon Cream Sauce

Le Pigeon aux Petits Pois en Cocotte Lutée
Pigeon and Baby Peas in a Sealed Casserole

Les Profiterolles à la Glace à la Vanille et au Coulis de Fraises
Profiterolles with Vanilla Ice Cream and Strawberry Sauce

had prevented her from disturbing our idyll after the *fraises au sucre* (strawberries sprinkled with sugar).

I think that since our marriage she hasn't had too much to complain about—at least on that score.

Doing the Marketing

Order the pigeon and the lobsters a few days in advance. The lobsters should be alive when you cook them.

(In a pinch, you could use frozen lobsters, although they won't be nearly as good.) Choose medium-size eggs.

What to Drink

For the apéritif and the first courses, it's hard to imagine anything other than Champagne for a lovers' dinner. With the pigeon, you can serve a fine

Bordeaux (such as Saint Emilion or a Saint Estèphe). You'll need an ice bucket for the Champagne and a basket for the Bordeaux.

Table Linens and Decoration

Choose elegant and refined pastels for this dinner. Decorate the table with beautiful candelabra and flowers that harmonize with the linen.

Write the menu on one of those lovers' postcards that you roll up, tie with ribbon, and slip a rose into.

If possible, choose a table that isn't too large, so your knees will touch. And don't forget the music or the moonlight streaming through the curtains. Or, failing that, a fire in the fireplace. And, most important: take the telephone off the hook.

Tableware

2	egg cups and 2 small plates for the eggs and caviar
4	large dinner plates
1	large platter with a folded

white napkin on which to place the pigeon casserole
| 2 | dessert plates for the profiterolles |

Silverware

| 2 | teaspoons for the scrambled eggs |
| 4 | dinner forks and knives (or you can use fish forks and knives for the lobster, although it is not easily cut with a fish |

knife)
4	dessert or sauce spoons for the sauce of the lobster and pigeon
2	dessert spoons for the profiterolles
1	serving knife and fork

Glassware

| 2 | Champagne glasses |
| 2 | Bordeaux glasses |

| 2 | water goblets |

Getting Organized

Many things in this menu can be prepared in advance. They are indicated in each recipe with the symbol ***. The symbol ** indicates those tasks that must be done just before serving.

Put the Champagne in the refrigerator to chill several hours in advance.

Twenty minutes before sitting down to eat, leave your guest, return to the kitchen, and set the oven to 400 degrees F. Warm 4 dinner plates on the back of the stove. Fill the choux pastries with the ice cream and put them in the freezer until time for dessert. Spoon the strawberry coulis onto 2 dessert plates and put them in the refrigerator.

Prepare the scrambled eggs and caviar. Just before serving the eggs, put the pigeon in the oven to bake and warm the lobster in its saucepan set in a bain marie for 20 minutes.

Before serving the lobster, add a few leaves of coarsely chopped tarragon and a grind of fresh pepper.

The pigeon can be taken to the table straight from the oven in its casserole.

Remove the profiterolles from the freezer, place on the plates of strawberry coulis, and serve.

overleaf: *A very special dinner for two.*

La Coquille de Brouillade d'Oeufs au Caviar

SCRAMBLED EGGS IN THEIR SHELLS WITH
CAVIAR

Time required: *10 minutes*
advance preparation
10 minutes just
before serving
Difficulty: *Very easy*
Cost: *Expensive*

Ingredients

2   extra large eggs
    Salt
    Freshly ground pepper
2   teaspoons unsalted butter
1   teaspoon crème fraîche (see
    Appendix), or heavy cream
8   blades fresh chives
1   ounce fresh caviar
1   large slice white bread

Utensils

    Small heavy skillet
    Small mixing bowl
    Small sharp knife
    Fine sieve
    Wooden spoon
    2 egg cups
    Measuring spoons
    Whisk

Preparation

***Begin by preparing the egg shells: Using a small sharp knife, cleanly slice off the top of the rounded end of each egg, discarding the tops. Empty the contents of both egg shells into a small mixing bowl. Gently rinse the egg shells and invert on a cloth to dry.

Season the eggs with salt and pepper and beat with a whisk. Strain the eggs through a fine sieve to remove any pieces of shell.

If preparing this dish in advance, stop here and refrigerate the eggs.

**Ten minutes before serving, heat the butter in a small skillet over low heat. Add the eggs and cook over low heat, until the eggs are thick and creamy.

Meanwhile, remove the crust from

the bread and toast it.

Remove the skillet from the heat and stir the crème fraîche into the eggs. Adjust the seasoning if necessary.

To serve, place the shells in the egg cups and fill each with the scrambled eggs. Stick 4 chive blades in each portion, then spoon ½ ounce (about 2 teaspoons) of the caviar on top of each. Cut the toast into *mouillettes*, or ½-inch-wide "fingers," and serve next to the eggs.

Note: If you wish, replace these fingers of white bread with small wild asparagus spears that have been boiled for one minute in salted water.

La Fricassée d'Homard à la Crème d'Estragon

FRICASSEE OF LOBSTER WITH TARRAGON
CREAM SAUCE

Time required: *1 hour
advance preparation
15 minutes before serving*
Difficulty: *Easy*
Cost: *Expensive*

Ingredients

2	lobsters (about 1 pound each)
1	shallot
2	sprigs fresh tarragon
2	tablespoons unsalted butter

1¼ cups crème fraîche (see Appendix)
Salt
Freshly ground pepper

Utensils

Large skillet with a tight cover
Medium saucepan
Fine sieve
Large knife
Paring knife
Nutcracker

Wooden spoon
Bain-marie, or a shallow roasting pan large enough to hold the saucepan (optional)
Measuring cups and spoons

Preparation

***When it comes to preparing lobsters, the essential question is, Are you a sensitive person or a brute like me?

If the former applies, you'll want to preheat the oven to 500 degrees F and place the lobsters in the hot oven for 4 minutes before halving them. (They won't even have time to think before they are in gourmets' heaven.) Remove them from the oven and cut each in half lengthwise: place the point of a large sharp knife at the joint of the body and tail shells and make a quick, clean cut through the middle. If you're less sensitive (or less hypocritical?), simply cut the live lobsters cleanly

down the middle in the same manner. It's quicker—for you and for them! Crack the claws lightly with a nut-cracker, being careful not to crush the meat.

Peel and finely chop the shallot. Separate the tarragon leaves from their stems, reserving both leaves and stems.

Place the butter in a skillet large enough to hold the lobster halves snugly. Add the shallot and sauté until softened and lightly golden. Add the lobster halves, shell side down, and pour the crème fraîche over them. Add the tarragon stems and simmer over low heat until the cream comes to a boil. Cover the skillet tightly and simmer over very low heat for 10 minutes.

Remove the lobsters from the cream, shaking the excess cream into the skillet. Carefully pull the tail meat

out of the shells all in one piece. Remove the claw meat. Place all of the lobster meat in a medium saucepan and set aside.

Reserve 2 legs and the upper body of two lobster halves for garnish. Crack or cut up all of the remaining lobster shells, including the legs, tail and claw shells, and the 2 remaining body halves. Add the shells to the cream in the skillet. Bring to a boil over moderate heat. Remove from the heat and strain the cream through a fine sieve held over the saucepan containing the lobster meat. Season with salt, if necessary, and the fricassee is ready to garnish and serve.

If you're preparing this well in advance, let cool slightly and refrigerate until shortly before serving.

❧

**To reheat, place the saucepan with the lobster in a bain marie (or a large, shallow roasting pan half-filled with warm water) and warm over low heat for 20 minutes. Or, warm the lobster directly over very low heat for 10 minutes.

Coarsely chop the reserved tarragon leaves and add to the lobster along with a grind of fresh pepper. Divide the lobster between the two warm plates and spoon the tarragon cream sauce generously over each. Decorate each plate with the reserved legs and bodies.

A romantic dinner should be beautiful as well as delicious.

Le Pigeon aux Petits Pois en Cocotte Lutée

PIGEON AND BABY PEAS IN A SEALED
CASSEROLE

Time required: *45 minutes*
advance preparation
30 minutes cooking
just before serving
Difficulty: *Moderately easy*
Cost: *Moderate*

Ingredients

1	pigeon (about 1½ pounds) or Cornish hen
½	shallot
3	tablespoons unsalted butter
¼	cup plus 1 tablespoon dry white wine
½	chicken bouillon cube
1	sprig fresh thyme
½	bay leaf
½	teaspoon tomato paste
	Salt

	Freshly ground pepper
2	slices thick-cut bacon, cut into 4 pieces
3	heaping tablespoons fresh shelled *petits pois* or baby peas (see Note)
10	white pearl onions
	Pinch of sugar
4	tender lettuce leaves
¾	cup flour

Utensils

	Small covered casserole or oval terrine with tight-fitting lid
3	small saucepans
2	medium skillets
	Fine sieve

2	bowls
	Cutting board
	Medium knife
	Large plate
	Measuring cup and spoons

Preparation

✳✳✳Clean and truss the pigeon or have your butcher do it, asking him to reserve the neck and wing ends for the pigeon stock (see Note).

To make the stock, peel and chop the shallot. Melt ½ tablespoon of the butter in a small saucepan, add the pigeon neck and wing ends, and sauté over medium heat until lightly browned. Add the shallot and sauté until softened. Stir in the wine and simmer over moderate heat until reduced by half. Add the half bouillon cube, thyme, bay leaf, tomato paste,

Cornish hen may be substituted for pigeon in this flavorful casserole.

and enough water to cover the bones. Simmer over low heat until the liquid has reduced to about 2 tablespoons. Strain through a sieve into a mixing bowl. Season with salt and pepper to taste and set aside.

Preheat the oven to 450 degrees F.

Season the pigeon inside and out with salt. Melt 1½ tablespoon of the butter in a medium skillet and add the pigeon, rolling it in the melted butter to coat thoroughly. Let the pigeon brown lightly on all sides. Place the skillet in the hot oven for 12 minutes, basting at least twice during the cooking.

While the pigeon cooks, place the bacon in a small saucepan of cold water. Bring to a boil, blanch briefly, and drain. Plunge the peas in a saucepan of salted boiling water and cook for 3 minutes. Drain. Set bacon and peas aside on a large plate.

Peel the pearl onions.

Melt ½ tablespoon butter in a medium skillet. Add the pearl onions and season with salt and pepper. Add a pinch of sugar and 3 tablespoons water

and cook over high heat until the water has completely evaporated and the onions are glazed, about 5 minutes. Set the onions aside with the bacon and peas.

Cut the lettuce leaves into small pieces and add to the skillet with the remaining ½ tablespoon butter. Sauté quickly over low heat just until wilted. Add the bacon, peas, and onions to the skillet, adjust the seasoning, and mix together well. Spread the mixture over the bottom of a small casserole or terrine.

Remove the pigeon from the oven and place on the bed of vegetables in the terrine. Spoon the stock over it and cover the casserole.

In a small bowl, combine the flour with enough cold water to make a wet paste. Generously dab this paste around the edge of the casserole. The mixture will harden and seal or "lute" the casserole so that steam does not escape during the cooking.

If you're preparing in advance, all the above can be done the day before or several hours ahead of the dinner.

**Forty-five minutes before serving, preheat the oven to 400 degrees F. Place the sealed casserole in the hot oven and bake for 30 minutes. Take the

casserole to the table still sealed with its beautiful golden crust. Then break open, lift the cover slowly, and inhale...!

Note: If fresh *petits pois* or baby peas are unavailable, fresh shelled sugar peas or frozen baby peas can be substituted.

If your butcher can't provide you with the neck and wing ends of the pigeon, substitute chicken necks and wing ends in the stock. Or, omit the neck and wing ends entirely, adding 1½ chicken bouillon cubes instead.

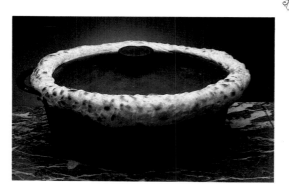

The golden crown makes this a sealed casserole.

Les Profiterolles à la Glace à la Vanille et au Coulis de Fraises

PROFITEROLLES WITH VANILLA ICE CREAM
AND STRAWBERRY SAUCE

Time required: *1 hour*
preparation
(at least 3 hours in advance)
Difficulty: *Moderately difficult*
Cost: *Moderate*

Ingredients

CHOUX PASTRY
⅓ cup milk
7 tablespoons unsalted butter
Pinch of salt

¾ cup water
1¼ cups flour
5 medium eggs
1 egg yolk

VANILLA ICE CREAM
½ cup plus 2 tablespoons super-fine sugar
1 cup milk
1¼ cups crème fraîche (see Appen-

dix), or heavy cream
2 tablespoons vanilla sugar (see Note)
8 egg yolks, at room temperature

STRAWBERRY COULIS
½ pint fresh strawberries, or 5 ounces quick-frozen

strawberries
1 tablespoon sugar

Utensils

Sorbet or ice cream machine
Blender or food processor
Medium saucepan
3 mixing bowls
Wooden spoon

Pastry bag
Baking sheet
Measuring cups and spoons
Pastry brush

Preparation

CHOUX PASTRY
***In a medium saucepan, combine the milk, butter, salt, and water and bring to a boil. Remove from the heat and gradually sift in the flour, stirring constantly with a wooden spoon until thoroughly incorporated. Return the pan to the heat and continue stirring for 2 to 3 minutes, until the dough is shiny and doesn't stick to the sides of the pan.

Transfer the dough to a large mixing bowl and add the eggs, one at a time, blending well after each addition, to obtain a smooth, glossy dough.

Preheat the oven to 350 degrees F and lightly oil a baking sheet.

Fit a pastry bag with a plain 1-inch tip and fill with the choux pastry. Pipe walnut-size mounds onto the baking sheet at regular intervals. (Six or 8 should suffice for two lovers.)

In a small bowl, beat the egg yolk with a few drops of water and brush over the top of each choux.

(With the remaining dough, you can make more choux balls and sprinkle them with sugar. Bake along with the others; they make excellent petits fours.)

Place in the oven and bake for a total of 25 minutes: For the first 15 minutes, bake with the oven door tightly closed, then open the oven door slightly and bake for the remaining 10 minutes so that the choux will dry out. Remove from the oven and let cool.

VANILLA ICE CREAM

While the choux cook, combine the superfine sugar and milk in a large mixing bowl, stirring until the sugar is completely dissolved. In a separate bowl, combine the crème fraîche, vanilla sugar, and egg yolks and blend thoroughly. Stir the sweetened milk into the cream and egg yolk mixture and blend well.

Pour the mixture into the container of an ice cream or sorbet machine and prepare according to the manufacturer's instructions. Place in the freezer for at least 3 hours.

(Any leftover ice cream can be stored in the freezer for 5 or 6 days, covered with plastic wrap to prevent ice crystals from forming. This ice cream is like nothing else you've eaten before. You won't find it in restaurants or ice cream shops because of its extremely fragile and perishable nature.)

STRAWBERRY COULIS

Wash, drain, and hull the strawberries. Place in a blender or food processor and process to a purée. That's all!

ASSEMBLING

**Before serving dinner, cut the choux in half horizontally. Fill the bottom half generously with ice cream and replace the top half. Place in the freezer.

Spoon the strawberry coulis onto two dessert plates and place in the refrigerator.

Just before serving, remove the choux from the freezer and place 3 or 4 on each plate on top of the strawberry coulis. Serve.

Note: Make your own vanilla sugar by placing 4 vanilla beans in a canister with 2 pounds of sugar and sealing it tightly. Let the sugar absorb the flavor of the vanilla for at least a week.

It's impossible to reduce this recipe to serve only two. So you'll have leftover choux pastry and ice cream. But believe me, it shouldn't be a problem!

Profiteroles, in which strawberry coulis replaces the usual chocolate sauce.

Menu for 6 People

Le Dîner de Ma Tante Celestine

Dinner at My Aunt Celestine's

Difficulty: *Moderate*
Cost: *Expensive*

When my Aunt Celestine had company, the party actually began for her with the invitations. She gathered steam during the shopping, really got underway during the preparation of the meal, and reached her apotheosis looking at the contented faces of her guests around the table. For Aunt Celestine, having guests was a whole series of happy moments—moments based solely on the pleasure of pleasing others.

That, I think, is the proper spirit for a dinner party. For if you consider the event as a series of efforts and responsibilities, then it is no longer a party but a chore. As long as your guests are made to feel that you are truly glad to see them and to offer them this feast, it doesn't matter about unforeseen difficulties or even a recipe that doesn't quite come off. You can all laugh about it together.

Les Goujonnettes de Soles et de St. Jacques à l'Huile de Citron
Goujonnettes of Sole and Scallops in Lemon Oil

La Terrine de Loup à l'Estragon
Terrines of Sea Bass with Tarragon

Le Carré de Veau Rôti au Sherry avec la Fondue de Champignons à la Crème
Sherried Loin of Veal with Mushrooms and Cream

La Charlotte Légère d'Abricots
Light Apricot Charlotte

A little glass of wine or Champagne before your guests arrive will give you an appreciable advantage over them and will help you put them at ease with your welcoming smile.

Doing the Marketing

Order the veal in advance.

Purchase the artichokes and the ingredients for the charlotte and prepare the day before. Everything else can be purchased the same day.

What to Drink

For an apéritif, serve a Champagne cocktail *aux pêches*. To prepare it, purée 2 ripe peaches in a food processor with 2 tablespoons sugar and 1 teaspoon lemon juice. Blend together, strain through a sieve, and chill. Just before serving, mix the peach purée with one bottle of well-chilled Champagne and serve in frosted glasses.

The peach cocktail that my Aunt Celestine liked so much.

What to Drink

For the wines, serve a dry, fruity white wine with the *goujonnettes* and the terrine of sea bass. I suggest a Jura or a Condrieu. With the veal, serve a full-bodied red wine such as a Bourgeuil, a Madiran, or a Cahors.

Table Linens and Decoration

My Aunt Celestine would have chosen a tablecloth and large napkins of white damask. In the center of the table she would have placed a large bouquet of garden or meadow flowers, arranged in a lovely tureen. She would have used brass candlesticks and rolled the napkins in silver rings. Finally, she would have written the menu on heavy white paper in her beautiful sloping handwriting.

Tableware

Choose an old-fashioned faïence style, such as a Faïence de Gien, for the dishes:

6	salad plates for the *goujonnettes*
6	individual terrines and 6 large plates for the sea bass terrines
6	large dinner plates for the veal
6	dessert plates for the charlotte
1	sauce boat for the Nantais butter
1	silver platter covered with a linen napkin for the sea bass terrines
1	large platter for the veal
1	shallow serving bowl for the mushrooms
1	large, round platter for the charlotte
1	sauce boat for the apricot compote

Silverware

12	fish forks and 12 fish knives for the *goujonnettes* and the sea bass
6	knives and 6 forks for the veal
6	dessert spoons and 6 dessert forks for the charlotte
2	serving spoons and 2 serving forks
2	sauce spoons
1	pie server and 1 knife for the charlotte

Glassware

18	goblets for water, white wine, and red wine
6	Champagne flutes for the apéritifs

Getting Organized

Many things in this menu can be prepared well in advance. They are indicated in each recipe with the symbol ✱✱✱. The symbol ✱✱ indicates those tasks that must be done just before serving.

The day before serving this dinner, you can prepare the charlotte and the artichokes for the *goujonnettes* of sole.

Several hours in advance, start preparing the fish terrines. About 2 hours before serving, put the white wine in the refrigerator to chill, as well as a large round platter and a sauce boat.

Preheat the oven to 400 degrees F. After preheating for 20 minutes, place the veal in the oven and prepare the garniture, as well as the mushrooms in cream. After cooking, keep everything warm in a bain-marie until serving time.

Warm 12 dessert plates, 12 dinner plates, 1 large platter, 1 deep serving platter, and 1 sauce boat on the back of the stove or over a pan filled with warm water.

Thirty minutes before the meal, set the oven temperature to 350 degrees F.

Finish preparing the *goujonnettes* Make the Nantais butter and keep it warm in a bain-marie.

Just before serving the *goujonnettes*, place the fish terrines in the oven to cook. (Be careful to cover them after 10 minutes of cooking.)

Serve the *goujonnettes*, then the terrines of sea bass. To serve the veal, simply put it on a large warmed platter or on the dinner plates. The charlotte requires only a few minutes just before serving for the finishing touches.

Les Goujonnettes de Soles et de Saint Jacques à l'Huile de Citron

GOUJONNETTES OF SOLE AND SCALLOPS IN
LEMON OIL

Time required: *25 minutes
advance preparation
20 minutes just before serving*
Difficulty: *Easy*
Cost: *Moderate*

Ingredients

6 purple or small green artichokes
½ lemon
   Salt
2 or 3 bunches mâche or other dark salad greens, such as arugula or watercress
1 small bunch chervil
⅔ cup virgin olive oil

¼ cup plus 1 tablespoon fresh lemon juice
   Freshly ground white pepper
3 celery ribs
6 to 8 fillets of sole (about 2 ounces each)
6 sea scallops (about 1¼ ounces each)

Utensils

Couscousière or large saucepan and large sieve or colander
Large saucepan
Paring knife

Chef's knife
Small mixing bowl
Cutting board
Whisk

Preparation

***The artichokes can be cooked the day before. To do so, break off the stems as close to the base as possible and remove all of the large outer leaves. Using a paring knife, trim off the bottom of each artichoke until the flesh of the heart is exposed. Cut off the top leaves even with the fibrous

choke and remove the choke. To prevent the artichokes from turning dark, rub them all over with the lemon half.

Bring a large saucepan filled with salted water to a boil. Add the artichoke hearts and boil for 15 to 20 minutes, depending on their size, until tender. To check for doneness, insert

the tip of a sharp knife into the hearts. If the knife slides in easily, they're done. Remove from the heat and set the artichokes aside in their cooking water.

**Thirty minutes before serving, wash the mâche and set aside to drain. Drain the artichoke hearts thoroughly, cut each into thin slices, and set aside. Separate the chervil leaves from the stems and set both aside separately.

In a small bowl, combine the olive oil and lemon juice, season with salt and pepper, and whisk until well blended.

Fill a couscousière or large saucepan with about 5 quarts of water. Add the chervil stems and celery ribs and bring to a gentle boil.

Meanwhile, cut the sole fillets into *goujonnettes*, or thin strips, by holding a sharp chef's knife at a slight angle and cutting lengthwise into ½-inch-wide strips. There should be about 4 *goujonnettes* per person. Cut each scallop into 3 slices. Season with salt and white pepper.

About 2 minutes before serving, place the *goujonnettes* and scallop slices into the top of the couscousière over the simmering water (or place in a large sieve or colander over a saucepan with the simmering water) and let steam for 1 minute or so. The celery and chervil-scented steam from the water will cook the fish. Keep an eye on the cooking, though; if the steam is hot, it won't take more than a minute to cook the fish.

Divide the mâche among 6 warmed plates. Arrange the sliced artichokes in a star shape on each plate. Arrange the steamed sole and scallops attractively on each plate. Spoon the dressing over each portion. Season with salt and pepper, if necessary. Sprinkle each salad with chervil leaves and serve.

La Terrine de Loup à l'Estragon

TERRINES OF SEA BASS WITH TARRAGON

Time required: *30 minutes advance preparation 25 minutes cooking and preparation just before serving*
Difficulty: *Moderate*
Cost: *Inexpensive*

Ingredients

1	cup unsalted butter
¾	pound sea bass fillets
	Salt
	Freshly ground pepper
7	egg yolks, at room temperature

⅔	cup crème fraîche (see Appendix), or heavy cream
25	fresh tarragon leaves, or 1 teaspoon dried tarragon

NANTAIS BUTTER

3	tablespoons white wine vinegar
½	cup dry white wine
2	tablespoons finely chopped shallots

1	teaspoon crushed black pepper
1½	tablespoons crème fraîche, or heavy cream
¾	cup unsalted butter

Utensils

Food processor
6 small earthenware terrines with covers or 6 individual soufflé molds
Small saucepan
Medium enamelled saucepan
Large saucepan
Roasting pan

Fine sieve
Chef's knife
Paring knife
Cutting board
Whisk
Small spatula
Wooden spoon

Preparation

***The first part of this recipe can be prepared several hours in advance.

Remove ⅔ cup of the butter from the refrigerator and let soften to room temperature.

Cut about one-third of the sea bass fillets into 6 *goujonnettes*, or thin strips, holding a sharp chef's knife at a slight angle and cutting the fillets lengthwise into ½-inch-wide strips.

Season the remaining sea bass with salt and pepper and place in a food processor. Process until finely chopped. Add the egg yolks and process for a few seconds. Add the softened butter and the crème fraîche and process briefly until very smooth.

Smooth a layer of the ground fish mixture over the bottom and sides of 6 well-buttered individual terrines or soufflé molds. Roll up each of the 6 *goujonnettes* of bass and place one in the center of each terrine. Season with salt and pepper and add 4 or 5 fresh tarragon leaves or a sprinkling of dried tarragon to each terrine. Spread a layer of the remaining ground fish mixture over the top of each terrine. Smooth the top of each with a small spatula.

In a small saucepan, melt the remaining ⅓ cup butter and drizzle over the top of the terrines to prevent them from drying out while cooking. Refrigerate the terrines until cooking time.

**Forty minutes before serving, preheat the oven to 350 degrees F. Fifteen minutes later, place the terrines in a shallow roasting pan and add enough water to come about halfway up the sides of the terrines. Place the roasting pan over high heat on top of the stove and bring the water to a boil. Place the terrines in the preheated oven and bake for 8 to 10 minutes.

Cover the terrines with their lids or with a sheet of aluminum foil and con-tinue baking for another 10 minutes.

While the terrines cook, prepare the Nantais butter. In a medium enamelled saucepan, combine the vinegar, wine, shallots, and crushed pepper and reduce over medium heat until only 1 tablespoon of liquid remains. Stir in the crème fraîche. Cut the butter into small pieces and add to the sauce, a little at a time, whisking constantly until the butter is thoroughly incorporated. Adjust the seasoning, if necessary.

Strain the sauce through a fine sieve.

(This sauce is very fragile and is best prepared at the last minute. If not serving immediately, however, return the sauce to the saucepan and keep warm in a bain-marie. To make the butter sauce a little more foamy, pour into a blender and whir for a few seconds just before serving.)

Turn the warm sauce into a sauce boat and arrange the terrines on a large silver platter covered with a linen napkin. Place a terrine on each guest's plate and pass the sauce to be spooned over the top.

Le Carré de Veau Rôti au Sherry avec la Fondue de Champignons à la Crème

SHERRIED LOIN OF VEAL WITH MUSHROOMS
AND CREAM

Time required: *1 hour and
10 minutes advance preparation
and cooking
20 minutes just before serving*
Difficulty: *Moderately difficult*
Cost: *Very expensive*

Ingredients

1	veal loin roast (about 5½ pounds before trimming; see Note)
	Salt
	Freshly ground pepper
⅔	cup vegetable oil
¾	cup plus 2 tablespoons unsalted butter
¾	to 1 cup dry sherry
2	celery ribs
3	small carrots
1	large onion
1	very ripe tomato

1	bouquet garni composed of 3 sprigs fresh thyme, 2 bay leaves, and 4 or 5 sprigs parsley
2½	pounds fresh mushrooms
¼	cup chopped shallots
1	teaspoon paprika
¼	cup plus 1 tablespoon crème fraîche (see Appendix), or heavy cream
1	cup water
1	tablespoon cornstarch
2	tablespoons parsley

Utensils

Large cast-iron casserole or roasting pan with cover
Large saucepan
Small saucepan
Cutting board
Chef's knife

Paring knife
Fine sieve

overleaf: *Dinner is served by a seascape of
the port of Toulon in 1870.*

Wooden spoon
Whisk

Aluminum foil

Preparation

✳✳✳Most of this recipe can be prepared 2 hours or more in advance. Preheat the oven to 400 degree F. Season the veal with salt and pepper on all sides. Heat the oil and 5 tablespoons butter in a large cast-iron casserole or roasting pan over medium-high heat. Add the veal and brown lightly on all sides. Remove the veal and set aside. Add the bones and trimmings to the pan and brown, stirring with a wooden spoon. Place the veal on top of the bones and trimmings, cover, and cook for 35 minutes, sprinkling frequently with small quantities of the sherry to keep the meat from drying out.

Meanwhile, trim the celery, scrape the carrots, and peel the onion. Coarsely chop the celery, carrots, onion, and tomato.

When the veal has cooked for 35 minutes, add the chopped vegetables

and bouquet garni. Cover and continue to roast for 20 to 25 minutes.

Meanwhile, prepare the mushrooms. Wipe off any dirt from the mushrooms and rinse quickly in cold water. Thinly slice the mushrooms, working as quickly as possible to prevent them from turning dark.

Melt 5 tablespoons butter in a large saucepan. Add the shallots and sauté until softened. Stir in the paprika. Add the mushrooms and cook until the liquid has completely evaporated. Season with salt and pepper.

Add the crème fraîche and simmer just until the crème thickens. Adjust the seasoning, if necessary.

If preparing in advance, set the mushrooms and cream and the veal aside in their pans until just before serving.

✳✳Twenty minutes before serving, preheat the oven to 400 degrees F. Place the mushrooms in a bain-marie to warm. Remove the veal from the pan, wrap in aluminum foil, and place in the oven to warm for 10 minutes.

Meanwhile, pour off the excess grease from the pan the veal cooked in. Add the water to the pan and reduce by two-thirds over medium-high heat.

Strain the sauce through a fine sieve into a small saucepan, discarding the bones and vegetables. If the sauce seems too thin, thicken it with cornstarch. To do so, dilute the cornstarch with a little cold water and stir until

smooth. Stir the cornstarch into the simmering sauce a drop or two at a time, just until the sauce thickens slightly and becomes creamy. Add the remaining 4 tablespoons butter to the sauce, stirring until fully incorporated. If you wish, add a little additional sherry at the last moment.

To serve, place the veal on a hot platter and surround it with the sauce. Serve the mushrooms separately in a large shallow bowl. Or, slice the veal and serve the slices on a bed of mushrooms on individual dinner plates. Surround with the sauce and sprinkle with the chopped parsley.

Note: Ask your butcher to trim and bone the roast and give you the trimmings and bones. The trimmed weight of the meat should be about 3 pounds.

La Charlotte Légère d'Abricots

LIGHT APRICOT CHARLOTTE

Time required: *1½ hours*
advance preparation
5 minutes preparation
just before serving
Difficulty: *Difficult*
Cost: *Moderate*

Ingredients

1 cup crème fraîche (see Appendix), or ⅔ cup heavy cream
2¼ pounds fresh ripe apricots, or 4 cans (17 ounces each) halved apricots in syrup
1⅓ cups sugar (plus ½ cup more, if using fresh apricots)
1 vanilla bean (if using fresh apricots)
3 tablespoons nonfat dry milk
2 tablespoons powdered unflavored gelatin
6 egg yolks, at room temperature
20 ladyfingers
½ cup plus 2 tablespoons apricot liqueur or kirsch

Utensils

Large saucepan with cover
Medium saucepan
Small saucepan
Food processor or food mill with fine disc
4 large mixing bowls
Small mixing bowl
Small bowl
Paring knife
Whisk
Wooden spoon
Electric mixer or egg beater
Candy thermometer (optional)
Charlotte mold or deep cake pan, 8 or 9 inches in diameter
Waxed paper
Saucer
Round plate
1 yard of 2-inch-wide orange ribbon
Measuring cups and spoons

Preparation

***This recipe should be prepared the day before serving for best results.

Place the crème fraîche in a large mixing bowl and chill the crème and the bowl in the refrigerator.

If using fresh apricots, wash and remove the stems, but do not remove the pits. Place the apricots in a large saucepan with the ½ cup of the sugar, the vanilla bean, and enough water to cover. Invert a saucer over the apricots to keep them submerged in the liquid. (If they are not completely covered with liquid, they will turn brown.) Bring the syrup to a boil, remove from the heat, cover, and set aside for 15 minutes. The apricots will continue to poach in the liquid.

Drain the apricots, reserving the liquid, and remove the pits.

If using canned apricots, drain well and reserve the syrup.

Place the apricots in a food processor along with about ¼ cup of the cooking liquid or syrup and purée. If the mixture seems too thick, add more liquid. Place half of the mixture in a mixing bowl and chill.

Pour the remaining apricot purée into a medium saucepan and stir in the nonfat dry milk. Sprinkle the gelatin over the apricot mixture and let stand for a minute or two to soften.

In a large mixing bowl, whisk together the egg yolks and ⅓ cup sugar. Beat well.

Stir the apricot and gelatin mixture over low heat until the gelatin dissolves, about 5 minutes. Bring to a boil, then pour a little of the hot mixture into the sweetened egg yolks, whisking constantly. Pour the egg yolk mixture back into the saucepan with the remaining apricot mixture and cook gently over low heat, stirring constantly, until thickened, *being careful not to let boil.* Rinse the large mixing bowl and pour the apricot crème anglaise back into it. Let cool, whisking from time to time.

Remove the chilled crème fraîche and bowl from the refrigerator and beat with a whisk until whipped. Chill.

Place the egg whites (without any traces of yolk) in the bowl of an electric mixer or in a mixing bowl (not plastic or aluminum; and the bowl must be very clean for the eggs to attain maximum volume).

In a small saucepan, combine the re-maining 1 cup of sugar with 3½ tablespoons water. Place the saucepan over low heat. At the same time, immediately begin to beat the egg whites, at first slowly, then faster.

Continue to beat the egg whites and cook the sugar syrup until the syrup reaches 250 degrees F, or the soft-ball stage, by which time the egg whites should be stiff.

Reduce the speed of the beater to low and pour a thin stream of the hot sugar syrup into the egg whites. Continue beating at low speed until the mixture has cooled. Chill.

Cut the ladyfingers into 2-inch lengths and sprinkle with ½ cup of the apricot liqueur.

Cut a round of waxed paper to fit the bottom of the charlotte mold and press in place. Arrange the ladyfingers upright around the sides of the mold.

At this point you should have the following: a charlotte mold lined with ladyfingers; an apricot crème anglaise (i.e., apricots, gelatin, egg yolks, and sugar); an Italian meringue (i.e., egg whites and sugar syrup); whipped cream; and the chilled half of the puréed apricots. For best results, the crème anglaise, Italian meringue, and whipped cream should all be very well chilled before being combined.

To assemble, gently fold the whipped cream and Italian meringue into the crème anglaise with a rubber spatula and blend together well. Pour the mixture into the charlotte mold, being careful not to disturb the ladyfingers and filling the mold to the rim. Smooth the surface with a spatula, cover, and chill overnight.

(If there is any of the filling left, scrape into a bowl and chill. It will keep for 3 to 4 days in the refrigerator.)

Fresh or canned apricots produce delicious results in this charlotte.

**Just before serving, invert the charlotte onto a flat, very cold plate and unmold. Spoon a light layer of the reserved apricot purée on top of the charlotte. Wrap a wide orange ribbon around the charlotte and tie in a butterfly bow.

Stir the remaining 2 tablespoons apricot liqueur into the remaining apricot purée and scrape into a chilled sauce boat.

Bring the charlotte and sauce to the table and wait for acclamations of success!

Menu for 6 People

Autour d'un Navarin

A Spring Feast

Difficulty: *Moderate*
Cost: *Moderately expensive*

Paris in June. Early summer is evident in all the markets, with their tender young vegetables, fresh from the provinces.

One particularly fine spring day, several fellow chefs and I decided to have lunch at René Lasserre's, in his marvelous room opening onto an almost Mediterranean sky. After a glass of Champagne, René told us the menu: a few dozen beautiful Belon oysters and, to celebrate springtime, a Navarin Printanier (spring lamb stew). I have retained a doubly happy memory of that meal. First, because I was with good friends, which is a great happiness in itself. And secondly, because we dined on that classic dish of French cuisine, a dish we had all prepared many times, but which—we all agreed—had rarely found such a great interpreter.

Les Frisures d'Oeuf en Salade Mouginoise
Composed Mouginoise Salad

Le Filet de Poisson Doré au Vermouth, avec le Beurre de Champignons
Broiled Fish Fillets with Vermouth and Mushroom Butter

Le Navarin d'Agneau Printanier
Spring Lamb Stew with Baby Vegetables

Le Gratin d'Abricots aux Amandes avec le Sirop de Kirsch
Individual Apricot Gratins with Almonds and Kirsch

In this menu, I offer my adaptation of this classic.

Doing the Marketing

For the navarin of lamb you will need fresh, sweet baby vegetables. If you don't have a garden, try to find the tin-iest young fresh vegetables possible.

Order the fish and the lamb in advance.

What to Drink

For an apéritif, my advice is to serve a sherry, chilled to about 60 degrees F.

For the wines, choose a white wine such as a Cassis to accompany the composed salad and the fish. With the lamb, serve a young St. Estèphe at cool room temperature.

opposite: *To erase this menu, rub the plate with a cloth moistened with lighter fluid.*

overleaf: *I love cast iron for cooking rustic dishes. The navarin should definitely be served in the pot in which it is cooked, in order to savor all the delicious aromas.*

Menu
Friture d'oeufs en salade
Filet de poisson doré au vermouth.
Navarin d'agneau printanier.
Gratin d'abricots.
Café

Table Linens and Decoration

Choose a very simple tablecloth and large napkins. This menu calls for those big beautiful cloth napkins that our grandparents would tuck under their armpits to protect their dress shirts or evening gowns. Decorate the table with bouquets of wildflowers.

Write the menu with a felt-tip pen directly on six plates. These plates will be what we call in the restaurant trade "marker plates" (*assiettes de marque*), which show the guests where to sit; the serving plates are placed on top of these.

Tableware

Choose a heavy, rustic faïence, perhaps with a floral design, or simply plain white:

6   large plates for the composed salad
6   large plates for the fish fillets
6   large plates for the navarin

6   dessert plates for the apricot gratins
1   salad bowl for the composed salad
1   sauce boat or bowl for the apricot compote

Silverware

6   forks for the salad
6   fish forks and 6 fish knives for the fish fillets
6   dinner knives and 6 dinner forks for the navarin

6   dessert forks for the apricot gratins
2   salad servers
1   serving spoon and 1 serving fork

Glassware

18   goblets for water, white wine, and red wine

Getting Organized

Many things in this menu can be prepared in advance. They are indicated in each recipe with the symbol ***. The symbol ** indicates those tasks that must be done just before serving.

Several hours in advance, put the white wine in the refrigerator to chill and begin preparing the composed salad, the apricot gratin, and the navarin.

One hour before sitting down to eat, warm 12 large plates on the back of the stove or over a large saucepan of hot water. Prepare the fish fillets and place them in the baking dish, ready to be cooked. Cook the mushrooms.

Thirty minutes before serving, assemble the salad and preheat the oven to 450 degrees F. Put the navarin in the oven to cook.

Twenty minutes later, put the fish fillets in to cook.

After serving the composed salad, return to the kitchen for 10 minutes. Set the oven to broil and prepare the mushroom butter. Place the fish under the boiler to brown. Remove them and reduce the oven temperature to 425 degrees.

Just before serving the fish, place the navarin over low heat to warm.

Twenty minutes before serving the apricot gratins, place them in the oven to bake.

Les Frisures d'Oeuf en Salade Mouginoise

COMPOSED MOUGINOISE SALAD

Time required: *30 minutes*
advance preparation
10 minutes to assemble
just before cooking
Difficulty: *Easy*
Cost: *Inexpensive*

Ingredients

1	sweet red pepper
2	large tomatoes
	Salt
1	cucumber
5	eggs
3	tablespoons virgin olive oil

DRESSING
1	clove garlic
2	anchovy fillets
1½	teaspoons strong mustard
2	tablespoons wine vinegar

1	tablespoon chopped fresh parsley
	Freshly ground pepper
1	head of lettuce
1	bunch chives
12	fresh basil leaves

¼	cup plus 1 tablespoon virgin olive oil
	Salt
	Freshly ground pepper
½	cup small black Niçoise olives

Utensils

	Medium saucepan
2	medium skillets
	Cutting board
	Chef's knife
	Paring knife

Shallow bowl
Small ladle
Colander
Whisk

Preparation

***Most of this recipe can be prepared several hours ahead.

Begin by preheating the broiler to roast the pepper.

Place the pepper under the broiler and let it roast, turning frequently, until blackened on all sides.

Meanwhile, bring a medium saucepan of water to a boil. Plunge the tomatoes into the boiling water for several seconds. Drain and rinse them under cold water and peel off the skin. Quarter the tomatoes and remove the core and seeds (reserving core and seeds for the preparation of the Navarin d'Agneau), so that all that remains are the 4 "petals" of each tomato. Cut the tomato petals into julienne, sprinkle with 1 teaspoon salt, and place in a colander to drain.

When the pepper is completely charred, hold it under cold water and peel off the skin. Cut it in half and remove the seeds and core. Cut lengthwise into julienne and drain in the colander with the tomatoes.

Strips of omelette for the Monginoise salad.

Peel the cucumber, cut it in half lengthwise, and scoop out the seeds. Cut into julienne the same size as the tomatoes and peppers; sprinkle generously with salt and add to the colander.

In a small bowl, beat the eggs with 2 tablespoons of the olive oil, the parsley, and salt and pepper.

Use the remaining 1 tablespoon oil to lightly coat the bottoms of 2 medium skillets. Place both over medium heat until hot. Pour a small ladleful of the egg mixture into each and tilt to distribute the egg evenly, as you would to make a crêpe. (The egg mixture should be about the thickness of a crêpe.) Cook the omelettes for about 1 minute, then turn and cook each for 1 minute on the other side. Slide the omelettes onto a plate, wipe out the skillets with an oil-soaked cloth, and continue to cook the remaining egg mixture in this manner.

Roll up the omelettes and cut crosswise into fine strips. Refrigerate until time to assemble the salad.

❖

**Shortly before dinner, wash and dry the lettuce. Shred into strips the size of the omelette strips. Cut the chives into 2-inch lengths. Shred the basil.

Make the dressing: Crush the garlic through a press into a large shallow bowl. Add the anchovies and crush them with a fork. Add the mustard and vinegar and blend thoroughly. Slowly whisk in the olive oil. Taste and season with salt, if necessary. (Be careful not to use too much; the anchovies are very salty.)

Add the tomato, pepper, cucumber,

and omelette strips to the salad bowl and toss well.

Cover the bottom of a large, shallow bowl or platter with the shredded let-tuce. Mound the vegetable mixture in a dome on top of the lettuce. Sprinkle the olives, chives, and basil leaves over the salad and serve.

Le Filet de Poisson Doré au Vermouth, avec le Beurre de Champignons

BROILED FISH FILLETS WITH VERMOUTH
AND MUSHROOM BUTTER

Time required: *30 to 40 minutes
advance preparation
5 to 10 minutes just before serving*
Difficulty: *Easy*
Cost: *Moderate*

Ingredients

6 fillets of white fish, such as sea bass, turbot, pike, hake, or cod (about 5 ounces each)
Salt
Freshly ground pepper
¼ cup plus 2 tablespoons dry vermouth
2 thick slices white bread, crusts removed
16 tablespoons unsalted butter
2 tablespoons chopped fresh parsley
⅔ pound fresh mushrooms
1 tablespoon fresh lemon juice
1 tablespoon water

Utensils

Baking dish large enough to hold 6 fish fillets
Small saucepan
Food processor
Mixing bowl
Cutting board
Paring knife
Chef's knife
Slotted spoon
Whisk
Large spatula
Measuring cups and spoons

Preparation

***This recipe can be started an hour before the meal.

Season the fish fillets with salt and pepper, arrange them in a single layer in a large buttered baking dish, and drizzle the vermouth over them.

Place the bread in the container of a food processor or blender and process to make fine crumbs. (Unlike ordinary dry breadcrumbs, these crumbs from fresh bread will be soft and white.)

Place 7 tablespoons of the butter in a mixing bowl to soften. Add the bread-crumbs and beat until well blended.

Preheat the oven to 450 degrees F.

Meanwhile, trim, rinse, and drain the mushrooms. Cut into thin slices.

In a small saucepan, combine the mushrooms, lemon juice, 1 tablespoon of the remaining butter, and water.

Season with salt and pepper. Bring to a boil over medium heat and boil for 1 minute.

Remove the mushrooms from the broth with a slotted spoon; set aside and keep warm. Reduce the mushroom broth over medium heat until only 3 tablespoons of liquid remain.

Place the fish in the hot oven and bake for 5 to 7 minutes.

Meanwhile, finish the mushroom butter: Cut the remaining 8 tablespoons butter into small pieces and whisk them, one at a time, into the reduced mushroom broth over low heat.

Remove the fillets from the oven and pour any juices from the bottom of the pan into the mushroom butter.

If not serving immediately, keep the fish, the mushrooms, and the mushroom butter warm in separate dishes.

**Fifteen minutes before serving, preheat the broiler.

Spread a thin layer of the breadcrumb mixture over the top of each fish fillet, patting it down gently into the fish.

Just before serving, place the fish fillets under the broiler for 2 minutes, until lightly browned.

Spoon a little of the mushroom butter over the bottom of 6 serving plates. Arrange a bouquet of mushrooms on each plate. Using a spatula, carefully place the browned fish fillets on the serving plates next to the mushrooms.

Le Navarin d'Agneau Printanier

SPRING LAMB STEW WITH BABY VEGETABLES

Time required: *1¾ hours
advance preparation and
cooking
20 minutes preparation
just before serving*
Difficulty: *Moderately easy*
Cost: *Moderate to expensive*

Ingredients

2½	to 3 pounds lean lamb shoulder
4	medium carrots
2	medium onions
3	or 4 ripe tomatoes
1	head of garlic
1	large bunch fresh thyme, or ½ tablespoon dried thyme

1	bay leaf
	Salt
1	tablespoon unsalted butter
1	tablespoon vegetable oil
2	tablespoons flour
	Freshly ground pepper

VEGETABLE GARNITURE
2   bunches baby carrots

A simple recipe, using good things from the earth.

2   bunches baby turnips
½   pound small white onions
1   pound small new potatoes
⅔   pound small green beans
5   tablespoons shelled baby peas

Salt
Pinch of sugar
1½   teaspoons unsalted butter
1   bunch parsley

Utensils

Dutch oven or cast-iron casserole with cover
2   medium saucepans
Fine sieve
Colander

Cutting board
Chef's knife
Paring knife
Slotted spoon
Wooden spoon

Preparation

*** All of this recipe can be prepared several hours in advance. Cut the lamb into 2-inch cubes. (Or ask your butcher to trim and cube the meat.)

Scrape the carrots and peel the onions. Cut both into ¼-inch dice. Core the tomatoes, cut them in half, and squeeze out the juice and seeds. Chop and set aside with the tomato trimmings reserved from the composed salad recipe.

Peel the garlic cloves and crush with the blade of a chef's knife. Separate the parsley leaves from the stems. Set the leaves aside and tie the stems in a bouquet garni with half of the bunch of thyme and the bay leaf.

Preheat the oven to 250 degrees F.

Season the lamb with salt.

Melt the butter with the oil in a Dutch oven or casserole over medium-high heat. As soon as the butter and oil start to sizzle, add the lamb and cook, turning with a wooden spoon, until seared but not brown. Remove the meat with a slotted spoon and let drain in a sieve set over a plate.

Add the carrots and onions to the casserole and sauté over medium heat until softened and lightly browned. Remove the vegetables and let drain with the meat. Pour off the cooking oil and return the meat and vegetables to the casserole.

Place over medium heat and add the garlic and tomatoes. Add the flour, stirring until well combined and no longer visible. Add the bouquet garni. Add enough water to just cover the meat and bring to a boil. Cover and place in the preheated oven to bake for 40 minutes; do not open the casserole or the oven door. This slow cooking keeps the meat from drying out.

While the meat cooks, prepare the vegetable garniture. Scrape the baby carrots. Peel the turnips, onions, and potatoes. String the beans. Rinse the vegetables quickly in a colander without letting them soak, except the potatoes, which you can keep in cold water to prevent from darkening.

Place the carrots in a medium saucepan of salted water, bring to a boil, and cook for 4 minutes. Drain in a colander. Place the turnips in a medium saucepan of salted water, bring to a boil, and cook for 5 minutes; drain. Place the onions in a saucepan, cover with water, add a pinch of salt, a pinch of sugar, and the butter and let boil over medium heat until all of the water evaporates. Place the potatoes in a medium saucepan of salted water, bring to a boil, and cook for 2 minutes; drain.

Remove the casserole with the lamb from the oven, but do not turn off the oven. Using a slotted spoon, remove the meat from the casserole; set aside on a plate and cover to keep warm.

Strain the lamb cooking juices through a sieve into a medium saucepan. Place over medium heat and reduce for 5 minutes. Discard the vegetables the lamb cooked with and skim off any grease that rises to the surface of the cooking juices.

Return the reduced sauce to the casserole, add the meat and the drained carrots, turnips, onions, peas, and potatoes.

Season with salt and pepper and sprinkle with the remaining sprigs of

thyme. Bring to a boil over medium heat, cover, and place in the oven to bake for 20 minutes longer.

Meanwhile, bring a medium saucepan of salted water to a boil. Add the green beans and cook just until tender, but still bright green and slightly crunchy. Drain immediately. Coarsely chop the parsley leaves.

Remove the casserole from the oven and discard the sprigs of thyme. Add the green beans and parsley, gently stirring them into the navarin.

If preparing in advance, cover and set the navarin aside.

**Just before sitting down to eat, place the casserole over low heat to warm while you serve the fish course. Bring the navarin to the table in the Dutch

oven or casserole.

When you taste this navarin, you won't begrudge the time spent on its preparation.

Le Gratin d'Abricots aux Amandes avec le Sirop de Kirsch

INDIVIDUAL APRICOT GRATINS WITH
ALMONDS AND KIRSCH

Time required: *15 minutes*
preparation (24 hours in advance)
35 minutes advance preparation
20 minutes cooking
Difficulty: *Easy*
Cost: *Moderate*

Ingredients

Using fresh fruit:
- 1 cup superfine sugar
- ½ cup honey
- 1 vanilla bean
- 2½ cups water

TOPPING
- ¾ cup powdered sugar
- 1¼ cups almond powder (see

- 2¼ pounds fresh apricots

Using canned fruit in syrup:
- 4 cans (17 ounces each) apricot halves in syrup

Appendix)
- 10 tablespoons unsalted butter, softened

2	egg yolks	3	tablespoons apricot brandy or kirsch
1	whole egg		
¼	cup slivered almonds		

❧

Utensils

Large saucepan with cover
Medium saucepan
Food processor or food mill
Large mixing bowl

Whisk
6 small gratin dishes, 4 to 4½ inches in diameter
Sugar sifter or fine sieve

❧

Preparation

✳✳✳If you are using fresh apricots, the preparation should be begun at least 24 hours ahead. If using canned, eliminate the first step and start the preparation several hours ahead.

For fresh apricots, combine 1 cup sugar, the honey, vanilla bean, and the water in a medium saucepan and bring to a boil.

Place the whole apricots in a large saucepan. Pour the boiling syrup over them, and bring back to a boil over medium-high heat. Remove from the heat; the apricots should be completely submerged in the syrup. If not, they will discolor. If necessary, invert a saucer on top of the fruit to keep it submerged. Cover the saucepan and let

The apricots in this gratin can be replaced by peaches, pears, prunes, or other fruits of your choice.

stand for 24 hours. During this overnight marinating, the pits will impart an almond flavor to the apricots and their syrup.

Drain the fruit, reserving the syrup and being careful not to crush the apricots. Halve the apricots. Remove and discard the pits. Place 4 or 5 apricot halves in the bottom of each gratin dish, arranging them to just cover the bottoms of the dishes.

If using canned apricots, begin the preparation at this point. Drain the fruit, reserving the syrup. Arrange 4 or 5 apricot halves in the bottom of each gratin dish, or enough to cover the bottoms of the dishes. Place the re-

maining fresh or canned apricots in a food processor or food mill with a little of the syrup and process to a thick purée; set aside.

To make the topping, combine ½ cup of the powdered sugar, the almond powder, butter, egg yolks, and whole egg in a mixing bowl and beat with a whisk until thoroughly blended.

Divide the batter among the 6 gratin dishes, spreading it evenly over the top of the apricots. (If the batter is too thick to spread, heat slightly to soften.) Sprinkle the top of the batter with slivered almonds. Sprinkle the remaining ¼ cup sugar over the top of the gratin dishes with a sugar sifter or fine sieve.

**Forty-five minutes before serving, preheat the oven to 425 degrees F. Twenty minutes later, place the gratins in the oven and bake for 15 to 20 minutes, until lightly browned on top.

Just before serving, place the apricot purée in a small saucepan and warm

over low heat. Add the apricot brandy and pour the sauce into a warmed sauce boat.

Serve the gratins on dessert plates lined with paper doilies or folded linen napkins. Pass the apricot topping separately.

Appendix
Conversion Chart

Liquid Measures

Fluid ounces	U.S. measures	Imperial measures	Milliliters
	1 tsp	1 tsp	5
¼	2 tsp	1 dessert-spoon	7
½	1 tbs	1 tbs	15
1	2 tbs	2 tbs	28
2	¼ cup	4 tbs	56
4	½ cup or ¼ pint		110
5		¼ pint or 1 gill	140
6	¾ cup		170
8	1 cup or ½ pint		225
9			250, ¼ liter
10	1¼ cups	½ pint	280
12	1½ cups or ¾ pint		240
15		¾ pint	420
16	2 cups or 1 pint		450
18	2¼ cups		500, ½ liter
20	2½ cups	1 pint	560
24	3 cups or 1½ pints		675

Fluid ounces	U.S. measures	Imperial measures	Milliliters
25		1¼ pints	700
27	3½ cups		750
30	3¾ cups	1½ pints	840
32	4 cups or 2 pints or 1 quart		900
35		1¾ pints	980
36	4½ cups		1000, 1 liter
40	5 cups or 2½ pints	2 pints or 1 quart	1120
48	6 cups or 3 pints		1350
50		2½ pints	1400
60	7½ cups	3 pints	1680
64	8 cups or 4 pints or 2 quarts		1800
72	9 cups		2000, 2 liters
80	10 cups or 5 pints	4 pints	2250
96	12 cups or 3 quarts		2700
100		5 pints	2800

Solid Measures

U.S. and Imperial measures ounces	pounds	Metric measures grams	kilos
1		28	
2		56	
3½		100	
4	¼	112	
5		140	
6		168	
8	½	225	
9		250	¼
12	¾	340	
16	1	450	
18		500	½
20	1¼	560	
24	1½	675	

U.S. and Imperial measures ounces	pounds	Metric measures grams	kilos
27		750	¾
28	1¾	780	
32	2	900	
36	2¼	1000	1
40	2½	1100	
48	3	1350	
54		1500	1½
64	4	1800	
72	4½	2000	2
80	5	2250	2¼
90		2500	2½
100	6	2800	2¾

Oven Temperature Equivalents	Fahrenheit	Gas Mark	Celsius	Heat of oven	Fahrenheit	Gas Mark	Celsius	Heat of oven
	225	¼	107	very cool	375	5	190	fairly hot
	250	½	121	very cool	400	6	204	fairly hot
	275	1	135	cool	425	7	218	hot
	300	2	148	cool	450	8	232	very hot
	325	3	163	moderate	475	9	246	very hot
	350	4	177	moderate				

Terminology Equivalents	U.S.	British	U.S.	British
	dry white beans	haricot beans	powdered sugar	icing sugar
	eggplant	aubergine	broil	grill
	zucchini	courgette	pit	stone
	heavy cream	double cream	skillet	frying pan
	sugar, granulated sugar	castor sugar		

Crème Fraîche

1 cup heavy cream, at room temperature

2 tablespoons buttermilk

Combine the cream and buttermilk in a clean, warm glass jar. Cover securely, and set the container in a warm place (over the pilot light or in the oven of a gas range or on the stove top, if elec- tric). Allow to thicken, 6 to 8 hours or more. Refrigerate and use as needed. This crème fraîche will keep up to 10 days.

Almond Powder

If almond powder is not available at your local gourmet shop, it can be easi- ly made in a nut grinder or a food pro- cessor. Process the nuts with an on-off pulsing action until just finely ground. Take care not to process them too long or they will reduce to an oily paste.

Vanilla Sugar

To make your own vanilla sugar, place several vanilla beans in large bottle and fill to the brim with superfine sugar. Close tightly and keep in a dry place. Refill with more sugar as you use it. Use this sugar in desserts, pastries, fruit salads, and creams—even in tea— to add a pleasant taste of vanilla.

Index

Acknowledgments

This book would not have seen the light of day without the work of the team of people who helped bring together all the key elements. I would like to thank all those who collaborated with me.

First, my gratitude goes to Charles-Henri Flammarion, who accepted this expansive project and gave me the opportunity to work with photographer Pierre Hussenot. Not only are the photos that Hussenot created superb, but his calmness and discretion made the long weeks of photography so agreeable. He was expertly assisted by photo stylist Laurence Mouton.

I would also like to thank Jean-Jacques Trilhe and Denis Mornet, who helped in testing the recipes. My thanks also to Danielle Schnapp, who helped us at the beginning of the photography.

This book is intended for home entertaining, but some of the photos were taken at Moulin de Mougins. Some were taken at my home, others at the homes of my friends, who willingly welcomed our invading team. My gratitude goes to Lynn and Roger Muhl, César, Bernard Chevry, Madam Costa, Monsieur Polverino, and Monsieur Chemit. Some of these names turn up again in the thanks I have reserved for that group of buddies who had the difficult job of dining under the linden tree: César, Roger Muhl, Bernard Chevry, José Albertini, and Patrick D'Humieres.

Thanks also to those who furnished the ingredients and props for many of the recipes: the great cheesemakers Robert and Edouard Ceneri of La Ferme Savoyarde and Georges Bruger of Le Roi du Charolais, and the following stores: Au Bain Marie (20 rue Herold, 75001 Paris), Ateliers de Segries (Moustiers Ste-Marie), Diners en Ville (27 rue de Varenne, 75007 Paris), Dior (30 avenue Montaigne, 75008 Paris), Frey (47 rue des Petits-Champs, 75002 Paris), Primerose Bordier, Descamps, La Tuile à Loup (35 rue Daubenton, 75005 Paris), G. Lethu (95 rue de Rennes, 75006 Paris), Pier Import (122 rue de Rivoli, 75004 Paris), Au Perou (Cannes), Soleiado (1 rue Lobineau, 75006 Paris), and Verreries de Biot (Biot).

The book was composed in Garamond Stempel by TGA Communications, Inc., New York, N.Y.

The book was printed and bound by Amilcare Pizzi s.p.a.-arti grafiche, Milan, Italy.